Everyman's

DICTIONARY OF PICTORIAL ART

VOLUME ONE

A Volume in
EVERYMAN'S REFERENCE LIBRARY

Other volumes in preparation

Everyman's Dictionary of
PICTORIAL
ART

Compiled by

WILLIAM GAUNT, M.A (Oxon.)

VOLUME ONE

LONDON: J. M. DENT & SONS LTD
NEW YORK: E. P. DUTTON & CO. INC.

Made in Great Britain
at the
Aldine Press · Letchworth · Herts
for
J. M. DENT & SONS LTD
Aldine House · Bedford Street · London
First published 1962
Reprinted 1969

SBN: 460 03006 x

INTRODUCTION

THE aim of this work is to provide in concise form and within the limits of 250,000 words and 1,000 illustrations a handy reference to painters and periods, forms and techniques of pictorial art in all parts of the world where pictorial art has flourished from the earliest times to the present. Immense though the subject is when so regarded, it cannot be said that any aspect of it is alien to modern interest and appreciation. Prehistoric art is living and comprehensible today; the landscape of a Zen Buddhist conveys its message to the western eye; abstract art needs its definition as well as Renaissance and baroque. It seemed desirable therefore to establish no arbitrary boundaries of place or time and, as in the volume on Architecture in Everyman's Reference Library, to take into account ancient and modern, East and West, though the European art of the Christian era figures largely and western development claims main attention.

From the virtually endless list of individual artists a choice has been made of some 1,200 for biographical entry. Exact dates and places of birth or death are given wherever this has proved possible, and though Old Master dates are frequently subject to the revisions of research the latter have been consulted and the findings of good authority used. While personal opinion cannot be freely intruded into a dictionary the attempt has been made to convey the nature and importance of individual achievement and to illustrate the latter by reference to characteristic works. In choosing for mention recent or living artists, the author has been guided by the following considerations: whether to the best of belief they have made some creative addition to pictorial art, are internationally known and are in general those about whom the public might reasonably be expected to require information. Supplementary lists are given of distinguished artists, British and American, represented, respectively, in public collections; the majority of the artists included being active in the nineteenth and the present century.

Descriptions of the main periods and schools of art are intended to summarize the character of these developments and at the same time to provide a channel of cross-reference with the biographical and individual entries, this operating in either direction. Thus one may turn from 'Florence' to 'Leonardo' or 'Michelangelo' or vice versa, and in the same way from or to 'Dutch Painting' and 'Rembrandt' and 'Ruisdael'. Art terms, used in technical description or in criticism and appreciation, e.g. 'impasto', 'Impressionism', are defined and as necessary given the shades or amplifications of meaning beyond the scope of the general dictionary, with historical reference and illustration where this seems to be called for. Descriptions are included of the various media in painting and graphic art (the latter extending to the various forms of print-making) and of mosaic, stained glass and enamel in their pictorial aspect.

The places where works of art are to be found have mention either in connection with a specific work or else in an entry dealing with some gallery of importance, though entries of the latter kind are purposely brief notes on the history, scope or specialization of the galleries in question.

It was thought desirable to include a certain number of descriptions of individual pictures, the history, subject-matter and significance of which seemed to need treatment in some detail. This does not profess to be a comprehensive list of masterpieces (though such a list is implicit in the examples mentioned together with the individual biographical entries), but appeared to be called for by, for instance, Titian's 'Sacred and Profane Love', or Manet's 'Déjeuner sur l'Herbe'. Titles are usually given in their English form, though some are so internationally familiar and recognizable in a language other than English that translation would be out of place. Thus the 'Déjeuner sur l'Herbe' would become less rather than more familiar if referred to as 'The Picnic'.

The illustrations have been gathered together from the great public collections and a number of private collections in various parts of the world: Italy, France, Spain, Germany, Holland, Belgium, Switzerland, the United States, the Commonwealth and Britain. They are placed near the account of the artist represented or alternatively near the article on a school, period or type of pictorial art which they exemplify.

In the preparation of the work the author has drawn upon his own experience and years of study as historian and critic though he wishes to express also his indebtedness to the many specialists in different fields by whose labours he has been able to profit.

W. G.

January 1962.

CONTENTS

VOLUME ONE

VOLUME TWO

SYSTEMATIC LIST OF ENTRIES

ART FORMS, MEDIA AND TECHNICAL TERMS

Alla Prima
Altar-piece
Aquatint
Arabesque
Atelier
Balance
Bistre
Bitumen
Bodegón
Body Colour
Cabinet Picture
Camera Obscura
Capriccio
Caricature
Cartoon
Cassone
-cento
Charcoal
Chiaroscuro
Codex
Collage
Composition
Contour
Contrapposto
Conversation Piece
Diptych
Distemper
Drawing
Drypoint
Enamel
Encaustic Painting
Engraving
Etching
Fête Champêtre
Foreshortening
Fresco Painting
Frottage
Gesso

Glaze
Gouache
Graphic Art
Grisaille
Ground
Hatching
Hue
Icon
Iconography
Iconostasis
Illumination of
    Manuscripts
Illustration
Impasto
Intaglio
Kakemono
Key
Kit-cat
Landscape Painting
Limner
Line Engraving
Lithography
Local Colour
Maestà
Mahlstick
Mass
Master
Medium
Mezzotint
Miniature Painting
Modelling
Monotype
Mosaic
Motif
Mural Painting
Niello
Oil Painting
Pastel

Pastiche
Pencil
Pentimento
Perspective
Pietà
Planes
Plastic
Polyptych
Portraiture
Poster
Predella
Primary Colours
Psalter
Retable
Sacra Conversazione
Sanguine
School
Sepia
Sfumato
Sgraffito
Signatures
Silhouette
Silverpoint
Soft Style
Sotto in sù
Stained Glass
Stanze
Steel Engraving
Still Life
Stipple
Tempera
Tone
Triptych
Underpainting
Values
Water-colour
Woodcuts and Wood
    Engraving

BIOGRAPHIES OF ARTISTS

American (United States)

Abbey, E. A.
Allston, W.
Audubon, J. J.
Bellows, G. W.

Benton, T. H.
Bierstadt, A.
Bingham, G. C.
Blume, P.

Burchfield, C.
Cassatt, M.
Chase, W. M.
Church, F E.

SYSTEMATIC LIST OF ENTRIES

Cole, T.
Copley, J. S.
Currier and Ives
Curry, J. S.
Davies, A. B.
Dove, A. G.
Eakins, T.
Earl, R.
Feininger, L.
Feke, R.
Glackens, W. J.
Grosz, G.
Harnett, W. M.
Hartley, M.
Hassam, C.
Hicks, E.
Homer, W.
Hopper, E.

Inness, G.
Johnson, E
Kensett, F.
Kent, R.
La Farge, J.
Lawson, E.
Malbone, E.G.
Marin, J.
Marsh, R.
Martin, H. D.
Morse, S. F. B.
Motherwell, R.
Mount, W. S.
O'Keefe, G.
Page, W.
Peale (family)
Pollock, J.
Prendergast, M.

Ryder, A. P.
Sargent, J. S.
Shahn, B.
Sheeler, C.
Sloan, J.
Stuart, G.
Sully, T.
Tobey, M.
Trumbull, J.
Vedder, E.
West, B.
Whistler, J. a. McN.
White, J.
Wollaston, J.
Wood, G.
Wyant, A. H.
Wyeth, A. N.
Supplementary List

Belgian

Delvaux, P.
Ensor, J.
Gallait, L.

Magritte, R.
Permeke, C.

Rops, F.
Smet, G. de

British

Abbott, L. F.
Adler, J.
Alken, H.
Allan, D.
Alma-Tadema, L.
Bacon, F.
Barker, T.
Barry, J.
Beardsley, A. V.
Beaumont, G. H.
Bewick, T.
Blake, W.
Bone, M.
Bonington, R. P.
Brangwyn, F.
Brett, J.
Brown, F. M.
Burne-Jones, E. C.
Caldecott, R.
Calvert, E.
Conder, C.
Constable, J.
Cooper, S.
Cosway, R.
Cotes, F.
Cotman, J. S.
Cox, D.

Cozens, A.
Cozens, J. R.
Craig, E. G.
Crawhall, J.
Crome, J.
Cruikshank, G.
Danby, F.
De Loutherbourg, P. J.
De Wint, P.
Dobson, W.
Dyce, W.
Eastlake, C. L.
Etty, W.
Farington, J.
Fielding (family)
Flaxman, J.
Frith, W. P.
Fry, R. E.
Fuseli, H.
Gainsborough, T.
Geddes, A.
Gilbert, J.
Gill, E.
Gillray, J.
Girtin, T.
Grant, D.

Greaves, W.
Haydon, B. R.
Hayman, F.
Highmore, J.
Hilliard, N.
Hogarth, W.
Hoppner, W.
Hudson, T.
Hughes, A.
Hunt, W. H.
Innes, J. D.
John, A. E.
Kauffmann, A.
Keene, C. S.
Kneller, G.
Landseer, E.
Laroon, J. M.
Lawrence, T.
Legros, A.
Leighton, F.
Lely, P.
Leslie, C. R.
Lewis, J. F.
Lewis, P. W.
Linnell, J.
McEvoy, A.
Maclise, D.

SYSTEMATIC LIST OF ENTRIES

MARSHALL, B.
MARTIN, J.
MARTINEAU, R. B.
MILLAIS, J. E.
MONRO, T.
MOORE, A. J.
MOORE, H.
MORLAND, G.
MORRIS, W.
MÜLLER, W. J.
NASH, P.
NASMYTH (FAMILY)
NEVINSON, C. R. W.
NICHOLSON, B.
NICHOLSON, W. N. P.
NOLAN, S.
NORTHCOTE, J.
OPIE, J.
ORCHARDSON, W. Q.

ORPEN, W.
PALMER, S.
PASMORE, V.
POYNTER, E. J.
PRYDE, J.
RAEBURN, H.
RAMSAY, A.
REYNOLDS, J.
RILEY, J.
ROMNEY, G.
ROSSETTI, D. G.
ROWLANDSON, T.
RUSKIN, J.
SANDBY, P.
SCOTT, S.
SICKERT, W. R.
SMITH, M.
SPENCER, S.
STANFIELD, C.

STEER, P. W.
STEVENS, A.
STOTHARD, T.
STUBBS, G.
SUTHERLAND, G.
THORNHILL, J.
TOWNE, F.
TURNER, J. M. W.
VARLEY, J.
WARD, J.
WATTS, G. F.
WHEATLEY, F.
WILKIE, D.
WILSON, R.
WOOTTON, J.
WRIGHT, J.
YEATS, J. B.
ZOFFANY, J.
Supplementary List

Dutch (see also *Early Netherlandish*)

AERTZEN, P.
APPEL, K.
ARENTZ, A.
ASSELYN, J.
AVERCAMP, H.
BAAN, J. VAN
BABUREN, D. VAN
BACKER (BAKKER),
  J. A.
BAKHUYSEN, L.
BERCHEM (BERGHEM),
  C. P.
BERCKHEYDE, G.
BEYEREN, A. VAN
BLOEMAERT, A.
BOL, F.
BOTH, A. and J.
BREKELENKAM, Q.
BUYTEWECH, W.
CAPPELLE, J. VAN DE
CLAESZ, P.
CORNELISZ, C.
CORNELISZ, L.
CUYP, A.
DOESBURG, T. VAN
DONGEN, K. VAN
DOU, G.
DUJARDIN, K.
EECKHOUT, G. VAN DEN
EVERDINGEN, A. VAN
FABRITIUS, C.

GOGH, V. VAN
GOYEN, J. VAN
HALS, D.
HALS, F.
HEDA, W. C.
HEEM, J. D. DE
HEEMSKERK, M. J.
HELST, B. VAN DER
HEYDEN, J. VAN DER
HOBBEMA, M.
HONDECOETER, M. D'
HONTHORST, G. VAN
HOOCH, P. DE
HOOGSTRATEN, S. VAN
HUYSUM, J. VAN
ISRAELS, J.
JOHNSON (JANSSEN), C.
JONGKIND, J. B.
KALF, W.
KEYSER, T. DE
KONINCK, P.
LAER, P. VAN
LASTMAN, P.
LIEVENS, J.
MAES, N.
MANDER, K. VAN
MARIS, M. J. AND W.
MAUVE, A.
MESDAG, H. W.
METSU (METZU), G.
MIEREVELD, M. J. VAN

MIERIS, F. VAN (the
  elder)
MOLENAER, J. M. AND
  J. (LYSTER)
MONDRIAN, P.
MOR, A.
MOSTAERT, J.
MYTENS, D.
NEER, AERT VAN DER
NETSCHER, C.
OCHTERVELT, J.
OSTADE, A. VAN
OSTADE, I. VAN
POT, H. G.
POTTER, P.
PYNACKER, A.
PYNAS, JAN
REMBRANDT, H. VAN
  RIJN
RUIYSCH, R.
RUISDAEL, J. I. VAN
SAENREDAM, P.
SAFTLEVEN (SACHT-
  LEVEN), C.
SCOREL, J. VAN
SEGHERS, H.
STEEN, J. H.
TER BORCH (TER
  BURG), G.
TERBRUGGEN, H.
VAN MEEGEREN, H.

[xi]

SYSTEMATIC LIST OF ENTRIES

SYSTEMATIC LIST OF ENTRIES

PATER, J. B. J.
PERRÉAL, J.
PERRONNEAU, J. B.
PICABIA, F.
PISSARRO, C.
POUSSIN, N.
PRUD'HON, P. P.
PUVIS DE CHAVANNES
REDON, O.
RENOIR, P. A.
RIGAUD, H.
ROBERT, H.
ROUAULT, G.

ROUSSEAU, H.
ROUSSEAU, T.
ROUSSEL, K. X.
SEURAT, G.
SIGNAC, P.
SISLEY, A.
SOULAGES, P.
STEINLEN, T.
TANGUY, Y.
TISSOT, J.
TOULOUSE-LAUTREC,
  H. DE
TROY, J. F. DE

TROYON, C.
UTRILLO, M.
VALADON, S.
VALENTIN, LE
VAN LOO (FAMILY)
VERNET (FAMILY)
VIEN, J. M.
VIGÉE-LEBRUN,
  M. A. E.
VLAMINCK, M. DE
VOUET, S.
VUILLARD, E.
WATTEAU, J. A.

German

ALTDORFER, A.
AMBERGER, C.
BALDUNG (GRÜN), H.
BAUMEISTER, W.
BECKMANN, M.
BEHAM, B. AND H.
BERTRAM, MASTER
BÖCKLIN, A.
BURGKMAIR, H.
CHODOWIECKI, D.
CORINTH, L.
CORNELIUS, P. VON
CRANACH, L.
DIX, O.
DÜRER, A.
ELSHEIMER, A.
ERNST, M.
FEININGER, L.
FEUERBACH, A.
FRANCKE, MASTER
FRIEDRICH, C. D.
GROSZ, GEORGE
GRÜNEWALD, M.
HECKEL, E.
HOFER, K.

HOLBEIN, H. (the
  elder)
HOLBEIN, H. (the
  younger)
HUBER, W.
KANDINSKY, W.
KIRCHNER, E. L.
KLEE, P.
KOKOSCHKA, O.
KOLLWITZ, K.
LAIB, C.
LEIBL, W.
LIEBERMANN, M.
LOCHNER, S.
MACKE, A.
MARC, F.
MARÉES, H. VON
MASTER OF THE
  HOUSEBOOK
MASTER OF THE LIFE
  OF MARY
MASTER OF TREBON
MENGS, A. R.
MENZEL, A. VON
MODERSOHN-BECKER, P.

MOSER, L.
MULTSCHER, H.
MÜNTER, G.
NOLDE, E.
OVERBECK, J. F.
PACHER, M.
PECHSTEIN, M.
PLEYDENWURFF, H.
RETHEL, A.
ROTTENHAMMER, J.
RUNGE, P. O.
SANDRART, J. VON
SCHMIDT-ROTTLUFF,
  K.
SCHONGAUER, M.
SCHWIND, M. VON
SLEVOGT, M.
SOEST, K. VON
STRIGEL, B.
SÜSS, H. (VON KULM-
  BACH)
THOMA, H.
TISCHBEIN, W.
WOLGEMUT, M.

Greek (Ancient) and Byzantine

APELLES
APOLLODOROS
BRYGOS
DOURIS
EUPHRONIOS

EXEKIAS
KLITIAS
PAMPHILOS
PARRHASIOS
PHILOXENOS

POLYGNOTOS
THEOPHANES
TIMOMACHOS
ZEUXIS

Italian (artists working abroad)

ABBATE, N. DELL'
BARTOLOZZI, F.

CARDUCCI, B. AND V.
GELTILESCHI, O.

PRIMATICCIO, F.
ROSSO, IL

[xiii]

SYSTEMATIC LIST OF ENTRIES

Italian (Bologna, Modena)

ALBANI, F.
BIANCHI FERRARI, F.
CANTARINI, S.
CARRACCI (FAMILY)

CRESPI, G. M.
DOMENICHINO
FONTANA, P.
FRANCIA

GUERCINO, IL
RENI, G.
SASSOFERRATO

Italian (Ferrara)

BOCCACCINO, B.
COSSA, F.
COSTA, L.

DOSSI, D. AND B.
GAROFALO

ROBERTI, E.
TURA, C.

Italian (Florence)

ALBERTINELLI, M.
ANGELICO, FRA
BACCHIACCA (F.
    UBERTINI)
BALDINUCCI, F.
BALDOVINETTI, A.
BANDINELLI, B.
BARTOLOMMEO, FRA
BENOZZO DI LESE
    (GOZZOLI)
BOTTICELLI, S.
BOTTICINI, F.
BRONZINO, IL
BUFFALMACO, B.
CASTAGNO, A.
CENNINI, C.
CIMABUE, G.
CREDI, L. DI

DADDI, B.
DOLCI, C.
DOMENICO VENEZIANO
FRANCIABIGIO
GADDI (family)
GHIRLANDAIO, D.
GIOTTINO
GIOTTO
LEONARDO DA VINCI
LIPPI, FILIPPINO
LIPPI, FRA FILIPPO
LORENZO MONACO
MAINARDI, S.
MASACCIO
MASO DI BANCO
MASOLINO
MICHELANGELO
ORCAGNA

PERINO DEL VAGA
PESELLINO
PIERO DI COSIMO
POLLAIUOLO, A. AND
    P.
PONTORMO, J. DA
RAFFAELLINO DEL
    GARBO
ROSSELLI, C.
ROSSO, IL
SALVIATI
SARTO, A. DEL
SELLAIO, J. DEL
SPINELLO, ARETINO
UCCELLO, P.
VASARI, G.
VERROCCHIO, A. DEL

Italian (Genoa)

CAMBIASO, L.

CASTIGLIONE, G. B.

MAGNASCO, A.

Italian (Lombardy)

BARNABA DA MODENA
BOLTRAFFIO, G. A.
BORGOGNE, A.
BRAMANTINO
BUTINONE, B.

CRESPI, G. B.
FERRARI, G.
FOPPA, V.
LUINI, B.

PARMIGIANINO
PROCACCINI, E.
SODOMA, IL
ZENALE, B.

[xiv]

SYSTEMATIC LIST OF ENTRIES

Italian (Naples)

ARPINO, G. C.
DESIDERIO
GIORDANO, L.

LANFRANCO, G.
PRETI, M.

ROSA, S.
SOLIMENA, F

Italian (Rome and Central Italy)

BAGLIONE, G.
BAROCCI, F.
BATONI, P. G.
BONFIGLI, B.
CARAVAGGIO, M. A.
CAVALLINI, P.
CORTONA, P. DA
GAULLI, G. B.
MANFREDI, B.
MARATTA, C.
MARCANTONIO

MARGARITO
MELOZZO DA FORLI
NICCOLO DI
  LIBERATORE
PANINI, G. P.
PERUGINO, P.
PIERO DELLA
  FRANCESCA
PINTORICCHIO
PIRANESI, G. B.

POLIDORO DA
  CARAVAGGIO
POZZO, A.
RAPHAEL
ROMANO, G.
SACCHI, A.
SANTI, G.
SIGNORELLI, L.
VITI, T.
VOLTERRA, D. DA
ZUCCARO, F. AND T.

Italian (Siena)

BARNA (DA SIENA)
BARTOLI, D.
BARTOLI, T.
BARTOLO DI FREDI
BECCAFUMI, D.
DUCCIO
FRANCESCO DI
  GIORGIO

GIOVANNI DI PAOLO
GUIDO DA SIENA
LORENZETTI, P. AND A.
MARTINI, S.
MATTEO DI GIOVANNI
MEMMI, LIPPO
NEROCCIO
PERUZZI, B.

SANO DI PIETRO
SASSETTA
TRAINI, F.
UGOLINO
VANNI, A.
VECCHIETTA

Italian (Venetia, Verona, Padua, Mantua, Parma)

BONO DA FERRARA
BONSIGNORI, F.
CORREGGIO
FETI, D.

MANTEGNA
MONTAGNA, B.
PADOVANINO, IL
PISANELLO

SCHIAVONE, G.
SQUARCIONE, F.
ZOPPO, M.

Italian (Venice)

AMIGONI, J.
ANTONELLO DA
  MESSINA
BARBARI, J. DE'
BASAITI, M.
BASSANO (DA PONTE
  FAMILY)
BELLINI (FAMILY)
BELLOTTO, B.

BISSOLO, F.
BONIFAZIO DI PITATI
BORDONE, P.
BUONCONSIGLIO, G.
CAMPAGNOLA, D.
CANALETTO
CARIANI (G. BUSI)
CARLEVARIS, L.
CARPACCIO, V.

CARRIERA, R.
CATENA (DI BIAGIO)
CIMA, G. B.
CRIVELLI, C.
GENTILE DA FABRIANO
GIORGIONE
GUARDI, F.
LONGHI, P.
LOTTO, L.

[xv]

SYSTEMATIC LIST OF ENTRIES

MORETTO, IL
MORONI, G.
PALMA GIOVANE
PALMA VECCHIO
PIAZZETTA, G. B.
PITTONI, G. B.
PORDENONE
PREVITALI, A.

RICCI, S. AND M.
SAVOLDO, G.
SCHIAVONE, A.
SEBASTIANO DEL
PIOMBO
SOLARIO, ANDREA DA
SOLARIO, ANTONIO DA
STROZZI, B.

TIEPOLO, G. B.
TINTORETTO
TITIAN
VERONESE
VIVARINI (FAMILY)
ZUCCARELLI, F.

Italian (Modern)

BALLA, G.
CAMPIGLI, M.
CARRÀ, C.

CHIRICO, G. DE
GUTTUSO, R.
MODIGLIANI, A.

MORANDI, G.
SEVERINI, G.

Mexican

OROZCO, J. C.

RIVERA, D.

SIQUEIROS, D. A.

Early Netherlandish and Flemish

BEER, J. D.
BENSON, A.
BEUCKELAER, J.
BLES, H. MET DE
BOL, H.
BOSCH, J.
BOUTS, D.
BRIL, M. AND P.
BROUWER, A.
BRUEGHEL, P. (the
 elder) AND FAMILY
CALVAERT, D.
CAMPIN, R.
CHRISTUS, P.
CLEVE, J. VAN
CONINXLOO. G. VAN
COQUES, G.
CORNELISZ (VAN
 OOSTZANEN), J.
COXCIE, M.
CRAYER, G. DE
DAVID, G.
DYCK, A. VAN
EYCK, H. AND J. VAN
FLORIS, F.
FRANCKEN (FAMILY)
FYT, J.
GEERTGEN TOT SINT
 JANS

GOES, H. VAN DER
GOSSART, J. (MABUSE)
ISENBRANT, A.
JANSSENS, A.
JODE, P. DE
JORDAENS, J.
JUSTUS OF GHENT
KEY, A. T.
LEYDEN, L. VAN
LOMBARD, L.
MASSYS, Q
MASTER OF FLÉMALLE
MASTER OF 1499
MASTER OF ST GILES
MASTER OF SPES
 NOSTRA
MASTER OF THE DEATH
 OF THE VIRGIN
MASTER OF THE FE-
 MALE HALF-LENGTHS
MASTER OF THE
 HOUSEBOOK
MASTER OF THE
 LEGEND OF ST LUCY
MASTER OF THE LE-
 GEND OF ST URSULA
MASTER OF THE MAG-
 DALEN LEGEND

MASTER OF THE VIRGO
 INTER VIRGINES
MEMLINC(MEMLING),H.
MEULEN, A. F. VAN DER
MOMPER, J. DE
NOORT, A. VAN
ORLEY, B. VAN
OUWATER, A. VAN
PATENIER, J.
PEETERS (FAMILY)
POURBUS (FAMILY)
PROVOST, J.
REYMERSWAEL, M. VAN
RUBENS, P. P.
SAVERY, R.
SEGHERS, D.
SIBERECHTS, J.
SNYDERS, F.
SPRANGER, B.
SUTTERMAN (SUSTER-
 MANS), J.
TENIERS, D.
VALCKENBORGH, L. VAN
VEEN (VENIUS), O. VAN
VOS, C. DE
VOS, M. DE
VRANCKZ, S.
WEYDEN, R. VAN DER
WOUTERS, F.

SYSTEMATIC LIST OF ENTRIES

Norwegian
MUNCH, E.

Oriental
BIHZAD
CHU-TA
HIROSHIGE
HOKUSAI
HSIA KUEI

KORIN, O.
KU K'AI-CHIH
MA YUAN
SESSHŪ

UTAMARO
WANG WEI
WEN CHENG-MING
WU TAO-TZU

Russian
BAKST, L.
BENOIS, A. N.
CHAGALL, M.
DEINEKA, A. A.

FEDOTOV, P. A.
JAWLENSKY, A.
KANDINSKY, W.
MALEVICH, K.

REPIN, I. E.
ROUBLEV, A.
SEROV, V. A.
VERESCHCHAGIN, V.

Spanish and Portuguese
BASSA, FERRER
BAYEU, F.
BERMEJO, B.
BERRUGUETE, A.
BERRUGUETE, P.
BORÈS, F.
BORRASSA, L.
CANO, A.
CARDUCCI (CARDUCHO,)
  B. AND V.
CARREÑO DE MIRANDA,
  J.
CÉSPEDES, P. DE
COELLO, A. S.
COELLO, C.
COTÁN, J. S.
DALI, S.

DALMAU, L.
FORTUNY, M.
GALLEGO, F.
GONÇALVES, N.
GOYA, F. DE
GRECO, EL
GRIS, J.
HERRERA, F. DE ('EL
  MOZO')
HERRERA, F. DE ('EL
  VIEJO')
HUGUET, J.
JUAN DE FLANDES
MASIP, J. V.
MAZO, J. B. DEL
MELÉNDEZ, L. E.
MIRÓ, J.

MORALES, L. DE
MURILLO, B. E.
PACHECO, F.
PANTOJA DE LA CRUZ
PARÉJA, J.
PICASSO, P.
RIBALTA, F.
RIBERA, J. DE
ROELAS, J. DE
SERRA, J. AND P.
SERT, J. M.
VALDÉS-LEAL, J. DE
VARGAS, L. DE
VELAZQUEZ, D.
VERGÓS (FAMILY)
ZULOAGA, I.
ZURBARÁN, F. DE

Swiss
CORBUSIER, LE
GIACOMETTI (FAMILY)
GRAF, U.

HODLER, F.
KLEE, P.
MANUEL DEUTSCH, N.

TAEUBER-ARP, S.
VALLOTTON, F.
WITZ, C.

[xvii]

SYSTEMATIC LIST OF ENTRIES

ART MUSEUMS AND GALLERIES

FAMOUS WORKS INDIVIDUALLY DESCRIBED[1]

[1] A selective list where title and subject-matter as well as importance seemed to call for comment.

SYSTEMATIC LIST OF ENTRIES

PERIODS AND SCHOOLS OF PAINTING

SYSTEMATIC LIST OF ENTRIES

STYLE AND THEORY

Abstract Art
Academic
Academy
Action Painting
Armory Show
Art for Art's Sake
Art Nouveau
Ashcan School
Baroque
Bauhaus
Blaue Reiter, Der
Brücke, Die
Chinoiserie
Classicism
Constructivism
Cubism
Dada
Decadence
Decorative
Design
De Stijl
Divisionism
Eclecticism
Empire Style
Expressionism
Fauve
Fête Champêtre
Figurative
Folk Art
Found Object
Futurism
Genre
Golden Section
Grand Style
Grotesque
Hellenic, Hellenistic
History Painting

Ideal, Idealism
Illusionism
Impressionism
International Gothic
Intimism
Jugendstil
Kinetic Art
Mannerism
Metaphysical Painting
Nabis, The
Naturalism
Nazarener
Neue Sachlichkeit, Die
Nocturne
Non-figurative Art
Op Art
Picturesque
Plein Air
Post-Impressionism
Pre-Raphaelite
Realism
Renaissance
Rococo
Romanist
Romanticism
Royal Academy of Arts
Salon
Salon des Refusés
Sezession
Stijl, De
Suprematism
Surrealism
Symbolism
Tachisme
Tenebrist
Trompe l'Œil
Vorticism

COLOUR PLATES

VOLUME ONE

SANDRO BOTTICELLI
Primavera

GEORGES BRAQUE
Still Life

PAUL CÉZANNE
Curtain, Jug and Fruit-Dish

JOHN CONSTABLE
The Hay-wain

JAN VAN EYCK
The Marriage of Giovanni Arnolfini
and Giovanna Cenami

PAUL GAUGUIN
Riders on the Shore

GIORGIONE DA CASTELFRANCO
The Tempest

VINCENT VAN GOGH
Road with Cypress

BOTTICELLI—Primavera—Uffizi Gallery, Florence.

BRAQUE—Still Life—
Stuttgart Gallery.

CÉZANNE—Curtain, Jug and Fruit-dish—Whitney Collection.

CONSTABLE—The Hay-wain—National Gallery, London.

JAN VAN EYCK—The Marriage of Giovanni Arnolfini and Giovanna Cenami—National Gallery, London.

GAUGUIN—Riders on the Shore—Niarchos Collection.

GIORGIONE—The Tempest—Accademia, Venice.

VAN GOGH—Road with Cypresses—Kröller-Müller Museum.

A

Abbate, Niccolò dell' (*b.* Modena, 1512; *d.* Paris, 1571), Italian painter who worked at Modena and Bologna until, at the age of forty, he went to France, where he settled, collaborating with Primaticcio (q.v.) in the decoration of the palace at Fontainebleau. His graceful Mannerist style, closely allied to that of Primaticcio, is characteristic of the first, Italianate 'School of Fontainebleau' (q.v.). His 'Adventures of Ulysses' in the Galerie d'Ulysse was destroyed, although engravings were made in 1630. A principal easel picture is his 'Martyrdom of St Peter and St Paul', now at Dresden. His brother Pietro Paolo, his son Giulio Camillo, his grandson Ercole and his great-grandson Pietro Paolo were all painters.

Abbey, Edwin Austin (*b.* Philadelphia, 1 April 1852; *d.* London, 1 Aug. 1911), American painter and illustrator who worked in England and became R.A. in 1898. He was commissioned by Edward VII to paint the coronation and also decorated the Boston Public Library with a series of panels, 'The Quest of the Holy Grail', but his illustrative style is better seen in delicate pen drawings to Herrick, Goldsmith and Shakespeare.

Abbott, Lemuel Francis (*b.* Leicestershire, 1760; *d.* London, 1803), English portrait painter, the pupil of Francis Hayman (q.v.). He is best known by several versions, often reproduced, of Nelson's portrait (National Maritime Museum; National Portrait Gallery).

Abstract Art, painting or sculpture which does not represent the appearance of objects in nature but concentrates on harmonious or effective combinations of form and colour 'in themselves'. All great art has the abstract element, even when it is otherwise realistic or 'true to nature', but historically the motive behind and the degree of the abstraction varies. Thus it has been linked with religious precept, as in Islamic art with its proscription of the image. The pursuit of 'pure' or absolute values, first philosophically conceived by Plato, and

N. DELL' ABBATE—Scene from the Aeneid—Galleria Estense, Modena.

as free from imitation or story-telling as music, is, however, a modern development. The rivalry of the camera as a recording instrument has no doubt affected the painter's aim, impelling him in this other direction, though abstract art has its own logic, and is the longest lived of the modern tendencies, having passed through several phases since the advent of Cubism, c. 1907: the Cubist still life with its disruption of surface appearance (Picasso, Braque, Gris); the purely geometric design (Mondrian, Ben Nicholson); and the freer abstract expression of which Kandinsky was the pioneer, 'Tachisme' and 'action painting' being its later offshoots. These forms of 'expressionism' are to be distinguished from decoration or pattern by reason of the subconscious factor assumed to play a part in the final result. *See also* NON-FIGURATIVE ART.

Academic, term often used in a somewhat deprecatory sense to denote attachment to a style of the past in painting, such as that which conservative academies have been prone to favour; capable within its limits but not original.

Academy. The name, adapted from the grove of Academe in which Plato taught and applied to many learned bodies, signifies also the institutions devoted to training in the fine arts and maintaining their standards and prestige. Italy gives the first examples (an academy being founded at Florence by Brunetto Latini in 1207), and the Academy of St Luke (whom legend represents as painter of the Virgin), founded in Rome in 1593, largely through the efforts of the painter Muziano, was a model studied by Europe and inspiring the foundation of the Académie Royale in France in 1648. As organized by Colbert and Lebrun the Académie Royale implemented and monopolized the whole grandiose scheme of art and decoration under Louis XIV, while it had a 'finishing school' in the French Academy in Rome founded in 1666. In turn it helped to inspire the Royal Academy (q.v.), founded in London, 1768, though this was free of State control and has remained a self-governing body of artists: 40 academicians—painters, sculptors, engravers and architects; 30 associates, with provision for honorary membership. Its first president, Sir Joshua Reynolds, did much to establish its dignity and influence, and its schools of instruction, yearly summer exhibition of works by living artists and winter exhibition of some great period or phase of art are each of importance. Its history illustrates something of the conflict between conservatism and new ideas which created an unfortunate division in the late nineteenth and early twentieth centuries. This, however, has lessened at the present time.

The American Academy, the National Academy of Design, founded in 1826, admits 125 painters, 25 sculptors and 25 architects and engravers.

Accademia, Venice. Developed from the church and monastery buildings connected with the Scuola della Carità, converted to the use of the Venetian Academy in the eighteenth century, the Accademia has since become a great gallery of Venetian art from Lorenzo Veneziano to Canaletto and Guardi. Among its principal treasures are

Carpaccio's splendid series, The Legend of St Ursula, Giovanni Bellini's 'Madonna with the Magdalen and St Catherine', Titian's 'Presentation of the Virgin', Tintoretto's 'Miracle of St Mark', Giorgione's 'The Tempest' and Veronese's 'The Feast in the House of Levi'.

Action Painting, American contribution to abstract art, laying stress on uninhibited physical action in the application of paint and taking advantage of the unexpected and seemingly accidental results thus obtained. Jackson Pollock (q.v.) was its most remarkable practitioner, his work stimulating similar effort in Europe.

Adler, Jankel (*b.* Lodz, Poland, 26 July 1895; *d.* Aldbourne, Wiltshire, 25 April 1949), Polish-born painter who worked in Düsseldorf until 1933, when he fled to Paris from the Nazi regime. After many travels he arrived in England in 1940 and settled there, producing a large number of paintings and drawings. Picasso and Paul Klee (with whom he had a long acquaintance) were influential in his development and he made a number of interesting experiments in technique. Works by him are in the National Gallery, Berlin; Museum of Western Art, Moscow; Musée d'Art Moderne, Paris; Museum of Modern Art, New York; and elsewhere.

'Adoration of the Lamb', altar-piece in Ghent Cathedral, traditionally ascribed to both Hubert and Jan van Eyck (qq.v.) and completed in 1432. When open it displays two main sections, the upper with large and few figures showing God the Father with on either side the Virgin and John the Baptist, companies of angels and representations of Adam and Eve. The main panel beneath, with many smaller figures, represents an earthly paradise in which the Lamb, symbol of Christ, stands on an altar venerated by devout groups. On the side panels the Just Judges, the Soldiers of Christ, hermits and pilgrims face inwards

ACTION PAINTING—Jackson Pollock—Black Painting, 1952—Photo: Marlborough Fine Art.

[3]

AEGEAN PAINTING—
The Chieftain, fresco from
Knossos, Crete—From copy
in the Ashmolean Museum,
Oxford.

towards the central scene. The outer panels have an Annunciation and the portraits of the donors, Jodocus Vijd and his wife.

Aegean Painting, wall-painting and pottery decoration of the highly advanced civilization centred in Crete, of which the greatest period may be placed between about 2000 and 1400 B.C. This civilization, now generally known as Aegean, covers all that period of East Mediterranean culture before the beginning of the historic period of Greece which is usually dated from about 800 B.C. Its traces are found both in Crete and on the Greek mainland. The vast palace unearthed by Sir Arthur Evans at Knossos, site of the ancient metropolis in Crete, was lavishly decorated with frescoes, resembling the wall-paintings of Egypt in their flat bright colour and linear style but marked by a freer sense of life and movement. They represented the sports of the bullring, an amazing example showing the vault of a female acrobat over the horns of a bull; athletic contests; processional scenes, one showing women of life size with tight-belted waists and flounced skirts of curiously modern appearance; and vividly stylized floral and marine motives—lilies, dolphins, flying-fish. One famous fresco is of a youthful cup-bearer of almost Hellenic aspect. Other remains of painting in an area near the palace in what was called the 'House of Frescoes' included representations of landscape with plants, shrubs, birds and animals, and one painting showed a Minoan officer leading Negro soldiers. Frescoes of the same style as at Knossos, though less remarkable, were also found at Mycenae and Tiryns. Pottery, it is evident, was a great export industry. Characteristic vases have polychrome decoration on a white or dark ground or dark painting on a lighter ground, and are noted for the free representation of flowers, aquatic plants and animal form, a famous type being the octopus vase.

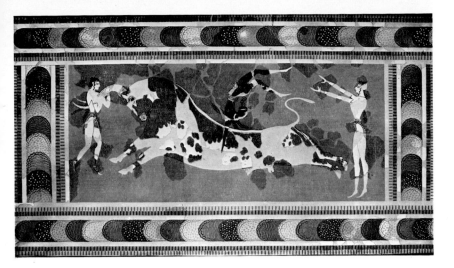

AEGEAN PAINTING—Fresco with Bull and Gymnasts from Knossos, Crete—From copy in the Ashmolean Museum, Oxford.

FRANCESCO ALBANI—The Rape of Europa—Uffizi Gallery, Florence.

Aertzen (Aartsen), Pieter (*b.* probably Amsterdam, *c.* 1509; *d.* there, 3 June 1575), Dutch painter, a pupil of Allaert Claesz, who worked at Amsterdam and also, *c.* 1535-56, at Antwerp. He excelled in interiors and homely scenes, though also producing historical and religious works. His 'Maidservant' (Brussels) is an original and early example of the Netherlandish domestic *genre*.

Agnolo, Andrea d', see SARTO.

Albani, Francesco (*b.* Bologna, 17 Mar. 1578; *d.* there, 4 Oct. 1660), Italian painter of religious and mythological subjects. He first studied in the school of the Flemish painter, Denis Calvaert (q.v.), at Bologna, then, like his contemporaries Guido Reni and Domenichino (qq.v.), with the Carracci (q.v.). His graceful compositions earned him the name of the 'Anacreon of painting' and he frequently introduced juvenile figures for which his own twelve children served as models. Popular in France in the reign of Louis XIV, he is well represented in the Louvre as well as in Italian and other galleries.

Albertina, art museum in Vienna famous for its collection of old master drawings, originally formed by Albert Casimir of Saxony (1737-1822).

Albertinelli, Mariotto (*b.* Florence, 13 Oct. 1474; *d.* there, 5 Nov. 1515), Italian painter of religious subjects, a pupil of Cosimo Rosselli (q.v.) and fellow student with Fra Bartolommeo (q.v.), with whom he collaborated in some works. He followed Bartolommeo in style, though a dignified simplicity of grouping was his own. 'The Visitation' (Uffizi) and 'Madonna and Child with Saints' (Louvre) are among his best-known works. Franciabigio (q.v.) was one of his several pupils.

M. ALBERTINELLI — The Visitation — Uffizi Gallery, Florence.

Alken, Henry (fl. 1816–31), English painter and graphic artist, said to have been stud-groom to the Duke of Beaufort, noted for many spirited paintings and engravings of hunting and other sporting subjects.

Alla Prima, direct method of painting in oils by which the final result is achieved without retouching.

Allan, David (b. Alloa, 13 Feb. 1744; d. Edinburgh, 6 Aug. 1796), Scottish painter who studied in Glasgow and at Rome, where in 1773 he won a gold medal for his 'Origin of Painting' and became a member of the Academy of St Luke. He settled at Edinburgh and was known as the 'Scottish Hogarth' for his water-colours and engravings of contemporary life, his subjects, e.g. 'The Penny Wedding' (Edinburgh), anticipating those of Wilkie.

Allston, Washington (b. South Carolina, 5 Nov. 1779; d. Cambridgeport, near Boston, 8 July 1843), American landscape painter, the first eminent representative of the Romantic spirit in American art. After graduating at Harvard, 1800, he went to Europe to study, first in London, then in Paris and Rome. He worked in London for a number of years, and was elected A.R.A., 1818, the year of his return to America. He was admired by Coleridge, whose portrait he painted

W. ALLSTON (attributed to)—The Deluge—Metropolitan Museum of Art, New York.

A. ALTDORFER—The Battle of Arbela—Pinakothek, Munich.

(National Portrait Gallery), and was a friend of John Martin (q.v.), with whose imagination he had much akin. His earlier work was grandiose and dramatic, 'The Deluge', 1804 (New York Metropolitan Museum), being an example. On one large picture, 'Belshazzar's Feast' (in which he gave a subject to Martin), he toiled unhappily for many years after he settled in Boston, though his work there is better represented by smaller paintings of dreamy reverie such as his 'Moonlit Landscape', 1819 (Boston).

Alma-Tadema, Sir Lawrence (*b.* Dronryp, Friesland, 8 Jan. 1836; *d.* Wiesbaden, 24 June 1912), painter of Dutch origin, who settled in London, *c.* 1870, and became a naturalized Englishman. Trained in the Belgian historical school of Wappers and Leys and influenced by the archaeologist, Ebers, he painted scenes from Merovingian history and reconstructions of life in ancient Egypt, Greece and Rome, accurate in archaeological detail but late Victorian in sentiment.

Altar-piece, screen, panel or series of panels on or behind the altar of a church or, in the past, a private chapel; adorned variously with paintings, sculptured ornament or other decoration. From a pictorial point of view it became important during the Gothic period as an alternative to wall-painting, partly because the diminished wall space of the Gothic church offered fewer opportunities for large-scale decoration, but also as the result of a growing desire for realistic representation, better achieved on a comparatively small scale. It often consisted of a set of hinged and folding panels, painted on either side (*see* DIPTYCH; POLYPTYCH; TRIPTYCH). Large polyptychs in elaborate Gothic frames, several storeys high and divided into a number of compartments, formed the retables which gave a special character to Spanish churches. An ancestral form of the easel picture, it ultimately became an oil-painting on canvas let into the wall behind the altar.

Altdorfer, Albrecht (*b.* Ratisbon, *c.* 1480; *d.* there, 1538), Bavarian painter, engraver and architect, a representative artist of the German Renaissance in the Danubian lands, probably the son of the Ratisbon painter, Ulrich Altdorfer. He is noted for his development of landscape as a main pictorial feature, being evidently impressed by the scenery of the Austrian Alps in 1511 when he journeyed down the Danube into Austria; or perhaps by journeys of earlier date. As well as forests and mountains he studied effects of light, and being city architect of Ratisbon his architectural tastes caused him to introduce elaborate buildings into some pictures. His most famous work is the 'Battle of Arbela' (Munich), in which vast numbers of small figures are set in a lake and mountain panorama. His engravings on wood and copper are second only to those of Dürer.

Alunno, Niccolò, *see* NICCOLÒ DI LIBERATORE.

Amberger, Christoph (*b.* Nuremberg, 1500; *d.* Augsburg, *c.* 1561), German painter, trained in portraiture at Augsburg, where he worked and was received into the Guild of Painters in 1530. He was influenced by the Venetian painter, Paris Bordone (q.v.), who was in Augsburg

C. AMBERGER — Portrait of Christoph Fugger—Pinakothek, Munich.

in 1540, and his colour has something of Venetian richness. His principal portrait is that of Charles V, 1532 (Berlin), another notable work being his 'Madonna' in the cathedral at Augsburg.

Ambrosiana, art museum and library in Milan containing a great collection of Leonardo drawings and Raphael's cartoon for the 'School of Athens' fresco in the Vatican.

American Art Museums. New York has one of the great museums of the world in the Metropolitan Museum of Art (q.v.). Other New York galleries are the Museum of Modern Art (q.v.); the Whitney Museum of American Art, specializing in modern American painting and sculpture; the Hispanic Museum of Spanish Art; the Guggenheim Museum (q.v.) and the Frick Collection. The National Gallery of Art (q.v.) is at Washington, D.C. Important collections are widely distributed and include the Boston Museum of Fine Arts (representing Far Eastern as well as European painting), the Art Institute of Chicago (paintings, drawings and prints and representing French, Dutch, Flemish, Italian and American artists), the Fogg Museum, Cambridge, and the Nelson Gallery of Art, Kansas, and there are fine collections at Philadelphia, Cleveland, San Francisco, Toledo, Buffalo (Albright Art Gallery) and Sarasota (Ringling Museum of Art). The Carnegie Institute, Pittsburgh, founded in 1896, holds an international exhibition of painting annually. The Barnes Foundation, Merion, Pennsylvania, founded as a private museum by Dr Albert C. Barnes, is noted for its paintings by modern French artists, Matisse in particular. In Brazil the São Paulo Museum of Art, founded in 1947, comprises a picture-gallery, strong in French Impressionist paintings, schools of art and exhibition halls for contemporary work.

'American Gothic', well-known painting of American rural types and their habitat by Grant Wood (q.v.). It is in the Art Institute of Chicago.

EDWARD HICKS—The Peaceable Kingdom—Charles J. Rosenbloom Collection.

W. HOMER—The Fox Hunt—Pennsylvania Academy of Fine Arts.

JOHN TRUMBULL—The Battle of Bunker Hill—Howland S. Warren Collection.

American Painting. Painting in America begins with the work of artist-explorers and naturalists, of whom the sixteenth-century water-colourist, John White (q.v.), is a notable example. A provincial form of portrait painting, Dutch and English, next developed as the colonies were settled, exemplified by the work of the 'Freake Limner' (painter of the Freake family), *c.* 1670–5, in New England. The early eighteenth century saw a more elaborate reflection of European portraiture in John Smibert (1688–1751), a Scot from Edinburgh who painted in the style of Kneller; Robert Feke (q.v.) and others. In the later eighteenth century London called to American-born painters, e.g. Benjamin West (q.v.) and J. S. Copley (q.v.), but both artists had much influence in America, e.g. on Charles Willson Peale (q.v.) and John Trumbull (q.v.). A native development of great interest in the eighteenth and nineteenth centuries was that of a 'primitive' or folk art, practised by sign painters and other craftsmen and amateurs, Edward Hicks (q.v.) being of note. Romanticism, more particularly in landscape, was a growth of the nineteenth century, first marked by the imaginative paintings of Washington Allston (q.v.), then by a succession of those incited to explore the vast continent artistically, e.g. Thomas Cole, Albert Bierstadt, Caleb Bingham (q.v.), Cole being one of a number of artists painting along the Hudson River and loosely comprised under the title of the 'Hudson River School'. The explorations of landscape painters were complemented by those of the artist-naturalist, Audubon (q.v.). The later nineteenth century saw many artists again turning back to

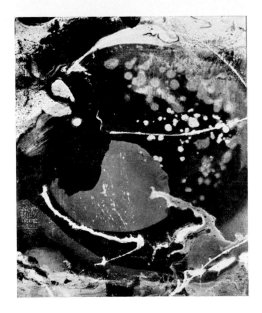

P. JENKINS—Uranus—
Photo: Arthur Tooth &
Sons.

Europe, Rome, Paris or
London, for training,
inspiration or sympathe-
tic environment, James
McNeill Whistler and
John Singer Sargent
(qq.v.) being the out-
standing examples, while
a host of others studied
in the academic *ateliers*
of Munich and Paris.
The high regard in which
Winslow Homer and
Thomas Eakins (qq.v.)
are held stems in part
from their sturdy inde-
pendence of this trend
and their portrayal of American life, and the early twentieth century
saw determined and courageous efforts to look at the United States
in an American way. 'The Eight', a group of 1908 (Henri, Glackens,
Luks, Prendergast, Lawson, Shinn, Sloan, q.v., Davies, q.v.), varied in
their individual styles, combined to make a gesture towards this end.
They were dubbed the 'Ashcan School' in reference to the liking that
appeared for city squalor. It has its continuance in the work of
Bellows, Hopper, Marsh (qq.v.) and others. The realism first applied
to New York expanded into the 'regionalism' of the 1930's, as in the
work of Benton, Curry and Grant Wood (qq.v.). Enthusiasm for a
modern art of international validity was quickened, however, by the
celebrated Armory Show of 1913 and by acquaintance with the School
of Paris in the expatriate 1920's (*vide* John Marin, Marsden Hartley).
The influence of modern European art was intensified by the Second
World War period, which brought many artists to the United States
from Europe, to visit or settle. Chagall, Léger, Grosz, Feininger
(qq.v.). While American art is still eclectic and varies from illustrative
minuteness to broad abstraction, it has in recent years notably
developed in the abstract and expressionist direction, the work, e.g.,
of Mark Tobey (q.v.), William de Kooning, Jackson Pollock (q.v.),
Sam Francis, Paul Jenkins, William Baziotes and Mark Rothko
showing a force and verve that have made their impression on
Europe.

Amigoni, Jacopo (*b.* Venice, 1675; *d.* Madrid, Sept. 1752), Italian
painter of mythological and decorative works and portraits. He
painted in a facile rococo style deriving from Ricci and Tiepolo

[13]

G. BELLOWS—The Cliff Dwellers—Los Angeles County Museum.

which gained him success in Germany, England and Spain, where he finally settled. He decorated some London mansions and produced an altar-piece for Emmanuel College, Cambridge, and a painting of 'Shakespeare and the Muses' for the Covent Garden Theatre.

'Anatomy Lesson, The', title of two paintings by Rembrandt (q.v.), 'The Anatomy Lesson of Dr Tulp', 1632, portrait group of the Amsterdam Guild of Surgeons (The Hague, Mauritshuis), and 'The Anatomy Lesson of Dr Joan Deyman', 1656 (Rijksmuseum), in which the cadaver is depicted with all Rembrandt's realistic power and the contrast of life and death impressively conveyed.

Angelico, Fra (b. Vicchio, Mugello, c. 1386–7; d. Rome, 1455), Italian painter whose real name was Guido di Pietro. In 1407 he entered the Dominican friary of St Dominic, near Fiesole, and was thenceforward known as Fra Giovanni, 'Angelico' being added to

[14]

this description as a term of praise. In full he is styled in Italy 'il Beato Fra Giovanni Angelico da Fiesole', 'the Blessed Brother John the Angelic of Fiesole'. Nothing is known of his training as a painter. He would no doubt share, 1409–18, in the displacement of the brethren at Foligno and Cortona during the papal schism, but returned to the monastery at Fiesole, of which he became prior in 1449. His first known work is the Madonna dei Linaiuoli (commissioned by the linen merchants), 1433 (Florence, San Marco Museum), and another principal undertaking was his frescoes for the monastery of San Marco in Florence on its architectural restoration by Michelozzo, 1436–43, these being intended as spiritual aids to the devotions of the monks. From 1445 he worked in Orvieto and Rome, to which Eugene IV summoned him, an existing chapel in the Vatican decorated by him with scenes from the lives of St Stephen and St Lawrence showing tendencies to a more elaborate style than that of his earlier works. This change may be attributed to his Renaissance surroundings in Rome. His art reflects the pure and devotional character for which he was always esteemed, and retains much that is Gothic rather than of the Renaissance in colour and conception. As a colourist and designer Fra Angelico was an exquisite master, and as well as the frescoes at Florence such works as the

FRA ANGELICO—Altar-piece—Christ Glorified (detail)—National Gallery.

FRA ANGELICO—The Annunciation—San Marco, Florence.

'Annunciation', painted for Fiesole and now in the Prado, and 'Christ Glorified' (National Gallery) show a resplendent beauty.

'Angelus, The', famous painting by Jean François Millet (q.v.), showing French peasants pausing in their work in the fields at the evening hour of prayer. It was painted 1858–9, exhibited at the Exposition Universelle of 1867 as 'L'Angelus du Soir', and is now in the Louvre.

'Ansidei Madonna, The', painting of the Virgin Enthroned, by Raphael (q.v.). It was executed for the Ansidei family of Perugia, whence its title, and was placed in the Servite Church of San Fiorenzo, 1506. It is now in the National Gallery.

Antonello da Messina (b. Messina, ?1414; d. Venice, ?1479), Italian painter of religious subjects and portraits. His youth was spent in Sicily and at Naples, where he seems to have been the pupil of the court painter Colantonio and like his master to have been strongly influenced by the works existing in Naples at that time of Jan van Eyck and Rogier van der Weyden. However he acquired it, he certainly followed the Flemish practice and technique of oil painting. Visiting Venice, 1475–6, he painted an altar-piece for the church of San Cassiano which deeply impressed Giovanni Bellini and others. He had much success in Venice, where he may be said to have initiated the new method of oil painting. His great gifts are seen

[16]

J. F. MILLET—The Angelus—Louvre.

in such boldly effective portraits as the 'Condottiere' (Louvre) and self-portrait (National Gallery) and that little masterpiece, the 'Crucifixion' (National Gallery).

Apelles (fourth century B.C.; *b.* Colophon, Ionia), Greek painter, court artist of Alexander the Great. He studied in the studio of Pamphilos (q.v.) at Sicyon, near Corinth, one of the centres of Greek painting, and was later employed by Philip of Macedon and Alexander, whose portrait Apelles alone was allowed to paint. No trace of his work remains and its nature can only be estimated by his reputation in the ancient world. Realism and an ability to convey three-dimensional effect are suggested by anecdote; thus in his 'Alexander wielding a Thunderbolt' the hand, according to Pliny, seemed to come out of the picture. His 'Aphrodite Anadyomene', showing Venus rising from the sea and wringing her wet hair, was one of his famous works, painted for the sanctuary of Aesculapius on the island of Cos. Augustus bought it from the island and brought it to Rome. Apelles wrote a treatise on painting which has also disappeared and was noted for his skill in using only four pigments—white, yellow, red and black.

[17]

ANTONELLO DA MESSINA—The Condottiere—Louvre.

Apollodoros (late fifth century B.C.), Athenian painter, the master of Zeuxis (q.v.), whose superiority he acclaimed. He introduced some innovations in perspective and seems to have been the first of Greek painters to study light and shade. His works included an 'Odysseus' and 'Ajax struck by Lightning by Minerva', which Pliny admired.

Appel, Karel (*b.* Amsterdam, 1921), Dutch painter of a forceful Expressionist character. He studied at the Royal Academy of Fine Arts, Amsterdam, and was one of the founders of an experimental group (Cobra) linking Dutch, Belgian and Danish painters. He painted a fresco for the Stedelijk Museum, Amsterdam, in 1951, and has exhibited in Paris, London and New York.

Aquatint, form of etching on copper or steel to produce pictures in imitation of sepia, Indian ink or wash drawings. The effect is obtained by biting a plate with acid through a granular ground. It was invented in the eighteenth century and Goya used it in combination with line etching in his 'Disasters of War' and other graphic works. It had a vogue in England in the early nineteenth century, as in the topographical prints published by Rudolph Ackermann, being used for colour as well as black-and-white prints. After long disuse it has had some revival in the twentieth century. The 'sugar process' of aquatint (an old trade recipe) was employed by Picasso in his illustrations to Buffon's *Histoire Naturelle*, 1942. Other artists in both France and England (e.g. John Piper in his *Brighton Aquatints*, 1940) have returned to the process with interesting results.

Arabesque, carved or painted panel in the Roman, Hellenistic or Renaissance style introducing human, animal, grotesque, symbolical or other elements in conjunction with flowing patterns of conventional foliage. In use since the seventeenth century, the term is really a misnomer, no relation with Arab art being involved. *See also* GROTESQUE.

[18]

Arentz, Arent (*b.* Amsterdam, 1585–6; *d.* there before Oct. 1635), Dutch painter who is noted for landscapes with lively groups of figures in the style of Hendrik Avercamp (q.v.).

Armory Show, exhibition held in New York at a regimental armoury in 1913; of historical note as introducing America to the modern developments of European painting. It included a number of works by contemporary American painters and retrospective examples of nineteenth-century French art, but the exhibits which caused great controversy and attracted the widest notice were the products of Fauvism and Cubism. On a larger scale it provides a parallel with the London exhibition of Post-Impressionist art in 1911.

'Arnolfini Marriage, The', famous masterpiece of Jan van Eyck (q.v.), assumed to depict the marriage of Giovanni Arnolfini and Giovanna Cenami at Bruges. It was once in the Spanish Royal Collection but fell into the hands of a French general, came into English possession in 1815 and is now one of the great treasures of the National Gallery. The persons depicted are an Italian merchant from Lucca, trading in Bruges, and his bride, the daughter of another Lucchese merchant. Arnolfini wears one of the tall beaver hats which were a special product of Bruges. Painted on an oak panel, the picture is signed ' Johannes de eyck fuit hic, 1434', which has been taken to mean that the painter 'was here'—as a witness to the

F. GOYA—Caprice—Etching and Aquatint—Victoria and Albert Museum.

A. ARENTZ—Fishermen on the Shore of an Estuary—National Gallery.

marriage ceremony. A statuette of St Margaret and a single candle burning in the chandelier are considered symbolic of the nuptials. The frame of the mirror on the rear wall, a marvel of detail, is painted with scenes illustrating the Passion (Colour).

Arpino, Giuseppe Cesari (*b.* Naples, 1560; *d.* Rome, 1640), Italian painter also called Il Cavaliere d'Arpino. He represents an insipid Mannerism, in contrast to the learned style of the Carracci and the new realism of Caravaggio, though he long outlived these contemporary rivals. He enjoyed great success in his own time in large decorative undertakings under a succession of popes, working also for foreign courts and princes.

Art for Art's Sake, idea that the beauty of a work of art is to be separated from religious, moral and other associations. It gained ground in the nineteenth century and, as a declaration of aesthetic independence, can be traced back to Baudelaire and Théophile Gautier. Its effect can be seen in the 'aestheticism' of the late nineteenth century in England. A useful corrective to the Philistine attitude, it has lost ground in the present century to the extent that art has again been deeply involved with social or psychological issues.

Art Museums and Galleries. The world's public art galleries of today are almost entirely of nineteenth-century or later foundation even when depending on works accumulated in the past. The principal collections in Britain include (1) *London*: British Museum (q.v.); Victoria and Albert Museum (q.v.); National Gallery (q.v.); National Portrait Gallery (q.v.); Tate Gallery (q.v.); Wallace Collection (q.v.); Sir John Soane's Museum (containing Hogarth's 'Rake's

H. MINDERHOUT—Battle of Lowestoft—National Maritime Museum, Greenwich.

Progress' and 'The Election'); Apsley House (Velazquez and other masters); Ken Wood House (mainly seventeenth- and eighteenth-century masters); Dulwich Gallery (a small but important collection, well representing the Dutch School); Hampton Court Palace (q.v.). It was decided in 1960 to create a small gallery at Buckingham Palace for the public exhibition of works from the Royal Collections. (2) *Provinces*: Notable collections are the Birmingham Museum and Art Gallery; the Walker Art Gallery, Liverpool; the Manchester Corporation Art Galleries; Norwich Castle Museum and Art Gallery (for the 'Norwich School'); Temple Newsam House, Leeds (pictures in period setting). The Ashmolean Museum, Oxford, and Fitzwilliam Museum, Cambridge, have excellent picture-galleries, and the former an important collection of old master drawings. The National Gallery of Scotland, Edinburgh, and Glasgow Art Gallery, the National Museum of Wales, Cardiff, and National Gallery of Ireland, Dublin, have collections of wide range. A new gallery at Coventry is the only addition to provincial art galleries subsequent to the Second World War.

The National Maritime Museum, Greenwich, founded in 1934 and occupying the Queen's House designed by Inigo Jones, contains many marine paintings of historical and artistic interest. Example above.

Commonwealth. See COMMONWEALTH ART MUSEUMS.

U.S.A. See AMERICAN ART MUSEUMS.

Europe. See Art Museums under the headings Belgian, Dutch,

[21]

J. ASSELYN—The Angry Swan—Rijksmuseum, Amsterdam.

French, German, Italian, U.S.S.R. *See*, for Spain, Prado, Escorial. Notable collections elsewhere in Europe are at Athens, Budapest, Copenhagen, Oslo, Stockholm and Zürich.

Art Nouveau, the 'new art' of the late Victorian, *c.* 1890, and Edwardian periods. It has two aspects. (1) As a decorative style noted for extravagant curvature it may in part be traced back to late Pre-Raphaelite floral pattern, as in the designs of William Morris, and even more to the 'decadence' or sophisticated adaptation of the style in the work of Aubrey Beardsley. (2) As a desire for a new simplicity in architecture, exterior and interior, with which decorative craftsmanship was, sometimes curiously, combined, it flourished particularly in Austria, Belgium, Britain and Germany, where the influence of Morris and Beardsley was strongly felt and was propogated by the early numbers of the *Studio*, the magazine in the first issue of which Beardsley's work appeared in 1893. In Germany it was called Jugendstil from the Beardsleyesque style characteristic of the Munich periodical *Jugend*, founded in 1896. In its decorative and linear aspect it is an element in the work of many painters and graphic artists of the period, among them **Edvard** Munch, Ferdinand Hodler and even Toulouse-Lautrec, Gauguin and van Gogh.

[22]

Ashcan School, name given to a group of American painters of realist aims in reference to their fondness for depicting city slums and squalor. An original group of eight led by Robert Henri was first active in Philadelphia in the 1890's and later in New York. Their healthy reaction against an artificial idealism had much influence and a number of later adherents included such vigorous artists as George Bellows and Edward Hopper.

Asselyn, Jan (*b.* Dieppe, 1610; *d.* Amsterdam, 1652), Dutch landscape and animal painter, perhaps a pupil of Esaias van de Velde (q.v.), who worked for some time in Rome and in landscape was a follower of Claude. His 'The Angry Swan' (Rijksmuseum) is a notable work, an allegory of the Dutch resistance which, however, may be appreciated as a vigorous study of nature.

Atelier refers not only to the studio of any French artist but to a type of informal academy where students draw from the life, either without tuition, as at the Académie Suisse (much frequented by artists in Paris in the early nineteenth century), or with the limited supervision of a teacher, as at the Académie Julian in Paris, founded in 1860. The *atelier* of the painter Gleyre (which he inherited from Delaroche) is famous as the meeting ground of the young Impressionists-to-be, Monet, Renoir and Sisley, and its casual mode of operation is vividly described in George du Maurier's *Trilby*.

Audubon, John James (*b.* ? Haiti, 4 May 1780; *d.* New York, 27 Jan. 1851), American artist-naturalist, of French parentage and

CONRAD MARTENS—Fort Macquarie, Bennelong Point. National Gallery of New South Wales.

educated in France, having a few lessons from David (q.v.). He came to the United States in 1804, married the daughter of a Pennsylvania farmer, lived in Kentucky and Louisiana and devoted himself to exploring the primeval forests of America and the study of bird life. His *The Birds of America*, 1827–38, is a classic for its 435 plates in which he showed an admirable sense of design and colour. It was followed by *The Quadrupeds of America*, 1845, in which he was greatly assisted by his sons, though *The Birds* remains his main title to fame as an artist. Many original water-colours and sketches are at Harvard and in the collection of the New York Historical Society.

Australian Art. Early settlers in Australia brought with them the English topographical tradition, a few painters in the 1830's and 1840's showing the influence of the English water-colourists, one of the best known being Conrad Martens, a pupil of Copley Fielding, who settled in Sydney in 1835. A break with this colonial tradition came in the 1880's when painters began to practise a form of Impressionism or open-air painting and looked for inspiration to France as well as England. Tom Roberts, Arthur Streeton, George Lambert, Max Meldrum and Elioth Gruner are painters illustrating this phase. From the mid-Victorian period onwards Australian artists have shown a special aptitude for illustration and caricature, Norman

R. DRYSDALE—The Walls of China—Art Gallery of New South Wales.

H. AVERCAMP—Winter Scene—Rijksmuseum, Amsterdam.

Lindsay and Will Dyson giving examples. A new vigour and independence came into Australian art after 1939. An exhibition of modern French art in that year encouraged freedom of style and expression. The large areas which the war made it necessary to traverse opened the eyes of artists to prospects previously unknown to them and produced a new spirit in landscape painting. Among the painters who have made a characteristically Australian contribution to modern art are William Dobell (*b.* 1899), in portraits and landscapes, Russell Drysdale (*b.* 1912), noted for his paintings of the 'outback', Arthur Boyd (*b.* 1920), who has interpreted aboriginal life and legend, and Sidney Nolan (q.v.). Nolan has shown a capacity for investing the early history of the continent with epic and legendary glamour and for vividly representing its strangeness and variety of landscape which has won international notice. Among abstract painters Godfrey Miller (*b.* 1893), John Passmore (*b.* 1904) and John Olsen (*b.* 1928) are notable. Australian art in a variety of forms seems to have come to a flourishing stage at the present time.

Avercamp, Hendrik (*b.* Amsterdam, 1585; *d.* there, 1634), Dutch painter, perhaps the pupil of Gillis van Coninxloo, noted for his small landscapes with a multitude of figures, especially winter and skating scenes (e.g. in the Rijksmuseum and National Gallery). His nephew, Berend Avercamp (1612–79), imitated his style.

[25]

B

Baan, Jan van (*b.* Haarlem, 1633; *d.* Amsterdam, 1702), Dutch portrait painter, who was invited to England by Charles II and painted portraits of the king and queen and their court.

Baburen, Dirck van (*c.* 1590–1624), Dutch painter of the Utrecht School who studied under Paulus Moreelse and worked in Rome, where he was influenced by Caravaggio. He was one of the Dutch *tenebrosi* who brought Caravaggio's emphatic light and shade to Holland.

Bacchiacca (**Francesco Ubertini**) (*b.* Florence, 1494; *d.* 1557), Italian painter, a follower of Andrea del Sarto (q.v.), who painted religious subjects and some scenes of town life.

'**Bacchus and Ariadne**', famous masterpiece of Titian, representing the legendary story of Ariadne, daughter of Minos, King of Crete, forsaken by Theseus on the island of Naxos and there startled by the advent of Bacchus and his crew. Bacchus, who was fabled to have become her lover, gave her the crown of seven stars, appearing overhead in the picture, which after Ariadne's death was changed into a constellation. The car of Bacchus is drawn by cheetahs and he is accompanied by Silenus, a Bacchanal brandishing a goat's leg, and the little faun who drags a calf's head. Painted *c.* 1520 at Ferrara for Alfonso I, the picture is signed 'Ticianus. F'. It was brought to England in 1806 and is one of the great treasures of the National Gallery. (Colour)

Backer (**Bakker**), **Jakob Adriaenz** (*b.* Harlingen, *c.* 1609; *d.* Amsterdam, 27 Aug. 1651), Dutch painter, one of Rembrandt's earlier pupils, the author of many powerful life-size and group portraits which also show the influence of van der Helst. He is well represented

BACCHIACCA—The Baptism of Christ—Staatliche Museum, Berlin.

L. BAKHUYSEN—Dutch Ship Wrecked on a Rocky Coast—National Maritime Museum, Greenwich.

in the Rijksmuseum. His nephew, Adriaen Backer (*b.* Amsterdam, *c.* 1636; *d.* there, 23 May 1684), was a painter of portraits and historical compositions who worked for a long time in Rome.

Bacon, Francis (*b.* Dublin, 1909), British painter, self-taught, whose work is noted for a dramatic and macabre quality. A retrospective exhibition was held at the Venice Biennale, 1954, and paintings by him are in the Tate Gallery, Galleria d'Arte Moderna, Turin, Museum of Modern Art, New York, and other galleries.

Baglione, Giovanni (*b.* Rome, 1571; *d.* there, 1644), Italian painter and art historian remembered mainly by his *Lives of Painters, Sculptors and Architects*, 1642, which includes a prejudiced account of his earlier contemporary, Caravaggio.

Bakhuysen, Ludolf (*b.* Emden, Hanover, 18 Dec. 1631; *d.* Amsterdam, 17 Nov. 1708), Dutch marine painter and etcher, the pupil of van Everdingen (q.v.) at Amsterdam, where his life was mainly spent. He worked for Peter the Great and in his own day was as highly esteemed for 'storms' ('Boats in a Storm' in the Dulwich Gallery being an example) as Willem van de Velde for 'calms'. He is well represented in the National Gallery.

[27]

Bakst, Léon (*b.* St Petersburg, 1866; *d.* Paris, 1924), Russian painter and designer whose real name was Rosenberg. He studied for a time at the Imperial Academy of Arts and was associated with Benois (q.v.) and Diaghilev in the World of Art group and the movement for reviving native Russian art. He exhibited in Paris, 1906, and became famous as designer of settings and costumes for Diaghilev's ballets, *Scheherazade*, 1909, being one of his triumphs. He went to Russia in 1922 but returned soon after to Paris. His brilliant and exotic *décors* for ballet had an influence extending to fashion in dress and interior decoration.

Balance, in a painting the equilibrium between forms or areas of light and shade or colour of unequal extent.

Baldinucci, Filippo (*b.* Florence, *c.* 1624; *d. c.* 1696), Italian art historian, who wrote a history of painters from Cimabue to the seventeenth century (1260–1670) published in six volumes (1681–8, 1767–74), giving main emphasis to Florentine art. He also produced a history of the most celebrated engravers and their work.

Baldovinetti, Alesso (*b.* Florence, *c.* 1426; *d.* there, 29 Aug. 1499), Italian painter and worker in mosaic and stained glass, born of a well-to-do family. Formative influences in his paintings were those

of Domenico Veneziano, Fra Angelico and Andrea del Castagno (qq.v.), and he was an eminent master of the early Florentine Renaissance. His extant frescoes are in imperfect condition owing apparently to the experiments with a painting vehicle (which Vasari describes), but outstanding works attributed to him are the 'Virgin and Child' (Louvre), with its beautiful landscape background, and the profile 'Portrait of a Lady' (National Gallery). Other

A. BALDOVINETTI—Virgin and Child—Louvre.

H. BALDUNG—The Birth of Christ—Pinakothek, Munich.

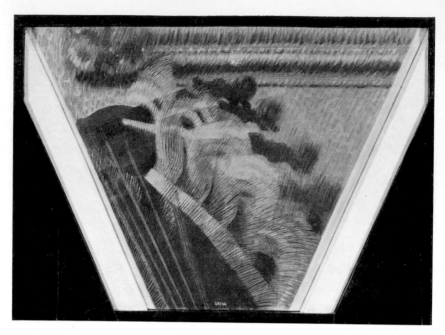

G. BALLA—Rhythm of the Violinist—Estorik Collection.

works are his 'Enthroned Virgin and Child with Saints' and the 'Nativity', 1460, a large fresco in the cloisters of the Santa Annunziata at Florence. He was the master of Ghirlandaio (q.v.).

Baldung (Baldung Grün), Hans (*b.* Gmünd, Swabia, *c.* 1484; *d.* Strasburg, 1545), German painter of religious subjects, portraits and allegories, designer of woodcuts, church windows and tapestries. He was a friend of Dürer, who had some influence on his work and may have been his master during his early stay at Nuremberg, *c.* 1502. His principal religious paintings were his altar-piece for the cathedral at Freiburg, 'The Adoration of the Kings' (Berlin) and 'Crucifixion' (Basel), showing an ornate invention. The fantastic and sombre element recurrent in German art appears in such an allegory as his 'Death and the Maiden' (Basel). His woodcuts are variously signed H. B., H. B. G. and H. G.

Balla, Giacomo (*b.* Turin, 21 July 1871; *d.* 1958), Italian painter, one of the leaders of the Futurist movement. He cultivated its theory of dynamic movement as a visual aim, this being represented characteristically by his 'Dog on a Leash', New York, Museum of Modern Art, in which various phases of movement simultaneously appear.

Bamboccio, *see* LAER, PIETER VAN.

Bandinelli, Baccio (*b.* Florence, 1488; *d.* there, 1560), Florentine sculptor, goldsmith and painter, an imitator of Michelangelo, whom

[30]

he tried to outdo by exaggerations of his style, as in his 'Hercules and Cacus' (Florence, Piazza della Signoria), based on Michelangelo's 'David'. Francesco Salviati (q.v.) and Giorgio Vasari (q.v.) were his pupils.

Barbari, Jacopo de' (*b.* ? Venice, *c.* 1440–50; *d.* Brussels before 1516), Italian painter who in 1500 went to Nuremberg in the service of the Emperor Maximilian and after 1504 worked for the Archduke Frederick III of Saxony and Joachim I of Brandenburg under the name of Jacob Walch. In 1510 he became court painter to the Regent of the Netherlands, Margaret of Austria. His studies of human proportions turned Dürer towards this research, though he seems to have followed Dürer and Cranach in his later style. A notable work is the exquisite still life (considered the earliest of its kind) of a dead bird and pieces of armour (Munich).

Barbieri, Giovanni Francesco, *see* GUERCINO, IL.

Barbizon School, name given to a group of French painters who from about 1830 lived and painted in the village of Barbizon on the borders of the forest of Fontainebleau. Friendship and poverty brought them together and first prompted their 'return to nature'. They were not, however, merely romantic exiles from the city but were devoted to the realistic study of landscape, and in this respect were the forerunners of the Impressionists. Their attitude seems to have been somewhat influenced by Constable and other English landscapists, though Théodore Rousseau, a leader of the group, was strongly influenced by the Dutch. Rousseau, Diaz de la Peña, Jules Dupré and Charles Daubigny (qq.v.) formed the nucleus of the school, and Corot and Millet became associated with them, though Barbizon represents only a part of Corot's career and Millet is distinct from the rest in the emotional significance he sought to attach to the life of the peasant. Daubigny in his practice of *plein-air* painting approached nearest to Impressionism. Among other Barbizon painters were Constant Troyon, Henri Harpignies (qq.v.), Antoine Chintreuil and Charles Émile Jacque. By the middle of the nineteenth century the village, through the prestige of its original settlers, had become a much-patronized resort of artists.

Barker, Thomas (*b.* Pontypool, Monmouthshire, 1769; *d.* Bath, 11 Dec. 1847), English landscape painter, the son of Thomas Barker, animal painter. He studied in Rome, 1790–4, then settled at Bath, being commonly known as 'Barker of Bath', A minor and imitative artist, he was very popular for his 'The Woodman', engraved by Bartolozzi, and his rustic scenes were much reproduced on china and pottery.

Barna (da Siena) (active mid fourteenth century), Sienese painter, a follower of Simone Martini (q.v.). His principal work is the series of frescoes illustrative of the Life of Christ in the Collegiata, San Gimignano, showing great qualities of imaginative design.

Barnaba da Modena (active 1362–83), Italian painter of a Milanese family settled in Modena, who according to records worked at

[31]

Genoa. His painting contains elements of the Byzantine tradition of Venice and of the Sienese School and is notable for its enamel-like brilliance of colour, as in the four scenes showing the Coronation of the Virgin, The Trinity, Virgin and Child and Crucifixion, 1374 (National Gallery).

Barocci (Baroccio), **Federigo** (b. Urbino, 1526; d. there 1612), Italian painter, the son of a sculptor. He studied under Battista Franco and worked at both Urbino and Rome, where he had ecclesiastical patronage. He decorated the palace of the Cardinal della Rovere with frescoes and at the invitation of Pope Pius IV assisted in the decoration of the Belvedere. He developed a soft and mannered style from the study of Raphael and Correggio but combined it with a sense of 'theatre' in which the development of baroque and seventeenth-century religious painting is foreshadowed. His 'Madonna del Popolo' (Uffizi) is a famous and characteristic painting.

Baroque, international development in art, arising towards the end of the sixteenth century and the period of Mannerism in Italy and shading off into the rococo period of the eighteenth century, its highest point being reached in the seventeenth century. The derivation of the term (from the Portuguese *barroco*, a rough pearl) to some extent suggests its calculated irregularities of form, but in essence the baroque was grandiose and theatrical. The description applies equally to architecture, sculpture and painting, and indeed it is in their conjunction that its maximum and most typical effect is to be seen. In dramatic effects of movement in space Michelangelo already forecast the development in the 'Last Judgment'. Caravaggio's oppositions of light and shade contributed to it, though merged with other influences. Rome in the age of Bernini saw its full expansion, which may be studied in the works of such painters as Lanfranco, Pietro da Cortona, Carlo Maratta and Andrea Pozzo: not among the greatest Italian artists but remarkable in their affinity with architecture and sculpture and the feats of illusionist daring they achieved (in baroque as in Gothic the style was more

T. BARTOLI—Virgin and Child with Saints—Galleria Nazionale, Perugia.

important than the man). It cannot, however, be looked on simply from an aesthetic point of view; it is bound up with religious, social and political circumstances, especially the Counter-Reformation movement. Thus its impressive theatricality was propagandist in aim and baroque may be termed an emotional statement of Catholicism. From a secular point of view it was an assertion of princely authority and consequently it is found not only in Italy but in other Catholic and aristocratically governed states, spreading to south Germany, the southern Netherlands, Spain and Portugal and appearing in the New World in Brazil and Mexico. Rubens may be considered a baroque painter, and in Spain Murillo. In the France of Louis XIV the style was also applied to authoritarian service.

Barry, James (*b.* Cork, 11 Oct. 1741; *d.* London, 22 Feb. 1806), Irish painter, encouraged by Edmund Burke. He studied in Italy and acquired large classical ambitions. His principal work was the 'Progress of Human Culture', wall paintings for the Royal Society of Arts, Adelphi, London (1777–83).

Bartoli, Domenico (Domenico di Bartolo) (*b.* Asciano, *c.* 1400; *d.* Siena ?), Italian painter of the Sienese School. His principal work is the fresco paintings in the Scala hospital, Siena, and his art, while

[33]

retaining the charm of the earlier Sienese style, shows the advance of Renaissance science in effects of perspective and realistic expression.

Bartoli, Taddeo (Taddeo di Bartolo) (*b.* Siena, *c.* 1363; *d. c.* 1436), Italian painter of the Sienese School, the last eminent representative of its great medieval period. He worked in the style of Simone Martini (q.v.), mainly in fresco. Examples of his best work are to be found in the Palazzo Pubblico of Siena and the cathedrals of Pisa, Perugia and Genoa. His nephew Domenico Bartoli was his pupil.

Bartolo di Fredi (active 1353 at Siena; *d.* 1410), Italian painter of the Sienese School, who also worked at San Gimignano and Volterra. He is noted mainly for his frescoes in the Collegiata of San Gimignano.

Bartolommeo di Paolo, Fra (also known as **Baccio della Porta**) (*b.* Savignano, nr Florence, 28 Mar. 1475; *d.* Pian' di Mugnone, 31 Oct. 1517), Italian painter of the Florentine School (called 'della Porta' because he dwelt in early life by the gate of San Piero Gattolino. With Albertinelli (q.v.), whose friend and collaborator he became, he was a pupil of Cosimo Rosselli (q.v.). Greatly affected by the preaching of Savonarola, he consigned all his nude studies to the flames and on Savonarola's death became a Dominican monk at San Marco. After

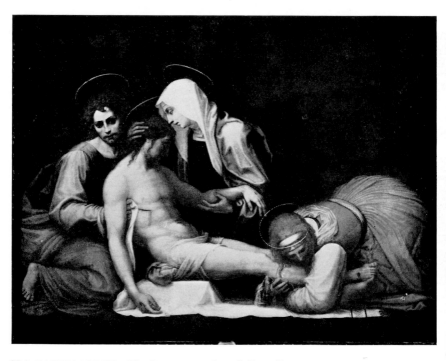

FRA BARTOLOMMEO—The Deposition—Pitti Gallery, Florence.

A. BARYE—Lion and Serpent—Louvre.

an interval due to this disturbance he resumed religious painting and when Raphael visited Florence in 1506 he made Fra Bartolommeo's acquaintance, each artist influencing the other's work. Bartolommeo made use of a life-size wooden lay figure, and to this some attribute the artificialities of pose and lack of real construction beneath the ample draperies of the figures which have also been criticized in Raphael. He again worked with Albertinelli after 1508 and visited Rome in 1514, when he was impressed by Michelangelo and Leonardo, his 'Deposition', 1516 (Pitti Palace), showing Leonardo's influence. Among the works in which he collaborated with Albertinelli are the fresco of the 'Last Judgment', 1498 (Santa Maria Nuova), 'Madonna and Saints' (Pitti) and 'Assumption' (Berlin). Some of his best work is at Lucca, including the 'Madonna della Misericordia' of 1515.

Bartolozzi, Francesco (*b*. Florence, 1725; *d*. Lisbon, 1815), Italian engraver who studied at Venice, worked for a while in Rome and settled in England in 1764, becoming one of the founder members of the Royal Academy. He was noted for his stipple engravings after Cipriani and Angelica Kauffmann. In 1802, at the invitation of the Prince Regent of Portugal, he became head of an engraving school at Lisbon.

Barye, Antoine Louis (*b*. Paris, 24 Sept. 1796; *d*. there, 25 June 1875), French sculptor and painter. He studied painting under Gros (q.v.), and though primarily a sculptor of animals is famous also for his water-colours and drawings of wild animals, especially beasts of prey, in which there is the Romantic energy that Delacroix (q.v.) admired and tried to emulate. He studied lions, tigers and other felines in the

Jardin des Plantes but
represented them imag-
inatively, at liberty and
often springing on and
devouring their quarry.
He frequently used the
forest of Fontainebleau
as a background and
there also observed and
drew deer in their free
habitat. Though he dis-
liked teaching, the post
of Professor of Zoological
Drawing at the Museum
of Natural History in
Paris, 1854, was congen-
ial in its opportunities
for further animal study.
Both the Louvre and
Bayonne are rich in his
water-colours and he
executed some notable
lithographs.

Basaiti, Marco (active
at Venice, 1496–1530),
Italian painter, born
at Venice or Friuli and
perhaps of Greek origin.
His works were usually signed 'Baxaiti'. He was perhaps assistant to
Alvise Vivarini (q.v.), finishing an altar-piece by Alvise in the Frari
at Venice after the latter's death, but his work often approximates
closely to that of Giovanni Bellini. The 'pseudo-Basaiti' (somewhat
between the two) seems a baseless invention of scholarship. There is a
distinct character in his masterpiece, 'The Vocation of St Peter and
St Andrew', 1510 (Venice, Accademia), and another fine work is his
'Descent from the Cross' (Munich).

Bassa, Ferrer (*c.* 1290–1348+), Spanish painter of the early
Catalan School, known by his one surviving work, the fresco decoration of the chapel of the Franciscan convent of Pedralbes, painted for
the King of Aragon, 1345–6. The style of these frescoes (discovered
early in the twentieth century) reveals him as a follower of Simone
Martini (q.v.). It is likely that he was trained in Italy or at all events
was acquainted with Sienese art as represented at Avignon, then the

J. BASSANO—The Good Samaritan—National Gallery.

papal headquarters (where Martini had worked and where he died in 1344).

Bassano, name adopted by a family of painters of the Venetian School (properly called **da Ponte**) from their place of origin on the Venetian mainland. First of them was **Francesco da Ponte the elder** (*b*. Vicenza, *c*. 1475; *d*. Bassano, 1530), a painter of altar-pieces and follower of the Bellini. His son **Jacopo da Ponte** (*b*. Bassano, 1510; *d*. there, 1592), the principal artist member of the family, was the pupil of his father and sent by him to study in Venice. Though he had success there (and Tasso and Ariosto sat to him for their portraits) he returned to work in his native town and introduced its peasants, animals and landscape into his religious compositions, which show great power and originality. In strong effects of lighting he had considerable influence, and El Greco would seem to have been among those who studied his work. Among his best works are the 'Entombment' at Padua and the 'Family Concert' (Uffizi). He had four sons assisting him in the family workshop, which was prolific in output, though many of its products were far below Jacopo's personal standard. **Francesco the younger** (1548–92) worked in the branch of the business in Venice itself. He committed suicide. **Giovanni** (1553–1613) copied his father's paintings. **Leandro** (1558–1623) worked with Francesco in Venice, carrying on the workshop there after his brother's death. He was mainly distinguished as a portrait painter. **Girolamo** (1560–1622) was employed by his father in making copies, though an original work of his own was the 'Virgin and St Barbara' at Bassano.

Batoni, Pompeo Girolamo (*b*. Lucca, 25 Jan. 1708; *d*. Rome, 4 Feb. 1787), Italian painter, the son of a goldsmith. He settled in Rome, first making a living by painting copies. He did some work for Roman churches and painted some academic subject pictures but is best known as a painter of elegant and dignified portraits. The desire for a souvenir of their Grand Tour brought many visitors to Rome to his studio, English visitors among them, whom he would often depict against a background of classical ruins. His only rival for popularity in Rome as a portraitist was Anton Raffael Mengs (q.v.).

Bauchant, André (*b*. Chateaurenault, Indre-et-Loire, 24 April 1873; *d*. Paris, 1958), French 'Sunday painter', self-taught farm labourer who started to draw when a soldier in the First World War. After 1922 he devoted himself entirely to painting, becoming noted for landscapes and flower-pieces seen with a fresh eye and delicate in colour.

Bauhaus, The, celebrated German school of modern design, founded in 1919 at Weimar by the architect Walter Gropius, who was invited by the Grand Duke of Sachsen-Weimar-Eisenach to reorganize art teaching in the city. Its basic assumption was the need for a return to first principles in every form of visual art, this entailing a radical departure in method. Though architectural and industrial design figures largely in the programme, painters of new ideas and modern outlook were enlisted on the staff, notably Kandinsky, Klee and Feininger (qq.v.). In 1926 the Bauhaus was transferred to

A. BAUCHANT—Wild Flowers—Marlborough Fine Art.

Dessau and it was closed down in 1933 under the Hitler regime, but its influence on the teaching of design has since been widely diffused.

Baumeister, Willi (*b.* Stuttgart, 22 Jan. 1889; *d.* there, 31 Aug. 1955), German painter, a leading exponent of abstract art in Germany. He studied at Stuttgart and during the 1920's developed a style of geometric design influenced by his association with Le Corbusier, Léger and Ozenfant. He practised a purely abstract art after the Second World War.

Bayeu, Francisco (*b.* Saragossa, 9 Mar. 1734; *d.* Madrid, 4 Aug. 1795), Spanish painter who worked under Mengs in Madrid and was a prolific decorator of religious and secular buildings, also producing tapestry designs. He was Goya's master at Madrid and in 1775 helped him to obtain his important commission for tapestry cartoons. Goya married his sister, Josefa, in 1773. Bayeu's brother, Ramón (1746–93), was a painter and etcher who assisted Francisco and worked with Goya at Saragossa in 1780, both being then influenced by the rococo art of Tiepolo. Ramón produced both original etchings and etched reproductions of paintings.

Bazille, Frédéric (*b.* Montpellier, 6 Oct. 1841; *d.* Beaune-la-Rolande, 19 Oct. 1870), French painter who studied at the studio of Gleyre in Paris, and there became friendly with Monet, Sisley and Renoir. He is associated with them in the early stages of Impressionist development, but his promising career was cut short by the Franco-Prussian War, in which he was killed in action.

Bazzi, Giovanni Antonio, *see* SODOMA, IL.

Beardsley, Aubrey Vincent (*b.* Brighton, 21 Aug. 1872; *d.* Mentone, 16 Mar. 1898) English pen draughtsman. Influenced successively by the book decoration of William Morris and Burne-Jones, Japanese prints and French rococo design, he produced brilliant work in black and white which in its sophisticated character sums up a trend

A. BEARDSLEY—La Dame
aux Camélias.

of the nineties. His illustrations to the *Morte
d'Arthur*, in which Pre-
Raphaelitism merges
with 'Decadence', were
followed by dazzling
changes of style in the
Yellow Book and the
Savoy and drawings for
Wilde's *Salome, The
Rape of the Lock, Made-
moiselle de Maupin* and
Volpone. His work was
a factor in the develop-
ment of 'Art Nouveau'
and very influential in
Germany and Austria.
He died of tuberculosis.

**Beaumont, Sir George
Howland** (*b*. nr Dun-
mow, Essex, 6 Nov.
1753; *d*. Cole Orton,
Leicestershire, 7 Feb.
1827), English patron of
art and amateur artist, succeeding to an ancient baronetcy in 1762.
The friend of many painters, Constable among them (though with a
prejudice against Turner that can only be deprecated), he is noted
also for his gift of pictures, 1826, to the National Gallery, an important part of its basic collection.

Beccafumi, Domenico (*b*. Siena, 1486; *d*. there, May 1551), Italian
painter of the later Sienese School, the son of a peasant, Giacomo di
Pace, who was employed on the estate of Lorenzo Beccafumi,
Domenico's subsequent patron. Domenico was at one time known as
Il Mecherino from the name of an artist with whom he worked, but
was later known by the name of his patron. He worked mainly in
Siena in both fresco and oil, though a two-year stay in Rome impressed his style with Renaissance mannerisms. The delicate charm
typical of Siena was grafted with the influence of Raphael and Fra
Bartolommeo. He made a beautiful addition to the marble pavement
of the Duomo of Siena and also practised sculpture and produced
chiaroscuro wood-engravings, copperplate engravings and etchings.

Beckmann, Max (*b*. Leipzig, 12 Feb. 1884; *d*. New York, 27 Dec.
1950), German painter, a representative of 'die Neue Sachlichkeit'
(q.v.)—the 'New Objectivity'. He studied at Weimar and in Paris,

M. BECKMANN—Odysseus and Calypso—Kunsthalle, Hamburg.

J. DE BEER—The Madonna enthroned with Saints—Collection of the Earl of Radnor.

and worked in Frankfurt, 1925–33, subsequently in Paris, and Amsterdam, 1938–47, then taught in the United States. Implied social criticism takes on a fantastic and sometimes sinister character in his figure compositions, among the most notable in modern German art.

Beer, Jan de (*b. c.* 1475; *d.* Antwerp, 1536), Flemish Mannerist painter of religious subjects, formerly confused with Herri met de Bles because one of his pictures bore the same device (an owl) by way of signature. A large group of Antwerp Mannerist pictures was assembled under his name but many have been assigned to other artists.

Beham, name of two German artist brothers. **Bartel Beham** (*b.* Nuremberg, 1502; *d.* on a journey to Italy, 1540), painter and engraver, studied with his brother Hans and from 1527 was court painter to Duke William IV of Bavaria, executing a series of portraits of the ducal household. **Hans Sebald Beham** (*b.* Nuremberg, 1500; *d.* Frankfurt, 22 Nov. 1550), painter and engraver, was a pupil of Dürer, noted for his woodcuts, which give interesting detail of modes and manners in his time.

H. BELLECHOSE—Crucifixion and Martyrdom of St Denis—Louvre.

Belgian Art Museums. The Antwerp Museum of Fine Arts was built in 1890 to house the Rubens and van Dyck collections, paintings from suppressed religious foundations and other sources. It is rich also in paintings of the early Netherlandish School and of the seventeenth-century Dutch School. The Palais des Beaux Arts, Brussels, is a comparable collection of mainly Flemish and Dutch art. Both galleries include works by modern Belgian painters. Other galleries of note are the Musée Communal, Bruges, and the Musée des Beaux-Arts, Ghent.

'Belle Jardinière, La', one of Raphael's most famous early 'Madonnas', now in the Louvre, the title deriving from the garden-like beauty of its setting. It is signed 'Raffaello Urb. MDVII' and seems to have been the picture painted in 1507 for Filippo Sergardi of Siena and bought from him by Francis I. It was one of a group painted at Florence, the others being the 'Madonna del Prato' (Vienna) and the 'Madonna del Cardellino' (of the Goldfinch) in the Uffizi Gallery.

Bellechose, Henri (active early fifteenth century; *d. c.* 1444), painter, one of the outstanding 'primitives' of the Franco-Flemish school, who was born in Brabant and worked at Dijon. He was employed by the dukes of Burgundy in succession to Jean Malouel and is said to have completed the painting begun by Malouel, the 'Crucifixion and Martyrdom of St Denis' (Louvre), though the unity of style suggests his sole authorship. Another work attributed to him is the 'Trinity', *c.* 1420 (Louvre).

Bellini, Venetian family of artists, Jacopo Bellini and his two sons, Giovanni and Gentile. **Jacopo** (*b.* Venice, *c.* 1400; *d.* there, 1470–1), the father-in-law of Andrea Mantegna (q.v.), worked at Venice, Padua, Verona and Ferrara, his few surviving paintings being executed in a simple and austere style. He is principally known by the designs for compositions, comprising figures, landscape and

GENTILE BELLINI—Study of a Janissary (Pen Drawing)—British Museum.

[43]

architectural perspectives, in his sketch-books, of which his sons made use, now in the British Museum and Louvre. **Gentile** (*b. c.* 1429; *d.* 1507) was probably the elder son of Jacopo and trained by him. Now overshadowed by his brother, his fame in his own day was no less. He was made Count Palatine by the emperor in 1469 and chosen in 1479 to go to Constantinople to paint portraits for the sultan, Mehmet II (of whom the much-repainted portrait is in the National Gallery). Gentile's great ability in portraiture is shown by the 'Man with a Pair of Dividers' (National Gallery), though the superb 'St Dominic' long attributed to him is now assigned to Giovanni. He painted in 1474 a series of history pictures for the Doge's Palace which were later destroyed, but extant compositions are his paintings of Venetian ceremonies and pageants in which he gives a fascinating view of the city, his 'Procession in the Piazza San Marco' (Venice, Accademia) being famous. A beautiful drawing of a janissary from his Turkish voyage is in the British Museum. His 'St Mark preaching at Alexandria' (Milan, Brera) was left to be finished by his brother. **Giovanni** (*b.* Venice, ? *c.* 1430; *d.* there, 1516) contributed more than any painter of his time to the creation of the great Venetian School, though the numerous works attributed to him and coming from the workshop where he employed many assistants show wide

GIOVANNI BELLINI—The Madonna of the Meadow—National Gallery.

variations of style. A sculptural firmness derived from his brother-in-law, Mantegna, appears in the impressive early work, 'The Agony in the Garden' (National Gallery). Antonello da Messina, who visited Venice, 1475–6, contributed no doubt to the richness of colour and the development of his oil technique (as seen in the famous portrait of Doge Leonardo Loredan, *c.* 1500, National Gallery). One of the great Renaissance compositions is the altarpiece of San Giobbe, 1479 (Venice, Accademia), while in its soft fullness of modelling the 'Madonna degli Alberetti' (Accademia) links Bellini with his pupils, Giorgione and Titian. He worked to an advanced age on paintings for public buildings and churches in Venice and other cities, including numerous versions of the Madonna and Child. Altar-pieces for San Pietro Martire, Murano, the church of the Frari and the church of San Zaccaria are notable, as also is a late mythological composition, 'The Feast of the Gods', 1514 (Washington), in which Titian may have had a hand.

Bellotto, Bernardo (*b.* Venice, 30 Jan, 1720; *d.* Warsaw, 16–17 Nov. 1780), Italian topographical painter, nephew and pupil of Canaletto, whose name he adopted. They were not long associated, though Bellotto worked in a similar if less animated style, more distinctly individual after he left Italy. He painted in Rome, 1740, and after travel in North Italy went to Munich, and from 1747 to 1766 was court painter in Dresden with an interlude, 1759–60, spent in Vienna because of the Seven Years War. Thirteen views of Vienna date from this latter stay. He visited St Petersburg in 1766 and from 1767 was employed by King Stanislaus Poniatowsky of Poland at Warsaw, where he was always known as Canaletto. His carefully detailed views of Warsaw helped in the rebuilding of the city after the Second World War.

[45]

B. BELLOTTO—A View of Dresden—National Gallery of Ireland, Dublin.

Bellows, George Wesley (*b*. Columbus, Ohio, 12 Aug. 1882; *d*. New York, 8 Jan. 1925), American painter and lithographer, who came to New York in 1904 and is noted for pictures of city life, prize-fights and other scenes in which his own energy of method and attitude is associated with violent or dramatic spectacle. Bold and coarse in execution, his work represents a movement towards realism already launched by the Ashcan School (*see* AMERICAN PAINTING). 'The Cliff Dwellers', 1913 (Los Angeles), and 'Stag at Sharkey's' (Cleveland) are characteristic.

Benci, Antonio and Piero di, *see* POLLAIUOLO.

Benois, Alexander (Alexandre) Nicolayevich (*b*, Russia, 1870; *d*. Paris, Feb. 1960), Russian artist of French descent, painter of historical subjects, illustrator, theatrical designer, art historian and critic. With Diaghilev he was one of the founders of the influential art review, *Mir Iskusstva*.

Benozzo di Lese (Gozzoli) (*b*. Florence, *c*. 1421; *d*. Pistoia, 1497), Italian painter known as Gozzoli from Vasari's rendering of his name. As a young man he worked for Ghiberti on the bronze doors of the Baptistery of Florence, but is more especially of note as the principal assistant of Fra Angelico in Rome and Orvieto. He painted mainly in fresco, principal works being his 'Journey of the Magi' (Florence, Palazzo Riccardi), with its portraits of Lorenzo de' Medici, the Byzantine emperor John Palaeologus and others; and a series of scenes from the Old Testament for a wall of the Campo Santo, Pisa (much damaged in the Second World War). The octagonal 'Rape of Helen' (National Gallery) which shows so much charm and skill on a small scale, is no longer definitely ascribed to him.

[46]

B. DI LESE (GOZZOLI)—Procession of the Magi (portraying Lorenzo de' Medici)—Palazzo Riccardi, Florence.

T. H. BENTON—Roasting Ears—Metropolitan Museum of Art, New York.

Benson, Ambrosius (*d.* 1550), painter of religious subjects and portraits, a native of Lombardy but belonging to the Flemish School. He was elected to the Guild of St Luke in Bruges in 1519 and was a follower of Gerard David (q.v.). Works signed with his monogram, AB, are in Belgium (the 'Deipara Virgo'—Antwerp, portrait of Baron Hastings—Brussels), though the number of his pictures in Spain, especially Segovia, formerly caused him to be known as the Master of Segovia.

Benton, Thomas Hart (*b.* Neosho, Missouri, 15 April 1889), American *genre* and mural painter, who studied in Chicago and Paris and was notable among those in the 1930's who protested against the dominance of Paris and the expatriate tendency of American art, upholding 'regionalism' and the 'American scene'. Both mural paintings and easel pictures (e.g. his 'Cattle Loading, West Texas'—Andover, Mass.) show his attachment to native subject-matter.

Berchem (Berghem), Nicholas (*b.* Haarlem, Sept. 1620; *d.* Amsterdam, 18 Feb. 1683), Dutch painter, the son and pupil of Pieter Claesz Berchem. He worked in the studios of several Dutch artists but in subject and style his pictures reveal the influence of Italy and his stay there, his warmly toned views of the Campagna, and of

N. BERCHEM—Italian Landscape with Figures—Reproduced by Gracious Permission of Her Majesty the Queen, Buckingham Palace.

G. BERCKHEYDE—The Flower Market at Amsterdam—Rijksmuseum, Amsterdam.

mountain scenery with ruins and peasants tending their flocks, answering to a contemporary vogue for Italian landscape. He also executed some etchings in the same vein.

Berckheyde, Gerrit Adriaensz (*b.* Haarlem, baptized 6 June 1638; *d.* (drowned) there, **10** June 1698), Dutch painter of town views who studied at Haarlem with his brother Job (1630–93), travelling with him also in Germany. Both settled at Haarlem, of which Gerrit has left charming pictures such as his 'Central Market-place and Town Hall' (Frans Hals Museum, Haarlem); also of Amsterdam.

Berettini, Pietro, *see* CORTONA.

Bermejo, Bartolomé (*b.* ? Cordova, active 1474–94), Spanish painter, one of the most powerful of the Spanish primitives. He worked at Saragossa and Barcelona, producing altar-pieces strongly influenced by Flemish example but with an individual realism. Principal works are the magnificent 'St Dominic of Silos enthroned', 1474–7 (Prado), and his 'Pieta', 1490, in Barcelona Cathedral.

Berruguete, Alonzo (1480–1561), Spanish painter, sculptor and architect, son of the painter, Pedro Berruguete (q.v.). He studied in Italy, gaining some inspiration from Michelangelo, and was appointed court painter and sculptor by Charles V.

P. BERRUGUETE—St. Dominic burning the Books —Prado.

Berruguete, Pedro (*b.* Paredes de Nava, Castile; *d. c.* 1504), Spanish painter who worked in the latter half of the fifteenth century, the first outstanding artist of Castile. He has been identified as the 'Pietro Spagnuolo' who worked at Urbino with the Flemish artist, Joos

B. BERMEJO—St. Michael overcoming Satan—Wernher
Collection.

J. BEUCKELAER—The Cook—Kunsthistorisches Museum, Vienna.

van Wassenhove, for Federigo da Montefeltro. By 1483 he had returned to Spain and painted frescoes (which have since disappeared) for the cathedral at Toledo, afterwards settling, and painting altarpieces, at Avila. His principal work is the series of panels from the Convent of St Thomas at Avila, painted for the Grand Inquisitor, Torquemada, one of the most impressive depicting St Dominic presiding at the burning of heretical books. While Flemish and Italian influence may be detected, his art has an austere dignity belonging to his own country.

Bertram, Master (b. Minden; d. Hamburg, before 1415), German painter, trained in the fourteenth-century School of Prague, who settled at Hamburg, c. 1367, where he had a busy workshop. His principal work is the altar-piece for the Petrikirche, Hamburg, 1383 (now in the Hamburg Kunsthalle), other examples being six paintings in the Musée des Arts Decoratifs, Paris, and a large altar-piece with forty-five scenes of the Apocalypse (Victoria and Albert Museum). His naïve realism shows a tendency towards the Gothic manner.

Beuckelaer, Joachim (b. Antwerp, c. 1535, d. there, 1574), Flemish painter, the pupil of his uncle, Pieter Aertzen. He produced market scenes, kitchen interiors and still life in Aertzen's manner. He took to painting accessories for Anthonis Mor and other artists, an unremunerative labour, and died in poverty.

Bewick, Thomas (b. Ovingham, Northumberland, 10 Aug. 1753; d. Gateshead, 8 Nov. 1828), English wood-engraver who worked at Newcastle. His fame rests principally on his engraved illustrations to the *History of Quadrupeds*, 1790, *History of British Birds*, 1797, 1804, and *Fables of Aesop*, 1818. The lively observation shown in his small vignettes and tail-pieces is accompanied by the exquisite technical

MASTER BERTRAM—The Creation of Beasts (Altar-piece of the Petrikirche, Hamburg)—Kunsthalle, Hamburg.

quality of his 'white-
line' method in which
he set an example to
modern wood-engraving.

**Beyeren, Abraham
Hendrickz van** (*b.* The
Hague, 1620–1; *d.* Alk-
maar, ? 1675), Dutch
still-life painter who worked in Leiden, Delft and Amsterdam. His
art well conveys richness of surface texture, as e.g. in his 'Still Life
with Lobster' (Ashmolean Museum, Oxford).

Biagio, Vincenzo, *see* CATENA.

Bianchi Ferrari, Francesco (*b.* Modena 1460, *d.* 1510), Italian
painter of the School of Modena, whose style is related to that of
Mantegna (q.v.). He is said to have been the master of Correggio.

He executed church
paintings in Modena,
though his 'Idyll' (Wal-
lace Collection), a work
of exceptional charm,
shows him apt to con-
vey the pagan mood of
the Renaissance. *See*
FERRARI.

Bierstadt, Albert (*b.*
Solingen, 1830; *d.* New
York, 10 Feb. 1902),
American landscape
painter, one of the
pictorial discoverers of
mountain and prairie.
Brought by his parents
to America when two

[54]

years old, he returned to Düsseldorf to study, 1853–7, and going back to the United States in 1858 took part in General Lander's expedition across the Rockies to map an overland wagon route to the Pacific. Paintings such as his 'Thunderstorm in the Rocky Mountains' (Boston), presenting vast novelties of scene in a German Romantic style, were long popular. His 'Discovery of the Hudson River' is in the Capitol, Washington.

Bihzad (Kemal ed din) (c. 1440–1527), Persian painter and court artist to Sultan Husein Mirza at Herat and Shah Isma'il at Tabriz. He is the greatest of the Persian manuscript painters, carrying colour harmonies and contrasts to the furthest point of brilliance and showing magnificent qualities of design and composition. Masterpieces by him are the Zafarnama, 1467, and Khamsa of Nizami, 1478, in the British Museum.

Bingham, George Caleb (b. Augusta county, Virginia, 20 Mar. 1811; d. Kansas City, 7 July 1879), American painter of pioneer life. Taken by his parents to the edge of settlement in Missouri, he drew as a boy, had some training at the Pennsylvania Academy of Fine Arts and

G. C. BINGHAM—Fur Traders descending the Missouri—Metropolitan Museum of Art, New York.

BOTTICELLI—The Birth of Venus—Uffizi.

CLAUDE LORRAINE—View of the Tiber (Bistre Wash Drawing)—British Museum.

after a period of travel returned to Missouri to make excellent pictures of trappers and traders, raftsmen and steamboat crews, conveying all the picturesqueness of the frontier in original fashion. 'The Fur Traders descending the Missouri' (New York Metropolitan Museum) is an example.

'**Birth of Venus, The**', 'La Nascita di Venere', painted by Botticelli (q.v.) *c.* 1478 for the villa at Castello near Florence belonging to Lorenzo di Pier Francesco de' Medici. It passed from the *guardaroba* of the Grand Duke into the Uffizi Gallery, Florence, in 1780. The world-famous painting exquisitely interprets the story of ancient mythologists, according to which Venus arose from the sea near the island of Cyprus, to which she was wafted by the zephyrs, being received on the shore by the Seasons (represented by a single figure ready to throw a cloak round Venus's nakedness).

Bissolo, Francesco (active at Venice, 1492; *d.* 1554), Italian painter of the Venetian School, a follower of Giovanni Bellini (q.v.). He made frequent use of Bellini's later religious compositions in versions of the Madonna and Child.

Bistre, warm brown-coloured pigment, generally prepared from beechwood soot and used by many old masters as both a pen line and wash. Claude provides fine examples. *See* opposite page.

Bitumen, medium made from pitch, formerly used to add richness to oil-paintings but liable to ruin a picture because of its radioactive componency. The cracks, blisters and blackened condition of some pictures by Sir Joshua Reynolds, are sad witness to its disastrous effect.

Blake, William (*b.* London, 28 Nov. 1757; *d.* there, 12 Aug. 1827), English painter, engraver, poet and an imaginative genius of a unique kind. Engraving was his chosen means of earning a living. He was first apprenticed to the engraver, Basire, making drawings of

W. BLAKE—The Spiritual Form of Nelson guiding Leviathan—Tate Gallery.

[57]

W. BLAKE—The Wise and Foolish Virgins (Pen and Water-colour)—Tate Gallery.

monuments in Westminster Abbey, thus acquiring early a deep feeling for medieval art. Prints after Michelangelo seem to have influenced him rather as the work of that master influenced the Italian Mannerists, i.e. to exaggerations of proportion and emphasis of design. He had a print-seller's shop with his brother Robert until the latter's death in 1787, and much of his early work was reproductive, after Stothard, Fuseli and Flaxman. The *Songs of Innocence*, 1789, was the first of many beautiful works written by him but never set up in type and commercially published. Text and its decoration were etched in relief and coloured by hand, his devoted wife, Catherine, whom he married in 1782, helping him; the effect being

W. BLAKE—Vignette from the 'Pastorals' of Virgil (Wood-engraving)—Victoria and Albert Museum.

comparable with that of medieval illumination but with its own freshness and originality of design. There followed the long series of 'prophetic' (i.e. 'poetic') books, culminating in the strange, powerful and visually beautiful *Jerusalem* of 1804. The period 1800–3 was a pivot in Blake's career, when he left London to live at Felpham in Sussex near the poet Hayley, hoping much from his patronage. Disappointed in this, he returned to London in 1803 to find little work from the publishers who had formerly employed him. He lived, he said, 'by miracle', but these later years produced his greatest works and saw an unremitting industry. He painted both in water-colour and a modification of tempera (using gum instead of egg as a vehicle) which he called 'fresco', a famous example of the latter being 'Sir Jeffery Chaucer and the Nine and Twenty Pilgrims on their Journey to Canterbury', 1808. In pure water-colour he achieved the final triumph of his designs for the *Divina Commedia*, 1827. In line engraving (in a style happily inspired by Marcantonio) he executed the wonderful 'Illustrations to the Book of Job', 1820. His woodcuts, 1820, for Dr Thornton's edition of Virgil's *Pastorals* inspired the best efforts of the little group of young artists, Samuel Palmer (q.v.), Edward Calvert (q.v.) and George Richmond, who attached themselves to him towards the end of his life.

W. BLAKE—The Morning Stars, from the Illustrations to the Book of Job (Line Engraving)—Victoria and Albert Museum.

Blake's 'visionary heads', e.g. 'The Ghost of a Flea', were a by-product of his imagination, not to be taken as proof of an unbalanced mind. He had a consistent view of art as imaginative expression and not realistic imitation, traceable in his witty epigrams and firmly stated critical utterances and realized in his superb creations.

Blaue Reiter, Der, 'The Blue Rider', group of Expressionist artists in Germany, founded at Munich in 1911 by Kandinsky in close association with Franz Marc and August Macke, taking its name from the title of one of Kandinsky's pictures. It was joined in 1912 by Paul Klee and French Cubists, notably Delaunay, and other artists from outside Germany were associated with 'Blue Rider' exhibitions. Wider in scope than the earlier Expressionist group 'Die Brücke' (q.v.), it was less strongly national and represents an abstract tendency which had much influence.

Bles, Herri met de (b. Bouvines, c. 1480; d. Liège, ? c. 1550), Flemish painter of the Antwerp School, generally identified with Herri Patenier, nephew of Joachim Patenier (q.v.). He worked in Italy, being there known as 'civetta' from the owl with which he signed his paintings, his Flemish name coming from his forelock of white hair. He is noted for small landscapes and religious pictures with many delicately executed figures.

Bloemaert, Abraham (b. Gorkum, 1564; d. Utrecht, 27 Jan. 1651), Dutch painter, who worked in Paris and Amsterdam and later in Utrecht. He produced biblical and historical pictures, portraits, still life and etchings, his style being influenced by the Italian Mannerists and by Caravaggio. He had many pupils, among them Gerard van Honthorst and Jakob Cuyp. Of his six children four were painters or engravers.

T. GAINSBOROUGH—
The Blue Boy—Huntington
Collection, California.

P. BLUME—South of Scranton—Metropolitan Museum of Art, New York.

'Blue Boy, The', portrait of Master Jonathan Buttall by Gainsborough (q.v.), painted *c.* 1770 during the artist's residence at Bath and when he was considerably influenced by van Dyck. This appears in the elegance of style, and Gainsborough, it is to be noted, also chose to paint Master Buttall in the dress of van Dyck's day. It was long supposed that he made blue predominant in the colour scheme to refute a dictum of Sir Joshua Reynolds that blue was unsuitable for this use, but Gainsborough's original use of cool colour seems to antedate and be independent of any such irritant or stimulation. 'The Blue Boy' acquired some of its exceptional fame for nonaesthetic reasons. It was sold from the Duke of Westminster's collection in 1921 for the Huntington collection in California for over £100,000, and is now in the Huntington Library and Art Gallery, San Marino, California.

Blume, Peter (*b.* Russia, 27 Oct. 1906), American painter of imaginative subjects who studied art in New York and derived from Surrealism a style of precise detail applied to, and emphasizing, unreality of subject-matter and strangeness of symbolism. A

[62]

well-known example is his 'South of Scranton', 1934 (New York Metropolitan Museum).

Boccaccino, Boccaccio (*b.* Ferrara, *c.* 1467; *d.* 1524–5), Italian painter, perhaps the pupil of Perugino (q.v.). He worked in Genoa, Ferrara and Venice, where he was influenced by Giovanni Bellini (q.v.), and settled at Cremona, his main work being frescoes in the cathedral there. A beautiful 'Marriage of St Catherine', with a background of the country round Ferrara, is in the Accademia, Venice. His son Camillo and a grandson (also called Boccaccio Boccaccino) were painters.

Böcklin, Arnold (*b.* Basel, 16 Oct. 1827; *d.* San Dominico, nr Florence, 16 Jan. 1901), German-Swiss painter of fantastic and mythological subjects. He studied at the Düsseldorf Academy, stayed in Rome, 1850–7, and in 1893 settled permanently near Florence. A famous picture is the 'Island of the Dead' (Basel), which might be called 'Surrealist' in its macabre suggestion.

Bodegón, in Spanish, literally an inn or eating-house, but applied to a type of Spanish painting which depicted various eatables and still-life properties in a kitchen interior. Such early works of Velazquez as 'The Cook' (National Gallery of Scotland) come under the heading of 'bodegónes'.

Body Colour, *see* GOUACHE.

Bol, Ferdinand (*b.* Dordrecht, baptized 24 June 1616; *d.* Antwerp,

F. BOL—Four Governors of the Leper Hospital—Rijksmuseum, Amsterdam.

G. A. BOLTRAFFIO—Narcissus—National Gallery.

buried 24 July 1680), Dutch painter, a pupil (before 1640) of Rembrandt in Amsterdam and probably the most prolific of his followers in portraiture, his works sometimes being confused with those of his master. In his later style he tended towards a baroque elegance and painted a number of civic group portraits, of which the Rijksmuseum has several examples.

Bol, Hans (*b*. Malines, 1535; *d*. Amsterdam, 1593), Flemish painter of landscape and *genre*, the pupil of his uncles, Jacob and Jan Bol. He worked in Malines and Antwerp and also in Holland. In addition to oil paintings he produced water-colours, miniatures, cartoons for tapestry and drawings for engravers.

Bologna became an important centre of art teaching and theory in the sixteenth and seventeenth centuries. This development was largely due to the Carracci (Annibale, Agostino and Ludovico), who founded their famous academy in 1585. Painters native to Bologna or else trained there in its principles were Guido Reni, Francesco Albani, Domenichino, Guercino, Lanfranco, Sassoferrato and others. *See also* BAROQUE; MANNERISM.

C. BOMBOIS—The Wrest-
ling Match—Photo, Bing.

**Boltraffio (Beltraffio),
Giovanni Antonio** (*b.*
Milan, 1467; *d.* there,
1516), Italian painter, a
pupil of Leonardo. He
came of a distinguished
Milanese family and for
most of his life occupied
various civic offices
in Milan. He painted
religious subjects and
portraits in a hard and
somewhat phlegmatic
style, showing, however,
a faint reflection of the
beauty of Leonardo's
facial type. The 'Casio'
Madonna, 1500 (Louvre),
includes an angel musi-
cian which according to a later tradition was painted by Leonardo
himself.

Bombois, Camille (*b.* Venaray-les-Launes, Côte d'Or, 3 Feb. 1883),
French 'Sunday painter', an ex-roadman, who became noted for the
vivid 'primitive' fashion in which he painted aspects of Paris and
circuses and fairs and their sideshows.

Bone, Sir Muirhead (*b.* Glasgow, 23 Mar. 1876; *d.* Ferry Hinksey,
Oxford, 21 Oct 1953), Scottish draughtsman and etcher, who studied
art at Glasgow. Drawings and etchings of buildings and building
operations in London established his reputation, causing him to be
compared with Piranesi. He produced many drawings of the Western
Front and of battleships as official war artist from 1916 to 1918
(Imperial War Museum and Tate Gallery) and recorded the aspect
of bombed London in the Second World War. Illustrations to *The
London Perambulator*, written by his brother James, are good
examples of his ability as a graphic artist.

Bonfigli, Benedetto (*b.* Perugia, *c.* 1420; *d.* 1496), Italian painter
who worked mainly at Perugia, a follower of Benozzo di Lese (q.v.) in
style. His main work was a series of frescoes for the Priors' Chapel in
the town hall of Perugia, not entirely finished at the time of his death.

Bonifazio di Pitati (*b.* Verona, 1487; *d.* Venice, 19 Oct. 1553),
Italian painter of the Venetian School, possibly a pupil of Palma
Vecchio, to whom a number of pictures after the manner of Giorgione
and Titian have been attributed. The only signed work by him is a

R. P. BONINGTON—A Sea Piece—Wallace Collection.

'Madonna and Child with Saints', 1533 (Venice, Palazzo Reale), but records show that he had a flourishing workshop.

Bonington, Richard Parkes (*b.* Arnold, nr Nottingham, 25 Oct. 1802; *d.* London, 23 Sept. 1828), English painter of landscape and historical subjects. Taken as a boy to France, he studied with the water-colourist, Louis Francia, at Calais and in Paris in the studio of Gros, his precocious talent attracting the admiration of Delacroix. He gained wider notice in the famous Salon of 1824, at which he won a gold medal. He worked mainly in France, where he has always been accounted a leading spirit in the formation of the French Romantic School, though visiting Venice, of which he painted some views in 1826. Beginning with water-colour, he took readily to oils and also executed some brilliant lithographs (q.v.). His historico-romantic costume pieces are of less note than the landscapes to which his sparkling touch gives atmospheric life. The freshness of impression is beautifully conveyed in one of his best oil-paintings, the 'Sea Piece' (Wallace Collection). His short life ended in England, where he had returned in failing health.

Bonnard, Pierre (*b.* Fontenay-aux-Roses, 13 Oct 1867; *d.* Le Cannet, 23 Jan. 1947), French painter and lithographer, a distinguished late follower of the Impressionist tradition. He studied at the Académie Julian at the same time as Maurice Denis, Paul Sérusier, Vuillard and Roussel and was associated with them in the 'Nabi' movement (q.v.). He began with various forms of design for furniture, screens, stage sets and posters, but, influenced by Degas, Renoir, Lautrec and Japanese art, became celebrated for pictures of Paris

[66]

streets and domestic interiors. With Vuillard (q.v.) he is sometimes described as an 'Intimist'. He is equally noted for the large decorative feeling of his work and for warm and beautiful colour. He produced lithographs in colour which are triumphs of graphic art. His free handling of colour was an inspiration to the abstract painters of the post-Second World War period. Bonnard was made honorary member of the Royal Academy in 1940. Works by him are in the principal modern galleries.

Bono da Ferrara (active mid fifteenth century), Italian painter, a pupil of Pisanello (q.v.) at Verona. He also worked in the studio of Squarcione (q.v.) at Padua and contributed a fresco of St Christopher carrying the Infant Christ to the paintings by Mantegna and others in the chapel of the Eremitani at Padua (destroyed in the Second World War). There is a signed work by him, 'St Jerome in a Landscape', in the National Gallery.

Bonsignori, Francesco (*b.* Verona, ?1455; *d.* ?1519), Italian painter of religious works and portraits, influenced by Mantegna in style. There are several of his works in Verona and he was a court painter to the Gonzagas in Mantua from about 1490.

Bonvicino, Alessandro, *see* MORETTO, IL.

Bordone (Bordon), Paris (*b.* Treviso, baptized 5 July 1500; *d.* 19 Jan. 1571), Italian painter of the Venetian School, a pupil of Titian. He was noted for his portraits and in 1538 was invited to France by Francis I, whose portrait he painted. He also worked at Augsburg. In addition to portraits he produced religious, mythological and allegorical paintings. His best and most famous work is 'The Fisherman presenting the Ring of St Mark to the Doge', *c.* 1535 (Venice, Accademia), with its splendid architectural setting adapted from the Doge's Palace.

P. BORDONE—A Lady of the Brignole Family, Genoa —National Gallery.

VELAZQUEZ—Los Borrachos—Prado.

Borès, Francisco (*b*. Madrid, 1898), Spanish painter associated with the modern School of Paris. He studied in Madrid and settled in Paris in 1925, first exhibiting there in 1927. His work has figured in many exhibitions representing the more recent trends of art in France.

Borgogne (Bergognone), Ambrogio (active 1481; *d*. 1523), Italian painter of religious subjects, born at Fossano or Milan. His original name was Ambrogio di Stefano da Fossano. He was probably the pupil of Vincenzo Foppa (q.v.), and though a contemporary of Leonardo was not influenced by him. He spent a number of years on altar-pieces and frescoes for the Certosa, the convent of the Carthusians at Pavia, being assisted by his brother Bernadino. On his return to Milan he painted a series of frescoes for the church of San Simpliciano. Two examples of his work at the Certosa are in the National Gallery.

'Borrachos, Los', 'The Topers', painting by Velazquez in the Prado, executed in 1629. A superbly realistic study of a group of Spanish peasants, its theme was ostensibly mythological and its actual title 'The Triumph of Bacchus'.

Borrassa, Luis (active 1380–1424), Spanish painter of the early Catalan School. He worked for Juan I of Aragon and produced elaborate altar-pieces for churches and convents in Barcelona and its neighbourhood, comparable with those of his contemporaries, Jaime and Pedro Serra (q.v.).

[68]

J. BOSCH—The Temptation of St Anthony—Prado.

Bosch, Jerome (active 1480–1; *d.* 1516), a uniquely individual painter whom it is usual to include with the Flemish School, though he was born and worked at 's Hertogenbosch (Bois-le-Duc), North Brabant. He is otherwise known as Jerome or Hieronymus van Aeken (being a member of an artist family that came from Aix-la-Chapelle). The source of his fantastic art, to which there is nothing comparable in the early Netherlandish School, cannot be exactly stated, though it evidently derives from the satire, humour, popular symbolism and folklore of the later Middle Ages. Thus 'The Ship of Fools' (Louvre) is a decidedly medieval conception and 'The Haywain' (Madrid) is clearly an allegory satirizing the pursuit of wealth and material aims. Well known and highly appreciated during his lifetime and in the sixteenth century, Philip the Fair of Burgundy commissioning a 'Last Judgment' from him and Philip II delighting in his works, Bosch was suspected of heresy by some Spanish writers and unexplained elements in his paintings have led to a modern theory that he was a member of a heretical (Adamite) sect, this mainly referring to his masterpiece, the triptych 'Paradise, Earth and Hell' now in the Prado, though the theory is not supported by any definite evidence. In this marvellous work, however, the strange symbolism, the erotic fancy of its 'Garden of Terrestrial Delights' (q.v.), the extraordinary goblins, the ruins silhouetted in flame, reveal perhaps the most fantastically inventive power in the history of painting. He was acclaimed by Surrealists of the twentieth century as a classic precursor. Historically, however, apart from his marked influence on Pieter Brueghel (q.v.), he stands alone. Some forty paintings remain, the 'Christ Mocked' of the National Gallery being probably an early work, the Madrid triptych and the 'Temptation of St Anthony' (Lisbon) being outstanding late works.

Boscoreale Paintings, Roman mural paintings of the first century B.C. discovered in 1900 in an excavated villa at Boscoreale near Pompeii. The walls were decorated with landscapes and perspectives and also with figure compositions on a large scale. There are sections of the paintings in the Naples Museum and the Metropolitan Museum, New York.

Both, name of two Dutch painter brothers, **Andries** (*b.* Utrecht, *c.* 1608; *d.* Venice, 1649) and **Jan** (*b.* Utrecht, *c.* 1618; *d.* there, 9 Aug. 1652), sons of a glass painter at Utrecht and pupils of Abraham Bloemaert (q.v.). They worked together in Rome and at Venice, where Andries was drowned, falling, it is said, from his gondola after a convivial party. While Andries was interested in peasant life, Jan specialized in landscape, being influenced by the golden light of Claude. He returned to Holland and became head of the Painters' Guild at Utrecht.

Botticelli, Sandro (more properly **Alessandro di Mariano dei Filipepi**) (*b.* Florence, *c.* 1445; *d.* there, 17 May 1510), Italian painter of the Florentine School, perhaps the most poetic of the great Renaissance artists. The nickname 'Botticello', given to his brother Giovanni, who seems to have taken charge of the boy, accounts for the name by which he is best known. From the goldsmith's shop of his

J. BOTH—Figures in the Forum Romanum—Rijksmuseum, Amsterdam.

S. BOTTICELLI—Venus and Mars—National Gallery.

brother Antonio he seems to have gone to the studio of Fra Filippo Lippi (q.v.), whom he imitated in his early work. He had his own studio when little over twenty and profited by the study of other masters, Verrocchio and Antonio Pollaiuolo (qq.v.) especially, as may be seen in his 'Fortitude', 1470 (Uffizi), and 'Judith', c. 1472 (Uffizi). In 1475 he entered the service of the Medici and his art shows the effect of the humanism and classical culture of this environment. His 'Adoration of the Magi', c. 1477 (Uffizi), contains a number of Medicean portraits (as well as his own), and soon after he painted for Lorenzo, son of Pierfrancesco de' Medici, his famous allegory, 'Primavera' (Uffizi) (q.v.), representing the seaons. The years 1481–2 were spent in Rome, where he worked with other artists on the decoration of the Sistine Chapel, to which he contributed frescoes of the Life of Moses, the Destruction of Korah, Dathan and Abiram, and the Temptation of Christ by Satan. Prolific years followed in Florence, both religious and pagan subjects occupying him, including his Madonna of the Magnificat, c. 1485, 'Pallas and the Centaur' and the famous 'Birth of Venus', c. 1485 (Uffizi) (q.v.). A change is perceptible in his work from about 1490, a religious disquiet almost certainly produced or intensified by the exhortations of Savonarola. He seems to have consigned a number of his pagan subjects to the reformer's bonfire, and the triumph of religious enthusiasm over the happy sensuousness of the Renaissance can subsequently be traced in his work. He made his series of illustrations for Dante's *Inferno* (Berlin and Vatican) between 1492 and 1497, 'The Calumny of Apelles', 1495 (Uffizi), being his last secular masterpiece. The year 1498, in which Savonarola was put to death, saw the production of his tragically passionate 'Pietà' (Munich), and in the great 'Nativity' of 1500 (National Gallery) (signed with an inscription of exalted incoherence) he returned impressively to the medieval spirit and conception. His last works express melancholy and suffering with dramatic intensity, as in the 'Crucifixion' (Cambridge, U.S.A., Fogg Museum) and the four scenes from the life of St Zenobius (Dresden, London, New York). In the *tondo* of Madonna and Child, as well as in his superb allegories, Botticelli creates a distinct type of human beauty to the exquisite character of which some personal sadness of outlook seems to be transmitted. In composition and detail he shows an unrivalled poetic invention. The delicacy of his art (which imitators at various periods have vainly tried to recapture) is accompanied by a dynamic linear energy and dramatic power.

Botticini, Francesco (*b.* Florence, *c.* 1446; *d.* 1497), Italian painter and craftsman, who is assumed to have been a pupil of Neri di Bicci. A number of works imitating Florentine contemporaries, including Botticelli, have been attributed to him. The 'Assumption of the Virgin' (National Gallery) ascribed to him illustrates the heretical view expressed in a poem by the donor, Matteo Palmieri, that human souls are the angels who remained neutral when Lucifer fell, a number of saints (having merited salvation) being represented as returned to angelic status.

S. BOTTICELLI—Abbondanza (Chalk Drawing)—British Museum.

S. BOTTICELLI—Mystic Nativity—National Gallery.

F. BOUCHER—Madame de Pompadour—National Gallery of Scotland.

Boucher, François (b. Paris, 29 Sept. 1703; d. there, 30 May 1770), French painter and decorative artist. He studied under François Lemoyne and worked for the engraver, Laurent Cars, first earning his living by making engravings after Watteau. He won the first prize of the Académie in 1723 but made the customary visit to Italy rather late, 1729–31, admiring there the art of Pietro da Cortona and Tiepolo. On his return he was made Academician and rose to be the director of the Académie in 1765. He was appointed first painter to Louis XV on the death of van Loo and was also chief designer to the Royal Beauvais Tapestry works, designer for the Opéra and the favourite artist of Mme de Pompadour, whom he taught drawing and of whom he made a number of portraits, notable being the full-length in the Wallace Collection (where also are the panels of gods and goddesses he designed for her boudoir). Stemming from Watteau and perhaps owing something to his Italian contemporary Tiepolo, his art is the triumph of the rococo style in France, his frivolous mythologies and artificial pastorals being skilfully planned in relation to the Louis Quinze interior and expressing the spirit of the age in terms of decoration. Criticized by Diderot and others since for a want of

[75]

F. BOUCHER—Venus and Cupid with Doves—Wallace Collection.

L. E. BOUDIN—The Pier at Trouville—Glasgow Art Gallery.

J. BOURDICHON—The Angel appears to the Shepherds (Miniature from the 'Grandes Heures d'Anne de Bretagne', 1508)—Bibliothèque Nationale, Paris.

seriousness, he was capable of figure painting (like that of Louis XV's mistress, Louise O'Murphy) of a quality that aroused the admiration of Renoir. Fragonard was among his many pupils.

Boudin, Louis Eugène (*b.* Honfleur, 12 July 1824; *d.* Deauville, 8 Aug. 1898), French landscape and marine painter, the son of a ship's captain at Honfleur. He was encouraged to paint by artists of the Barbizon School, Isabey, Troyon and Corot (qq.v.) contributing to his development, and worked mainly on the Normandy coast and in Brittany, rendering vividly the breezy atmosphere and restless sea and sky of the region round the mouth of the Seine and Deauville and Trouville with their Second Empire and Victorian visitors. He initiated Claude Monet (q.v.) in open-air painting in 1858 and with Jongkind (q.v.), the friend of both, thus has a place in the development of Impressionism (he contributed to the first Impressionist exhibition in 1874). A typical and delightful work is his 'Pier at Trouville', 1869 (Glasgow).

Bourdichon, Jean (active late fifteenth–early sixteenth century), painter and miniaturist of the Loire School, a follower of Jean Fouquet (q.v.) in style and working as Fouquet did for Louis XI. He was court painter also to Louis XII and Francis I. His principal work as a miniaturist was a Book of Hours for the wife of Louis XII, Anne of Brittany (Bibliothèque Nationale). A triptych in the Pinacoteca at Naples is one of the few paintings attributed to him.

Bourdon, Sébastien (*b.* Montpellier, 2 Feb. 1616; *d.* Paris, 8 May

S. BOURDON—The Return of the Ark from Captivity—National Gallery.

1671), French history painter and painter of landscape. He stayed in Rome, 1634–7, and seems to have been employed in painting pastiches after such contemporaries as Pieter van Laer, Claude and Poussin. Contrasting trends appear in his work, one aspect of it being scenes of popular life ('Bambochades') and the other decorative composition derived from Poussin, the latter becoming dominant. He worked in Sweden, 1652–4, but otherwise mainly in Paris and is well represented in the Louvre.

Bouts, Dieric (Dirck) (*b.* probably Haarlem, *c.* 1410; *d.* Louvain, 6 May 1475), Netherlandish painter, probably identical with Dirck van Haarlem, who settled at Louvain and worked there with his two sons, Dieric and Aelbrecht, and in some association with another painter family of Louvain, Hubrecht Stuerbout and his sons. His style reflects that of Rogier van der Weyden (q.v.) and the landscape backgrounds of his religious pictures show much originality and distinction, as in his 'Adoration of the Kings' (Munich, Pinakothek). Principal authentic works are 'The Last Supper', *c.* 1463, and the 'Martyrdom of St Erasmus', datable before 1466, for St Peter's, Louvain, and the panels with life-size figures for the Hôtel de Ville, Louvain (now in the Brussels Gallery), representing the virtue of justice as exemplified in a judgment of Otho III. Bouts's Christian name, variously spelt, also appears in French form as Thierry.

D. BOUTS—Virgin and Child—National Gallery.

Bramantino (*b.* Milan, ?*c.* 1450; *d.* 1536), Italian painter whose real name was Bartolommeo Suardi, a pupil of Foppa (q.v.) and follower of Bramante, either as painter or architect, whence his nickname. In 1525 he was made architect and painter to Francesco Sforza II. His religious paintings include the 'Holy Family' and 'Crucifixion' (Milan, Brera) and 'Pietà' in the church of San Sepolcro.

Brangwyn, Sir Frank (*b.* Bruges, 12 May 1867; *d.* Ditchling, 11 June 1956), decorative artist, born of Welsh parents. After an early period in the William Morris workshops he went to sea, Eastern voyages contributing to the sense of colour which attracted attention to his early work. He became highly successful and internationally esteemed as a mural painter, principal works being in the Royal Exchange, Lloyd's Registry and Skinner's Hall in London; the Court House, Cleveland, Ohio, Missouri State Capitol and the Rockefeller Centre, New York; while his British Empire panels, intended for the House of Lords but not so used, are now in the Guildhall, Swansea. An immensely prolific worker, he produced also many easel pictures in oils, water-colours, etchings, lithographs, woodcuts, posters and designs for pottery, furniture and textiles. There are Brangwyn museums at Bruges (about 400 works), Orange (about 300 works), and had it not been for the destruction by fire of 90 works in the Matsukata Collection, Tokyo would have had a similar museum.

Braque, Georges (*b.* Argenteuil, 13 May 1881; *d.* Paris, 1 Sept. 1963), one of the most eminent of modern French painters, with Picasso inventor of Cubism (q.v.). His father was a contractor for house-painting and Braque in boyhood observed his father's workmen's mode of mixing colours, 'graining' and 'marbling' to fruitful effect. He went to Paris to study art in 1904 and painted in the Fauve manner with free, bright colour until, under the stimulus of Cézanne and in association with Picasso, he evolved the 'new pictorial language' of Cubism. He

SIR F. BRANGWYN—Study of a Rhinoceros—Swansea Art Gallery.

G. BRAQUE—Still Life—Photo: Arts Council.

seems to have been the first to exhibit an entirely Cubist picture—at the Salon des Indépendants, 1908. His work shows the two stages of the movement, first 'analytic' and then 'synthetic', but believing that 'in art progress does not consist in extension but in knowledge of limits', he confined himself, unlike his restless colleague Picasso, to consolidating discovery. In the still lifes for which he is famous he shows how from some quite simple object such as a dish of fruit a whole set of novel relationships and harmonies can be derived. He has also produced designs for ballets, etched illustrations for Ambroise Vollard's fine editions, colour lithographs and incised plaster panels for decorative purpose. Works by him are in the world's principal modern galleries. (Colour)

Brekelenkam, Quirin (*b.* Zwammerdam, 1620+; *d.* Leyden, 1658), Dutch painter, probably a pupil of Gerard Dou, who became a member of the painters' guild at Leyden in 1648. He is noted for scenes of everyday life, such as the 'Old Woman by the Fire' (Prado) and the 'Confidential Talk' (Rijksmuseum).

Brera Gallery, Milan, the picture-gallery of the Brera Palace (badly damaged in 1943 but since reconstructed). It contains Raphael's 'Sposalizio', works by many Venetian masters, Tintoretto, Giovanni Bellini, Veronese, Tiepolo, Lotto, Crivelli, and by the Lombard followers of Leonardo, Luini, Boltraffio, Solario.

Brett, John (*b.* Liverpool, 1831; *d.* London 18 Jan. 1902), English

J. BRETT—The Stonebreaker—Walker Art Gallery, Liverpool.

landscape and marine painter, noted for early, minutely detailed pictures inspired by Pre-Raphaelite principles, e.g. 'The Stonebreaker' (Walker Gallery, Liverpool), highly praised by Ruskin. Later he specialized in Cornish seascapes, exhibiting regularly at the Academy and becoming A.R.A. in 1881.

Breuil, Henri (*b.* Mortain, 1877; *d.* 14 Aug. 1961), French archaeologist, an authority on palaeolithic cave painting and engraving. He studied archaeology under Father J. Guibert at Issy seminary. In 1902 he discovered the two famous caves of Font-de-Gaume and Les Combarelles, where he began the copies of cave art in which he showed great powers of interpretative draughtsmanship. His pastels of the Altamira paintings are celebrated and his record of Altamira was followed by detailed studies and published accounts of prehistoric works in France, Spain, China, Ethiopia and South Africa, pursued in the intervals of his work as professor at the Institute of Human Palaeontology in Paris and at the Collège de France. He was awarded the gold medal of the Society of Antiquaries of London in 1937. After the Second World War he closely studied and made copies of prehistoric art in South Africa.

Bril (Brill), name of two Flemish painter brothers, **Matheus** (*b.* Antwerp, 1550; *d.* Rome, 1584) and **Paul** (*b.* Antwerp, 1554; *d.* Rome, Oct. 1626). Both as young men studied and worked in Rome, painting landscapes and large frescoes, those of Matheus for the Vatican being completed after his death by his brother. Paul in particular brings us

P. BRIL—Italian Mountain Landscape—Glasgow Art Gallery.

THE CHICHESTER ROUNDEL (early English Gothic)—Bishop's
Palace, Chichester—Photo: Victoria and Albert Museum,

to that meeting point between the Flemish style of landscape and
that developed in Italy by Annibale Carracci and Domenichino
(qq.v.), from which stemmed the classical landscape of Poussin and
Claude (qq.v.). His small landscapes on copper influenced those of
Adam Elsheimer (q.v.), with whom he is to be associated in this
development.

British Museum, London, contains, together with its great collection of antiquities, magnificent collections of pictorial art, including
(1) Western illuminated manuscripts, among which are the Lindisfarne Gospels, the Luttrell Psalter, Queen Mary's Psalter, Bedford
Book of Hours, etc; (2) oriental manuscripts, Persian and Indian;
(3) one of the finest European collections of Chinese and Japanese
painting and graphic art; (4) a unique collection of prints and drawings of all the Western schools, including examples of the work of
Michelangelo, Leonardo, Rembrandt, Dürer, Watteau and a
splendid collection of Turner water-colours; (5) early illustrated
books.

British Painting is regarded as beginning to all intents and purposes
in the Tudor period, after the Reformation and the establishment of
a national Church had made a decisive break with medieval tradition.

[83]

W. BAKER—Fresco, Eton College—Photo: 'Country Life'.

A. DEVIS—The Thomlinson Family—Photo: Tooth Gallery.

MEDIEVAL ENGLISH PAINTING (Artist Unknown)—Lady Margaret Beaufort—National Portrait Gallery.

Few examples survive of medieval painting apart from the illuminated manuscripts produced in the monastic centres of Winchester, Canterbury and St Albans, among the few being the roundel of Virgin and Child, *c.* 1260 (Bishop's Palace, Chichester), and the fifteenth-century wall-paintings by William Baker in Eton College Chapel. The Tudor art was portraiture, and many foreign practitioners were called in, Hans Holbein at the court of Henry VIII being followed by Hans Eworth (active 1549–74), the Dutch painter, Cornelis Ketel (1548–1616), the Flemings Marcus Gheeraerts, father (*c.* 1510–90) and son (1561–1609), and the Italian Federigo Zuccaro (q.v.). An exquisite and native Elizabethan art, however, is that of the miniaturists Nicholas Hilliard, Isaac Oliver and his son Peter Oliver. The Stuart, Commonwealth and Restoration periods saw the continuance of foreign infiltration with van Dyck from Antwerp, Daniel Mytens and Sir Peter Lely from Holland, and Sir Godfrey Kneller from Germany. Native painting is represented by William Dobson, Robert Walker, John Riley and Robert Streater. After Kneller, however, British painting came into its own in the great eighteenth-century period of portraiture, *genre* and landscape. The 'conversation piece' as practised by Highmore, Hayman and Devis became a great picture of social life with William Hogarth. Portraiture had many eminent exponents—Hogarth, Gainsborough, Reynolds, Romney, Allan Ramsay, Raeburn, Hoppner, Opie, Sir Thomas Lawrence. Landscape, the great glory of British painting, was represented by Gainsborough, Richard Wilson, Crome (*see also* NORWICH SCHOOL), Constable and Turner. A rural and sporting *genre* is exemplified by George Morland, George Stubbs, James Ward and others. J. R. Cozens, Thomas Girtin and Turner mark the rise of a unique school of water-colour (q.v.). Blake and Fuseli in imaginative art and Rowlandson and Gillray in satire and humorous invention were also remarkable. In the nineteenth century after Wilkie and

ELIZABETHAN PAINT-
ING—Queen Elizabeth I—
the 'Rainbow Portrait'—
Collection of the Marquess
of Salisbury.   86

H. EWORTH—Portrait of
Lady Dacre—National
Gallery of Canada.

I. HITCHENS—Damp Autumn—Tate Gallery.

Etty came the Pre-Raphaelites (*see* PRE-RAPHAELITE). At the end of the nineteenth century British art was much influenced by France. *See* CAMDEN TOWN GROUP; NEW ENGLISH ART CLUB. Notable painters from that time onward are Wilson Steer, Walter Sickert, Augustus John, Frank Brangwyn, Matthew Smith, Wyndham Lewis, Stanley Spencer and Paul Nash. A form of new realism is to be found in the Euston Road School (q.v.), while abstract, Surrealist and Expressionist tendencies are variously to be found in recent British painting. Formal abstraction is represented notably by Ben Nicholson and by Victor Pasmore in his later productions. Other artists, abstract in trend, are Ivon Hitchens, William Scott, William Gear, Ceri Richards and Alan Davie. The sinister atmosphere of Surrealism reappears in the work of Francis Bacon, while Graham Sutherland has found that movement a stimulus to an imaginative interpretation of nature. In an intensified realism, Lucien Freud and John Bratby may be considered Expressionists. Sir William Coldstream, Carel Weight and Ruskin Spear are distinguished among painters of more orthodox style.

Broederlam, Melchior (active 1381–1409), painter of the Franco-Flemish School, born at Ypres, where he mainly worked. He became court painter and *valet de chambre* to the Duke of Burgundy, Philip the Bold, in 1385. His principal remaining work is the panels of an altar-piece commissioned by the duke for the Chartreuse of Champmol in 1392. The Annunciation and Visitation and the Presentation in the Temple and Flight into Egypt are the subjects of the panels now in the Musée de Dijon, in which Flemish realism, Parisian refinement and a certain Sienese influence are exquisitely combined.

Bronzino, Il (Agnolo di Cosimo di Mariano) (*b.* Monticelli, 17 Nov.

[87]

1503; *d*. Florence, 23 Nov. 1572), Italian painter of the Florentine School, a pupil of Jacopo da Pontormo (q.v.). He was employed as portrait painter at the court of Cosimo I, Duke of Tuscany, posing his sitters with a somewhat stiff dignity. One of his best portraits is that of Don Garzia de' Medici as a child holding a bird (Uffizi). His allegory 'Venus, Cupid, Folly and Time' (National Gallery) is an exceptional work, a 'thing of singular beauty' in Vasari's words, in its elaborately planned composition and bold contrasts of pale flesh tones with brilliant if metallic colour.

Brouwer (Brauwer), Adriaen (*b*. Oudenaerde, 1605; *d*. Antwerp, Jan. 1638), brilliant Flemish painter of *genre* who worked both in Flanders and Holland and was equally esteemed by Flemish and Dutch masters, both Rembrandt and Rubens possessing examples of his work. Beginning with highly coloured pictures of peasant scenes in the Brueghel manner, he progressed towards a more concentrated realism and simplicity of tone and colour, in this

BRONZINO—Venus, Cupid, Folly and Time—National Gallery.

the influence of Hals, whom he knew at Haarlem, being a factor. It is believed he led a dissolute life but this is not to be confused with the art and unflinching observation of his tavern scenes and such works as 'A Quarrel between Two Peasants' (Dresden) and 'Spanish Soldiers playing Dice' (Munich). He settled at Antwerp, and had both Dutch and Flemish followers, Ostade and Teniers (qq.v.) among them.

Brown, Ford Madox (*b.* Calais, 16 April 1821; *d.* London, 6 Oct. 1893), English painter, who studied in Belgium (at Antwerp under Wappers), worked for three years in Paris and was somewhat influenced by Overbeck and the German Pre-Raphaelite circle whom he met when visiting Rome in 1845. He settled in London and Rossetti was his pupil in 1848. Though not a member of the English Pre-Raphaelite Brotherhood he was drawn by Rossetti into its orbit and 'The Last of England' (Birmingham) and 'Work' (Manchester) reflect Pre-Raphaelite enthusiasms. His paintings for the Town Hall, Manchester, 1878–93, were a notable effort to interpret local and social history. His later subject pictures, romantically historico-literary, are not always harmonious in design and colour but as a colourist he excels in some small landscapes.

Brücke, Die, group of German Expressionist painters formed in Dresden in 1905, influenced by the Post-Impressionism of France but also by old German woodcuts and the discovery of primitive and Negro art. Ernst Ludwig Kirchner (q.v.) took the lead in its formation, other prominent members of the group being Erich Heckel, Karl Schmidt-Rottluff, Emil Nolde (qq.v.) and Max Pechstein. The group was dissolved in 1913 but largely contributed to spreading a ferment of ideas in German art and is historically linked with the 'Blaue Reiter' group (q.v.) of Munich.

Brueghel (Bruegel), Pieter the Elder (*b.* Brueghel, *c.* 1529; *d.* Brussels, 5 Sept. 1569), great Flemish painter and first of a long-continuing family succession of painters. Born at a village near

A. BROUWER—Portrait of Jan de Dood—Museum Boymans-van Beuningen, Rotterdam.

F. MADOX BROWN—The Last of England—Birmingham Art Gallery.

Bruges, he became pupil assistant of Pieter Coecke at Antwerp, paid a visit to Italy in 1552 (being impressed rather by Alpine landscape than Italian art) and on his return to Antwerp worked for the engraver Jerome Coecke, designing satirical and allegorical prints. These and some of his paintings, such as 'The Fall of the Rebel Angels' (Brussels), borrow fantasy from Jerome Bosch (q.v.), but between 1558 and 1569 (the date of his death) his personal genius was expressed in a series of masterpieces in which both peasant life and landscape have their part. They include such superb works as 'The Peasant Dance' and 'The Wedding Feast' (Vienna), the 'Massacre of the Innocents' (Vienna) and 'The Census of Bethlehem' (Brussels) —these perhaps a covert reference to Alva's reign of terror in the Netherlands—and the series of the months, of which five remain, including the splendid snow scene 'February' (Vienna). One could add a dozen more incomparable paintings. He himself spelt his name 'Bruegel'. His nickname 'Peasant Brueghel' refers to his subjects and not to the cultivated humanist of the urban Netherlands himself.

His eldest son, **Pieter Brueghel the Younger** (*b.* Brussels, *c.* 1564; *d.* Antwerp, 1638), known as 'Hell' Brueghel from the subjects of his pictures, copied many of his father's works in a more primitive style. His second son, **Jan** ('**Velvet**') **Brueghel** (*b.* Brussels, 1568; *d.* Antwerp, 13 Jan. 1625), painted flowers, fruit, animals, birds and landscape with a delicate finish that inspired a number of little masters, and was friend and collaborator of Rubens, the 'Paradise' (Mauritshuis) being a fine example of their collaboration. The sons of Jan and Pieter II, less distinguished in art, bring the painting history of the family down to the beginning of the eighteenth century.

Brygos (early fifth century B.C.), Greek vase painter in the red-figured style, with an exceptionally vigorous and decorative line. A fine work is the cup (Louvre) showing Helen's arrival at Troy.

Buffalmacco, Buonamico (*b.* Florence, 1262; *d.* 1340), Italian painter of the early Florentine School, a disciple of Andrea Tafi. He painted frescoes in the old Badia Church in Florence but is better known, from Boccaccio, as a wit and practical joker than as an artist.

P. BRUEGHEL (the Elder)—The 'Dulle Griet'—Musée Mayer van de Bergh, Antwerp.

P. BRUEGHEL (the Elder)—The Hunters' Return—February—Kunsthistorisches Museum, Vienna.

P. BRUEGHEL (the Elder)—The Peasant Dance—Kunsthistorisches Museum, Vienna.

J. BRUEGHEL—The Senses of Hearing, Taste and Touch—Prado.

Buffet, Bernard (*b*. Paris, 10 July 1928), French painter who achieved a remarkable success after the Second World War in landscapes and still lifes with a strongly marked linear style.

Buonaccorsi, Pietro, *see* PERINO DEL VAGA.

Buonconsiglio, Giovanni (active 1495; *d*. 1535–7), Italian painter of the School of Vicenza, called Il Marescalco. He worked both at Vicenza and in Venice, where he decorated a number of churches in association with Antonello da Messina (q.v.). He was influenced by Montagna and Bellini.

Burchfield, Charles Ephraim (*b*. Ashtabula, Ohio, 9 April, 1893; *d*. Gardenville, N.Y., 10 Jan. 1967), America painter, noted for his pictures, mainly in water-colour, of Middle West life and nature: a 'regionalist', though some of his works have a visionary character.

Burgkmair, Hans (*b*. Augsburg, 1473; *d*. 1531), German painter and wood-engraver, pupil of Martin Schongauer, friend of Dürer and father-in-law of Hans Holbein the Elder (qq.v.). As a painter he enriched his colour by the study of the Venetians, and his 'Esther in the House of Ahasuerus' (Munich) is an elaborate attempt to adapt an Italian type of composition, with profuse Renaissance detail of architecture and ornament. He is, however, more remarkable for his woodcuts, of which he made some seven hundred. These give a vivid presentation of contemporary life. He worked for the Emperor Maximilian and his 'Triumph of Maximilian' series is especially notable.

'Burial of Count Orgaz, The', masterpiece by El Greco (q.v.), painted in 1598 for the church of Santo Tomé, Toledo.

H. BURGKMAIR—John at Patmos (from the Johannes Altar)—Pinakothek, Munich.

[95]

how galahad sought the sangreal and found it because his
heart was single so he followed it to sarras the city of the spirit

The composition, divided between the earthly and the celestial, shows in the lower section the count in full armour being lowered into the grave by St Augustine and St Stephen before a concourse of nobles and ecclesiastics; and above his soul being received into heaven.

Burne - Jones, Sir Edward Coley (*b*. Birmingham, 28 Aug. 1833; *d*. London, 16 June 1898), English painter and designer. He and William Morris, whom he met when they were undergraduates at Exeter College, Oxford, in 1853, represent a second phase of the Pre-Raphaelite movement into which they were inducted by Dante Gabriel Rossetti, taking part with him in decorating the walls of the Oxford Union, 1857. Burne-Jones's work as a painter was guided by a love of the legendary past and after 1862, when he visited Italy in company with his wife and John Ruskin, by Italian models, in particular by Botticelli and Mantegna. A wistful nostalgia characterizes such paintings as his 'King Cophetua and the Beggar Maid' and 'The Golden Stairs' (Tate Gallery). More considerable, perhaps, as a designer, he collaborated with Morris in designing stained-glass windows, tapestries and book decorations for the Kelmscott Press. He was made a baronet in 1894.

Bushman Painting, paintings on rocks or cave walls in various districts of Southern Rhodesia, South-West Africa and South-East Africa, attributed to the aboriginal, nomadic hunting folk called bushmen. Some of these paintings may go back to the epoch of palaeolithic art in Europe (*see* PREHISTORIC AND PRIMITIVE ART), though the most recent come down to the beginning of the nineteenth century, and show the invasion of the Bantu people, armed with assagais and shields. Living the same kind of life as prehistoric man in Europe, the bushmen produced a strikingly similar art, remarkable for the skill with which animals were drawn and painted. The studies of Breuil (q.v.) and others indicate some thread of connection between prehistoric art in Spain and the North African deserts and the bushman's art. Some early penetration is assumed from the Nile valley of North African and Mediterranean peoples, though the rock paintings of the Sahara are not closely comparable with those of the bushmen, reflecting a different stage of social organization.

Busi, Giovanni, *see* CARIANI.

Butinone, Bernardino (active 1484 – 1507), Italian painter of the Milanese School, a native of Treviglio. He seems to have been a pupil of Foppa (q.v.) and was associated with Bernardo Zenale in painting frescoes in San Pietro in Gessate, Milan, and an altar-piece at Treviglio. His style has been traced in a number of religious panel paintings in various collections—National Gallery, London, Chicago, Edinburgh, Milan and elsewhere.

Buytewech, Willem Pietersz (*b.* Rotterdam, 1591–2; *d.* probably Rotterdam, *c.* 1625), Dutch painter of *genre* and etcher. He worked at Haarlem, 1613–17, and Rotterdam from 1617, with success, his 'Society Courtship' (Rijksmuseum) attractively illustrating his love of finery in costume and his ornateness of style.

Byzantine Painting comprises mosaics, wall painting, manuscript

BUSHMAN ART—Two Deer—Rock Painting, S.W. Africa.

W. BUYTEWECH—Amorous Conversation—Rijksmuseum, Amsterdam.

BYZANTINE MOSAIC (Sixth Century)—The Empress Theodora with Attendants (detail)—
Ravenna, Church of San Vitale.

illumination and panel painting, distributed over a wide area of the
eastern Mediterranean and ranging in date from the establishment of
the seat of Roman authority at Byzantium (Constantinople, the
present Istanbul) by Constantine the Great in A.D. 330 to the fall of
Constantinople to the Turks in 1472, and even later in such local
centres as Crete. Mosaic is the most wonderful and impressive form
of Byzantine pictorial art (*see* MOSAIC). Wall painting developed from
classical art (*see* EARLY CHRISTIAN PAINTING) and its later products
are to be seen in churches and monasteries in Greece, Yugoslavia and
other parts of the Balkans. Illustrated manuscripts are an important
feature of Byzantine painting (*see* ILLUMINATION OF MANUSCRIPTS).
Panel painting has its origin in the Greco-Roman style of portraiture
as practised in Egypt in the first century A.D. (*see* ROMAN PAINTING)
and its final development in icon painting as developed in various
local centres, the latter being more especially associated with Russia
(*see* RUSSIAN PAINTING), where it was practised by Greek artists or
artists working in the Greek manner. 'Our Lady of Vladimir' (twelfth
century, Moscow, Tretyakow Gallery) is an outstanding example of
Byzantine workmanship taken to Russia.

Several periods of Byzantine painting can be distinguished: (1)
330–528, the importation of the art of Imperial Rome into the new

BYZANTINE MOSAIC (Twelfth Century)—Christ with, below, the Virgin and Angels, and Apostles—Cefalu, Apse of the Cathedral.

A. BYZAYIOS—The Raising of Lazarus—Ashmolean Museum, Oxford.

capital, and its transformation there. (2) Sixth–seventh centuries, the first golden age of Byzantine art, fully developed in the reign of Justinian, exemplified in wonderful mosaics not only in Constantinople but in many different parts of the Empire, notably at Ravenna in Italy. Even Islamic conquest did not abolish Byzantine art in the Middle East, the mosaics in the Great Mosque at Damascus being an example. (3) Eighth to ninth centuries, a period of Iconoclasm (q.v.) forbidding the use of representational art in churches. This product of an oriental mysticism had the result of increasing the cleavage between east and west. Many artists repaired to Rome and revived the classical tradition in opposition to the orientalizing tendency of Constantinople. The rigid conventions of the icon may be looked on as a final result of Iconoclasm. (4) Ninth to twelfth centuries, a second golden age marked by the extreme luxury and splendour of the court art. The influence of Byzantine art was extended with conquest, e.g. in Bulgaria, which became a Byzantine province, or by the industry of Greek artists abroad, e.g. in Norman Sicily. The conflict of Roman and Byzantine traditions and the supersession of the latter are seen in Italian painting of the thirteenth century (*see* FLORENCE; SIENA; VENICE). (5) Twelfth to fifteenth centuries, a period of political decline finally marked by the Turkish conquest, but producing in art some evidence of a Byzantine Renaissance. It extended through Greece and the Balkans to Russia. Examples are the wall-paintings at Mileševo in Yugoslavia (thirteenth century), at Boiana, Bulgaria (thirteenth century), at Mistra, Greece (fourteenth century), also in Rumania. Though Russia developed its own school of icon painters, Byzantine Greek masters such as Theophanes (fourteenth century) and Dionysos (fifteenth–sixteenth centuries) worked there. The last great product of the Byzantine tradition was El Greco (q.v.), trained in the Byzantine monastic style of Crete.

[101]

C

Cabinet Picture, archaic term for the small easel picture, not intended to occupy one fixed or permanent position, suited to intimate surroundings.

Caldecott, Randolph (*b*. Chester, 22 Mar. 1846; *d*. St Augustine, Florida, 12 Feb. 1886), English graphic artist and book illustrator, noted for his illustrations to Washington Irving's *Sketch Book* and *Bracebridge Hall* and a series of coloured books for children, 1875–85, e.g. his *John Gilpin*.

Caliari (Cagliari), Paolo, *see* VERONESE.

Callot, Jacques (*b*. Nancy, 1592–3; *d*. there, 24 Mar. 1635), French graphic artist, and one of the great masters in engraving and etching. After early picaresque wandering, with Italy as the objective, he studied engraving in Rome and in 1611 went to Florence and worked at the court of Cosimo de' Medici, achieving great success with engravings of festival and characters of the Commedia dell' Arte. From 1622 onwards he worked at Nancy, with a short interlude, 1628–30, in Paris, being much in demand for scenes of battle and siege. In his preferred medium of etching he gives an intensely vivid view of his disturbed epoch, when Lorraine was ravaged by war, in the series (comparable with that of Goya) 'Les Grandes Misères de la Guerre', 1632, following the scenes of vagabondage of 'Les Barons' (tramps and displaced persons), 1622, and 'Les Bohémiens', 1631. A remarkable imagination is also seen in his renderings of the Temptation of St Anthony, which recall the visions of Bosch (q.v.). There are nearly 1,500 of his recorded etchings and a very large number of drawings, many of them studies for his plates.

J. CALLOT—The Tour de Nesle, Paris (Etching).

J. CALLOT—Temptation of St Anthony (Wash Drawing)—National Museum, Stockholm.

Calvaert, Denis (*b.* Antwerp, 1540; *d.* Bologna, 1619), Flemish painter who went to Italy as a young man, worked with Lorenzo Sabbatini in Rome and is mainly noted as having established a school at Bologna in rivalry with that of the Carracci; Domenichino, Guido Reni and Albani (qq.v.) being for a time among his pupils.

Calvert, Edward (*b.* Appledore, Devon, 20 Sept. 1789; *d.* London, 14 July 1883), English painter and engraver. After serving as a midshipman in the navy, he studied art at Plymouth and in the Royal Academy Schools and is associated with Samuel Palmer (q.v.) as an admirer of William Blake and one of the 'Ancients' of Shoreham, producing under this influence a few exquisite small works (e.g. 'The Primitive City', 'The Cyder Feast'). A visit to Greece changed the direction of his art, which in the pursuit of an ideal beauty lost its earlier quality.

Cambiaso, Luca (*b.* Moneglia, Oct 1527; *d.* Madrid, 1585), Italian painter and engraver who worked at Genoa, where his best works are to be found. He studied with his father and a painter of Bergamo, G. B. Castello, also travelling widely in Italy and absorbing a variety of Renaissance influences. In 1583 he was commissioned by Philip II to finish a series of frescoes in the Escorial begun by Castello.

Camden Town Group, association of English painters formed in 1911, largely reflecting and giving a local character to the Post-Impressionist trend of art in France, and later merged with the London Group. Inspired by Walter Sickert, it began with sixteen members, Spencer Gore, J. B. Manson, Walter Bayes, Robert Bevan,

Malcolm Drummond, Charles Ginner, J. D. Innes (q.v.), Augustus John (q.v.), Henry Lamb, Wyndham Lewis (q.v.), M. G. Lightfoot, Lucien Pissarro, W. Ratcliffe, Doman Turner, W. R. Sickert (q.v.) and Harold Gilman; Duncan Grant (q.v.) joining later. It is, however, most characteristically represented, in late- and Post-Impressionist colour (mainly applied to London themes), by Spencer Frederick Gore (1878–1914), its first president, Harold Gilman (1876–1919) and Robert Polhill Bevan 1865–1925), evolving styles of distinction) from the study of Cézanne, van Gogh and Gauguin respectively.

Camera Obscura, apparatus by which a reflected image is thrown on to the surface on which an artist works by means of lens and mirrors, enabling him to trace an accurate outline of a scene or number of objects. Its invention has been ascribed to Giovanni Battista della Porta, 1569, though in principle it was known and used earlier. The Venetian view-painters, Canaletto in particular, seem to have employed it. The camera lucida was a related device, incorporating a prism, and was mainly used in copying, reducing or enlarging drawings.

Campagnola, Domenico (*b.* Padua or Venice, *c.* 1482; *d. c.* 1562), Italian painter and engraver of the Venetian School, a follower and perhaps a pupil of Titian. He painted frescoes in the Scuola del Santo, and other paintings by him are in the Scuola del Carmine. He produced a large number of drawings, mostly done for sale or circulation and not as studies for pictures.

Campigli, Massimo (*b.* Florence, 1895), Italian painter who has worked in Paris for many years. He developed an original style from the study of Etruscan and Pompeian painting, modified by the

R. BEVAN—From the Artist's Window—Leicester Art Gallery.

M. CAMPIGLI—Two Seated Women—Estorick Collection.

R. CAMPIN—A Woman—National Gallery.

T. THOMSON—The West Wind—Art Gallery of Toronto.

influence of the School of Paris. In addition to oil-paintings he has produced frescoes, mosaics and lithographs.

Campin, Robert (1378/9–1444), painter of the early Netherlandish School, active at Tournai from 1406. He is regarded by many scholars as the centre of that shadowy nucleus of fifteenth-century Netherlandish art comprised under the name of the 'Master of Flémalle' (q.v.), the master of Jacques Daret (c. 1403–68) and of 'Rogier de la Pasture', i.e. Rogier van der Weyden (q.v.). In him a somewhat uncouth 'Gothic' style, as in the 'Virgin before a Firescreen' (National Gallery), seems to have been modified by the grace and realism of his pupil, van der Weyden.

Canadian Art. Both French and English tradition contributed to development of art in Canada from the seventeenth century onwards. In the colony of New France, c. 1670, Frère Luc (Claude François) transplanted the European style of religious painting. After the British conquest in 1759, contact with Europe is reflected in the work of François Beaucourt, who studied in France, and in the early

[107]

P. KANE—Indian Encampment on Lake Huron—Art Gallery of Toronto.

C. KRIEGHOFF—Settler's Log House—Art Gallery of Toronto.

nineteenth century in the portraits of Antoine Plamondon and Théophile Hamel. The British legacy was evident in the eighteenth century style of portraiture of Robert Field in Nova Scotia and also in landscape, in which Thomas Davies was a pioneer. The Canadian scene was romantically presented by Paul Kane (1810–71), Cornelius Krieghoff (1815–72) and Robert Whale (1805–87). About 1870 the romantic picturesque gave way to greater realism, as in the landscapes of John A. Fraser and others and the *genre* paintings of Robert Harris (1849–1919), who painted the first Canadian mural in 1881 'The Fathers of the Confederation'. A poetic style of landscape was practised in the 1890's by Horatio Walker (1858–1938). Homer Watson (1885–1936) and William Brymner (1855–1925). The influence of French Impressionism seen in Maurice Cullen (1866–1934) and James Wilson Morrice (1865–1924) led eventually to a national movement exemplified by a group of painters in Montreal from 1910 onwards, who developed a powerful regional style—Tom Thomson (1877–1917) is notable among them. Recent painting shows, besides the attachment to the Canadian scene, a response to abstract art, leading abstractionists being Paul Émile Borduas, Jean Paul Riopelle and Harold Town.

Canaletto (Giovanni Antonio Canal) (*b.* Venice, 18 Oct. 1697; *d.* there, 20 April 1768), Italian painter, son of the scene painter and

CANALETTO—A View in Venice, 'The Stonemason's Yard'—National Gallery.

CANALETTO—London from Richmond House—Collection of the Duke of Richmond and Gordon.

designer Bernardo Canal, with whom he worked as a scene painter in his early years. In 1719 he went to Rome and no doubt began to paint architectural views in emulation of Panini, though the 'perspectives' of Luca Carlevaris (q.v.) seem to have been a formative influence on his work. Returning to Venice he devoted himself to the views of the city for which he is famous, producing many for export to England. From 1730 Joseph Smith (later British consul) was a principal patron, the paintings and drawings executed for him now being mostly in the Royal Collection at Windsor. Canaletto's series of etchings of Venice and the lagoons, 1733, was dedicated to Smith. Encouraged to visit England, he worked mainly in London and its environs, with brief intervals at Venice, between 1746 and 1756, finally returning in the latter year to his native city. His style shows considerable variation, his early maturity being splendidly represented by the View of Venice, also known as 'The Stonemason's Yard', of about 1730 (National Gallery), and the 'Scuola di San

Rocco', probably a little later, this work showing Canaletto's great skill in figure painting as well as architecture. No doubt because of the sameness of his themes his style became mechanically dexterous as time went on and his use of the camera obscura inclined him to exact imitation rather than creative design. His work in England, though of great interest, shows a harder manner than his earlier productions, as remarked disapprovingly by Vertue, and he seems to have found English landscape a difficult problem, though his views of London and its river are superb. Allowance must be made for studio works and also for some confusion with paintings close in style by his nephew, Bernardo Bellotto (q.v.). At all times Canaletto showed wonderful skill, and his presence in England was influential on topographical artists and others—his brushwork may well have given its example to Hogarth and Wilson, while his drawings were models followed by Girtin and Turner. In Venice, Francesco Guardi (q.v.), somewhat younger, was his follower, though developing a freer, lighter manner.

Cano, Alonzo (*b.* Granada, 19 Mar. 1601; *d.* there, 3 Sept. 1667), Spanish painter, sculptor and architect. He studied painting under Francisco Pacheco (q.v.), the master of Velazquez, and sculpture under Juan Martinez Montanes. In 1637, after a duel, he left Seville for Madrid, where he was befriended by Velazquez, who obtained him a court appointment. Suspected of having killed his wife he again fled in 1652 to Granada. An able painter of portraits and religious subjects, he earned the title of the 'Michelangelo of Spain' from his practise of three arts. Examples of his work are at Granada and in the Prado.

Cantarini, Simone (*b.* Orpezzo, nr Pesaro, 1612; *d.* Verona, 15 Oct. 1648), Italian painter, also known as Pesarese and Simone da Pesaro. He was a disciple of Guido Reni (q.v.), whom he followed closely in style. It was supposed that he poisoned himself after an unsuccessful attempt to paint the portrait of the Duke of Mantua. Religious paintings by him are at Bologna, Naples and Dresden and a portrait of Guido at Pesaro.

Cappelle, Jan van de (*b.* Amsterdam, *c.* 1626; buried there, 22 Dec. 1679), Dutch marine painter who studied the work of Simon de Vlieger (1601–53—first of the celebrated Dutch marinists). Cappelle's paintings of ships are especially notable for their skies and he produced also some winter landscapes and etchings.

Capriccio (Caprice), usually a free or fantastic combination of architectural objects, real or imaginary, in a painted view. Panini, Piranesi, Guardi and Hubert Robert provide examples. Goya, however, in his 'Caprichos' gives the term a wider imaginative significance.

Caravaggio, Michelangelo Amerighi (or Merisi) da (*b.* Caravaggio, 1573; *d.* Porto d'Ercole on the Tuscan coast, 1610), Italian painter, a commanding influence on seventeenth-century European art. The son of a mason in a village near Milan, he had some early training in

[111]

J. VAN DE CAPPELLE—The State Barge greeted by the Home Fleet—Rijksmuseum, Amsterdam.

that city but was painting in Rome before he was twenty, quickly developing that famous 'Naturalism' which was in strong contrast to the prevailing Mannerism of Zuccaro and the Cavaliere d'Arpino. Instead of ideal figures he painted the types he saw and knew, delighting in plebeian traits of character, contemporary dress and carefully delineated still life. Early examples are the 'Bacchus' (Uffizi), the 'Fortune Teller' (Louvre) and the 'Fruit Basket' (Milan, Ambrosiana). The innovation which gave him fame and made him the centre of controversy was not only to apply this realistic method to religious painting but to intensify its effect by combining it with a depth and drama of light and shade which he may have adapted from Tintoretto. It appears in his first commission for the Contarelli Chapel of St Luigi dei Francesi: 'St Matthew and the Angel', the 'Vocation of St Matthew' and 'Martyrdom of the Apostle'. These and other works in Rome, painted between 1600 and 1607, including the 'Madonna of the Serpent' (Borghese Gallery), the 'Death of the Virgin' (Louvre) and the 'Madonna del Rosario' (Vienna), were either refused by his patrons or the subject of fierce argument. His short career, so brilliant in art, was otherwise violent and ill-starred. Involved in numerous brawls, he fled from Rome after killing a man, worked in Naples in 1607 and was received with honour at Malta, where he painted his masterly 'Decollation of St John' in the cathedral at Valetta and the magnificent portrait of Olaf de Wignacourt, Grand Master of the Order of the Knights of St John (Louvre). Again causing trouble in Malta, he was imprisoned

CARAVAGGIO—The Vocation of St Matthew—Contarelli Chapel of St Luigi dei Francesi, Rome

but escaped, working in Sicily at Syracuse, Messina and Palermo. He returned to Naples and thence embarked on a boat with the intention of working his way back to Rome and restoration to favour there. By some misunderstanding or ill intention he was left stranded on the malarial coast, where he died. The extent of his influence was extraordinary, both in the propagation of realism and in effects of lighting, touching Rubens, Velazquez and Rembrandt; evident in the 'Tenebrosi' of the Netherlands, e.g. Honthorst; and in France in Georges de la Tour and Le Valentin. In Italy itself the influence of his art was merged among others producing the dramatic effects of the baroque style.

'Card Players, The', one of the most famous of Cézanne's figure compositions, of which he produced five versions, depicting a peasant group. 'Les Joueurs de Cartes', now in the Louvre, is one version, painted *c.* 1885.

Carducci (Carducho), name of two painter brothers of Italian origin

[113]

who settled in Spain. **Bartolommeo** (**Bartolomé**) (*b*. Florence, 1560; *d*. Madrid, 1610) studied architecture and sculpture with Ammanati and painting with Zuccaro (q.v.), helping the latter to paint the cupola in the cathedral at Florence. He went with Zuccaro to Spain in 1585 and settled there, becoming painter to Philip II and Philip III. A principal work is 'The Descent from the Cross' (San Felipe el Real, Madrid). **Vincenzo** (**Vicente**) (*b*. 1568; *d*. Madrid, 1638) was trained by Zuccaro and his brother, whom he accompanied to Spain. After his brother's death he finished a series of frescoes begun by the latter for Philip III and painted many religious works, among them a series of fifty for the Carthusians of El Paular, representing scenes from the life of St Bruno and martyrdoms and miracles of monks of the order. He wrote in Castilian a *Diálogos de las Excelencias de la Pintura*, giving some account of both Italian and Spanish artists.

Cariani (**Giovanni Busi**) (active early sixteenth century), Italian painter of the Venetian School, coming from Bergamo. He worked in manners derived from Titian, Giorgione and Palma Vecchio and is mainly noted for bold, somewhat coarsely treated portraits, an example being the 'Member of the Albani Family' (National Gallery). His work, however, is often confused with that of contemporaries, his style being variable.

Caricature (It. *caricatura*), exaggerated representation of features or action, with a humorous or satirical intention. The word was first given its present meaning by Annibale Carracci, who applied it to his own drawings and others by members of the School of Bologna in the sixteenth century. Caricature, however, had a long previous history. Burlesque representation is found in some Greek vase paintings and in paintings at Pompeii and Herculaneum. It appears in the grotesques of medieval sculpture

AGOSTINO CARRACCI
—Caricature Heads.

SIR MAX BEERBOHM—Tosti, the composer, surrounded by imaginary stars of Italian Opera (Water-colour)—British Museum.

and illuminated manuscripts. Leonardo studied and emphasized ugliness and deformity with unsparing observation. It has a long history since the Reformation as a popular form of political and social criticism, and on a number of occasions has been associated with the work of great artists. It is an element in the work of Goya. Hogarth and Rowlandson are great examples in England, Honoré Daumier in France. Aesthetically the value of Carracci's excursions into caricature was to underline the fact that a likeness of either an individual or a type may survive, or even be made more vivid by, a considerable amount of exaggeration, which has its place even in serious portraiture.

Carlevaris, Luca (*b.* Udine, 1663; *d.* Venice, 1730), Italian painter and etcher, the father of Venetian eighteenth-century view painting. He studied painting at Rome under Flemish and Dutch artists and moved to Venice, 1679, where he worked for English and other foreign visitors. Canaletto may have been his pupil. A sketch-book (British Museum) contains studies of groups of figures as used in his views.

Carpaccio, Vittore (active 1490; *d.* 1523–6), Italian painter of the Venetian School. His real name was Scarpazza and he probably came

L. CARLEVARIS—Harbour with an Obelisk—Reproduced by Gracious Permission of Her Majesty the Queen—Windsor Castle.

from a family established in the Venetian islands. He is said to have been a pupil of Lorenzo Bastiani but was evidently influenced by Gentile Bellini (q.v.), with whom he vied in depicting the aspect and ceremony of Venice. He was much employed by the *scuole* or confraternities of Venice and his charm and narrative gift are beautifully displayed in his cycles of the Life of St Ursula, 1490–5, painted for the Scuola di Sant' Orsola and now in the Accademia, Venice, and the Life of St George and other saints for the Scuola di San Giorgio degli Schiavoni, 1502–7. The 'Dream of St Ursula' is a famous work in the earlier series. 'The Miracle of the Cross at Rialto' (Accademia) is remarkable for its typically Venetian background and, as a form of *genre* picture (though perhaps a fragment of a larger work), also famous is the so-called 'Courtesans' (Venice, Correr Museum).

Carrà, Carlo (*b.* Quargnento, nr Alessandria, 1881; *d.* Milan, 13 April 1966), Italian painter, in his work and theoretical writings one of the main promoters of the revival in modern Italian art. He studied at Milan and was one of the founders of the Futurist movement in 1910. He broke away from Futurism and in 1917 became associated with Giorgio de Chirico (*q.v.*) in the form of imaginative painting they called 'metaphysical'. From 1921 he reverted to more realistic subject-matter and style.

Carracci, name of three related Italian painters who represent an important phase of late-Renaissance art, Lodovico Carracci and his cousins (who were brothers) Agostino and Annibale. **Lodovico** (*b.* Bologna, 21 April 1555; *d.* there, 13 Nov. 1619), pupil of Prospero

[116]

CARPACCIO—The Dream of St Ursula—Accademia, Venice.

Fontana (q.v.) and in the school of Passignano at Florence, was an artist of scholarly inclination who made an extensive study of Renaissance masters, especially of Correggio and Titian. He was the founder of the famous academy at Bologna (both a teaching school and a centre of learned study), 1585, in which he enlisted the aid of his cousins. From 1600 he carried it on alone. Albani, Domenichino, Guido Reni, Guercino and Lanfranco were among the Carraccis' distinguished pupils. **Agostino** (b. Bologna, 15 Aug 1557; d. Parma, 25 Feb. 1602), painter and engraver, also studied under Fontana and at Parma and Venice and took a leading place in the Bologna academy and in directing its policy, which required, not the piecemeal assemblage of various excellences in celebrated masters but intelligent study, especially of Correggio and the Venetians, designed

[117]

ANNIBALE CARRACCI—Landscape with Figures—National Gallery.

to counteract a facile mannerism. He worked with his brother on the decorations commissioned by Cardinal Odoardo Farnese for the Farnese Palace in Rome, 1595–7, moving to Parma in 1600. **Annibale** (*b*. Bologna, 3 Nov. 1560; *d*. Rome, 15 July 1609) was the most original artist of the three. He studied Correggio's work and was an excellent draughtsman (drawing from the life being one of the Carraccis' tenets). His principal work was the decoration of the Farnese Palace, the Loves of the Gods being the theme of the paintings in its gallery, exuberant in movement, fancy and a light-hearted approach to the mythological subject. The idealism of the Carracci did not exclude humour or an element of caricature. With its two compositions by Domenichino of the legend of Perseus, the Farnese Gallery served as a model for the French painter decorators of the seventeenth century under Le Brun (q.v.). In religious painting, Annibale may be thought less inspired and more conventional in the attempt to convey the pious spirit prescribed by the Counter-Reformation. In landscape, however, he was an originator, and one can trace to him the 'classical' landscape with ruins developed by Claude and Poussin. His work and that of the Bolognese School as a whole have risen in estimation as a prelude to the age of baroque.

Carreño de Miranda, Juan (*b*. Avila, 1614; *d*. Madrid, 1685), Spanish painter whose style was formed by study of Rubens and Velazquez. He painted frescoes of religious subjects (Cathedral of Toledo) and

L. CARRACCI—The Holy Family (Pen and Wash Drawing)—The Courtauld Gallery, Witt Collection.

J. CARREÑO—Charles II of Spain—Staatliche Museum, Berlin.

mythological scenes (Alcazar, Madrid), but later specialized in portraiture. After the death of Velazquez he became court painter to Charles II (1669).

Carriera, Rosalba Giovanna (*b.* Venice, 7 Oct 1675; *d.* there, 15 April 1757), Italian woman painter of miniatures and pastel portraits, the prettiness of which had a European vogue. She worked in Paris and Vienna as well as Venice, and popularized the use of the medium by artists in eighteenth-century France.

Carrière, Eugène Anatole (*b.* Gournay-sur-Marne, 17 Jan. 1849; *d.* Paris, 27 Mar. 1906), French painter, a pupil of Cabanel and, in Edmond de Goncourt's phrase, 'the modern Madonna painter', his many pictures of motherhood and childhood being tenderly treated in melting tones. In these and his portraits he strictly limited colour in order to give a poetic and mysterious character to personality. His 'Verlaine', in the Luxembourg Collection, exemplifies this method in portraiture.

Cartoon (It. *cartone*, pasteboard), originally the large-scale design on strong paper traced by the fresco painter on a wall surface; also used of any comparable design for a large decorative undertaking, such as the superb cartoons of Raphael intended as a guide for the Flemish tapestry weavers, and painted in distemper. Famous as projects, though never completed in painting and now lost, are the cartoons of Leonardo da Vinci ('The Battle of the Standard') and Michelangelo ('Florentine Soldiers attacked while Bathing'). In England a nineteenth-century revival of design on this scale was produced by the competition for wall-paintings in the Houses of Parliament, 1843–4. This suggested the later application of the word in parody by *Punch* to its 'political pencillings' on a larger scale than its other drawings. 'Cartoon' has since been commonly used as a synonym for political or social caricature.

Cassatt, Mary (*b.* Pittsburgh, 1845; *d.* Château Beaufresne, Beauvais,

M. CASSATT—The Family —Photo: Marlborough Fine Art.

A. DEL CASTAGNO—The Last Supper—Convent of Sant' Apollonia, Florence.

19 June 1926), American painter, the daughter of a Pennsylvania banker, who in spite of family resistance took to art. Her childhood was spent in France, and after some training at the Philadelphia Academy and a period of travel about Europe, when she studied the old masters, she settled in Paris, 1874, becoming an adherent of the Impressionists. She contributed to the Impressionist exhibitions of 1879, 1880, 1881 and 1886, her work being much admired by Degas, who encouraged her efforts. From 1912 she suffered from a partial but increasing blindness. Her delicate studies of women and children relate her work to that of Berthe Morisot (q.v.), though she was not so free and adventurous in style as her French contemporary. She did much to arouse interest in Impressionist painting in America.

Cassone, Italian word for the marriage coffer, which in Renaissance Italy, among noble and wealthy families, assumed large proportions and was richly decorated with carving, inlay, gilded gesso and painted panels depicting some legendary subject or splendid scene of courtly life. Many beautiful examples of these painted panels, especially those by minor Florentine and Sienese painters and craftsmen, now hang in museums.

Castagno, Andrea del (*b.* nr Castagno, 1423; *d.* Florence, 19 Aug. 1457), Italian painter of the Florentine School. His full name was Andrea di Bartolo di Simone and he was called Castagno after the town where his early life was spent. He attracted the notice of Bernedetto de' Medici, who took him to Florence, where he mainly worked, though he stayed in Venice for a time and painted frescoes at San Zaccaria. The Convent of Sant' Apollonia, now a Castagno museum, has major works in fresco including his 'Last Supper', 'Crucifixion' and the series of Famous Men and Women, in which Dante, Petrarch and Boccaccio figure (originally a decoration for the Villa Carducci at Legnaia). Among his few other paintings are the equestrian portrait of Niccolo de Tolentino in the cathedral of Florence, an 'Assumption' (Berlin) and 'Crucifixion' (National

[121]

Gallery). His art develops from that of Masaccio and has a sculptural quality that seems to derive from Donatello, its grandeur of style fully appearing in the 'Last Supper', a worthy forerunner of Leonardo's great conception, and containing also remarkable passages of abstract decoration. It should perhaps be mentioned that Vasari's yarn of his having murdered Domenico Veneziano, long solemnly credited, was entirely without foundation.

Castiglione, Giovanni Benedetto (*b.* Genoa, 1616; *d.* 1670), Italian painter and etcher, known in Italy as Il Grechetto (the Little Greek) and in France as Le Bénédette. He studied under van Dyck and included much landscape, animal and still-life detail in religious and mythological subjects, 'The Animals entering the Ark' being one of his themes. His etchings were Rembrandtesque in light and shade.

Catena (properly **Vincenzo di Biagio**) (active 1506; *d.* 1531), Italian painter of the Venetian School, a disciple of Giovanni Bellini (q.v.). Some association with Giorgione (q.v.) is indicated by a contemporary inscription on the back of Giorgione's 'Laura' (Vienna), referring to 'Master Vicenzo Catena' as 'colleague' of Master Giorgio of Castelfranco. The 'Warrior adoring the Infant Christ and the Virgin' (National Gallery), formerly thought beyond his abilities and worthy of Giorgione, is now reattributed to Catena. The portrait of Doge Andrea Gritti (National Gallery), formerly attributed to Titian (and quoted as a perfect example of Titian's 'finish' in the Ruskin-Whistler libel action), is also assigned to this minor but problematic Venetian.

Cavallini, Pietro (*b. c.* 1250; *d. c.* 1330), Italian painter, sculptor, mosaicist and architect, a Roman master with whom the young Giotto worked at Rome, perhaps being his pupil. His importance lies in his having studied or returned in style to classical tradition (as distinct from Byzantine formula), thus helping to set the direction which leads from Giotto to the Renaissance. His mosaics in Santa Maria in Trastevere, 1291, are famous and the remains of his fresco, 'The Last Judgment', uncovered in the convent of Santa Cecilia in Rome, 1900, include impressive heads. The Roman style of Cavallini is seen in the 'Crucifixion' fresco at Assisi.

Cave Art, earliest known art of man, the paintings, drawings and rudimentary forms of sculpture of the Old Stone Age, found in a number of caves in southern France and north-eastern Spain. It covers an immense stretch of time, radio-carbon analysis suggesting a period of about 10,000 years, i.e. from about 20000 B.C. to about 10000 B.C., though the great student of caves, the Abbé Breuil (q.v.), has suggested that the earliest date should be put at about 50000 B.C. The period has been divided into two main cultural phases, Aurignacian (named after the site at Aurignac), of which three stages have been recognized, and Magdalenian (named after the La Madeleine site), subdivided into as many as six stages. Broadly speaking the main distinction between the two phases is that the Aurignacian represents an art of outline and monochrome (the great cave of Lascaux in the Dordogne containing its finest ultimate products) and

CAVE PAINTING, Font de Gaume, Dordogne—Two Reindeer—Copy by Abbé Breuil, Musée de l'Homme, Paris.

the Magdalenian the development of polychrome paintings, as at Altamira in Spain. The masterpieces of cave art are superbly naturalistic representations of animals—bison, mammoth, horse, ox, red deer and reindeer—known from datable deposits of their bones to be the food of Upper Palaeolithic man. The human form appears more rarely and diagrammatically, either as a hunter aiming his arrows or as a mysterious sorcerer-like figure. It is generally agreed that the purpose was magico-religious, to ensure success in the hunt by a pictorial 'spell' and also to make for fertility in the animals hunted. The paintings and engravings are found on the roofs and walls of deep caves where no natural light penetrated, and indications of torches and cup-like lamps providing artificial light have been seen. Animals are depicted in fresh and vigorous line, often enriched by red and yellow ochre, red haematite, manganese and graphite and sometimes emphasized by finely powdered colour, probably blown on through a pipe. The Magdalenian artist seems also to have used a stone palette and some form of brush. The first cave to be discovered, in 1879 at Altamira, eighteen miles from Santander, contains some of the finest late Magdalenian polychrome paintings, and its bison have been made famous by the Abbé Breuil's copies. Other well-known caves are in the Dordogne: Font-de-Gaume, where in addition to fine renderings of bison and reindeer there are curious signs ('tectiforms') supposed to represent huts with semicircular entrances; Les Eyzies; Les Combarelles; the latter in particular suggesting from the crowded overlay of drawings that magic and not decoration was intended; and, most famous of all, Lascaux, near Montignac, discovered in 1940, with its magnificent black bulls and spirited horses. In the 'Trois-Frères' cave, in the northern part of the central Pyrenees, the black rock was anciently covered with a white deposit caused by weathering and again coated with a yellow-clay-like skin, inciting the primitive artist to engraving with a cameo effect. A figure called 'The Sorcerer' in this cave, with a human body and the head of a deer, suggests a hunting spirit or witch-doctor. The Mid and New Stone Age saw the decline of the remarkable naturalism of the caves into a largely non-pictorial or schematized form of art. This may be associated with the appearance of agriculture and settled communities. The amazing and even 'modern' quality of cave art, however, has its later parallel in the work of hunting folk in Africa (*see also* BUSHMAN PAINTING; PREHISTORIC AND PRIMITIVE ART).

Cennini, Cennino (late fourteenth–early fifteenth century), Italian painter, *b.* Colle di Valdelsa, who worked with Agnolo Gaddi (q.v.) at Florence, though no paintings by him are now known. He is of importance as the author of the famous *Trattato della Pittura* (Eng. trans. ed. by Mrs Herringham, 1899), which details the methods and precepts of the school of Giotto and gives an early account of oil-painting technique.

-cento (It. 'hundred') preceded by a number indicates a particular century; thus trecento = the 1300's, i.e. the fourteenth century, quattrocento = the 1400's (fifteenth century), cinquecento = the 1500's (sixteenth century), seicento = the 1600's (seventeenth century), settecento = the 1700's (eighteenth century). In international usage this Italian form most frequently refers to the great periods of Italian art.

Cerano, Il, *see* CRESPI, G. B.

Céspedes, Pablo de (*b.* Cordova, 1548; *d.* there, 26 July 1608), Spanish painter, sculptor, architect and writer on art. He studied under the brothers Zuccaro (q.v.) in Rome, where he copied Michelangelo and Raphael, and returned to Spain in 1575. He produced crowded religious pictures in a Mannerist style, of which his 'Last Supper' (Seville) is characteristic.

Cézanne, Paul (*b.* Aix-en-Provence, 19 Jan. 1839; *d.* there, 22 Oct. 1906), French painter who has been called the 'father of modern painting', son of a wealthy provincial (at one time a hatter) who had built up a successful banking business. He was educated at the Collège Bourbon of Aix (where he became the friend of Zola) and was intended for the law, but persuaded his parents to allow him to study art in Paris. He had, however, no regular training, failing in the entrance examination of the École des Beaux-Arts, and his early work had an undisciplined and Romantic enthusiasm for Delacroix, Daumier and Courbet (qq.v.), sensational subject-matter ('L'Orgie', 'L'Enlèvement') being rendered with violent and dark colour, heavily plastered on the canvas. His real apprenticeship began in the 1870's when his friendship with Camille Pissarro (q.v.) brought him within the orbit of Impressionism. 'Never paint', Pissarro advised him, 'except with the three primary colours and their immediate derivatives', and though he did not follow this advice literally, it made him aware of the importance of pure colour. A further result of Impressionist influence was to wean him from Romantic ideas and to

P. CÉZANNE—Boy in Red Waistcoat—Collection of Mr & Mrs Paul Mellon.

confront him simply with the study of nature, 'La Maison du Pendu',
which he contributed to the first Impressionist exhibition of 1874,
marking a transitional stage in his art. Paris he found unsympathetic,
and his later life, the most creative phase, was spent largely in un-
sociable seclusion at Aix, though vivid descriptions of the sensitive
recluse have been written by several devotees, notably the dealer
Ambroise Vollard. Well-to-do and able to do what he liked after the
death of his father, with a passively domestic wife (his former model),
Hortense Fiquet, he absorbed himself in nature and the problems of
his art, which contains many interesting and fruitful contradictions,
the devotion to nature and a complete lack of interest in subject
primary among them. He wished to 'refashion Poussin after nature':
on the other hand, the Louvre, he remarked, was 'a good book but
only a means to an end'. A sense of structure, opposed to the atmospheric preoccupation of the Impressionists, dictated not only the
representation of an object by planes translated into colour but the
representation of space (as in his 'Montagne Ste Victoire'). The
beauty of his later paintings lies in the subtle gradations of transparent colour from cold to warm combined with and inseparable from
a grand simplicity of form. In the water-colour medium itself he
showed remarkable brilliance and successfully applied its trans-
parency in oil. As in his 'Joueurs de Cartes' the human element was
the result, but not the primary incentive, of his art, though he considered the study of the figure an important exercise and his many
'Bathers' show a desire, never completely realized, to achieve a great
nude composition. The logic of his ideas, however, inevitably tended
towards still life, in which he excelled, and ultimately towards
abstraction. In this respect he may be looked on as the progenitor of
Cubism (q.v.), which followed so soon after the retrospective exhibition of his work in 1907. (Colour)

Chagall, Marc (*b.* Vitebsk, 7 July 1887), Russian-born painter of
imaginative and poetic subjects. He studied painting under Bakst in
St Petersburg and in Paris, 1910–14. He worked in Russia during the
First World War but returned to Paris in 1922 and gained fame in the
School of Paris of the 1920's and 1930's for his fantasies inspired by
Russian peasant life and folklore. These were 'surreal' in the sense of
being dream-like, but quite distinct from the Surrealism practised by
Ernst or Dali. Chagall went to live in the United States in 1941.
Besides oil-paintings and water-colours he produced a number of
designs for the theatre (Jewish State Theatre in his Moscow period,
Aleko, Mexico City, 1942, *The Firebird* ballet, New York, 1945) and
etched illustrations for Ambroise Vollard to Gogol's *Dead Souls*, La
Fontaine's *Fables* and the Bible. Works by him are in the world's
principal galleries of modern art.

Champaigne, Philippe de (*b.* Brussels, 26 May 1602; *d.* Paris, 12
Sept. 1674), French painter of portraits and religious subjects. He
first studied landscape at Brussels and went to Paris in 1621, collaborating with the young Nicolas Poussin (q.v.) in the decoration of
the Luxembourg. He became painter to Marie de' Medici in 1628 and

P. DE CHAMPAIGNE—Louis XIII—Louvre.

won the favour of Louis XIII and Richelieu, of whom two of his portraits are famous, the three-fold head and shoulders (National Gallery), intended like van Dyck's triple portrait of Charles I to serve Bernini as a guide for a bust, and the large full-length (Louvre), formal and grandiose, which set a style for official French portraiture. Richelieu employed him in painting the dome of the Sorbonne. He became a member of the Académie in 1648. An austerity of style grew with his association from the 1640's onward with the severe Jansenist sect of Port-Royal where his daughter Catherine became a nun. His *ex voto* painting of the girl, miraculously cured of paralysis by the intercessions of the Mother Superior, 'Les Réligieuses' (Louvre), is considered a masterpiece, and the portraits of his Jansenist phase after he withdrew from court circles have a typical gravity of mood. He devoted himself to religious painting after 1659, decorating several Paris churches. His nephew, Jean Baptiste de Champaigne (1631–81), was also a painter and his collaborator.

'**Chapeau de Paille, Le**', painting by Rubens, *c.* 1620, of Susanna Fourment, sister of Rubens's second wife. She wears a plumed felt hat and not, as the title indicates, a straw hat. One reason given for the misnomer is that the term *chapeau de poil* was mistranscribed. The picture came to the National Gallery from Sir Robert Peel's collection in 1871.

Charcoal for artists' use consists usually of the carbonized residue of willow twigs, suitable for preliminary drawings and easily rubbed

A. DÜRER—Portrait of a Young Man (Charcoal Drawing)—British Museum.

J. B. S. CHARDIN—The Skate—Louvre.

out. The old masters found it convenient for the large-scale cartoon. It has never been extensively employed for finished drawings, but by the sixteenth century a method of fixing it had been found, and in Venice, charcoal, together with white chalk on blue paper, was a graphic medium of Titian and Tintoretto. Dürer made some powerful studies in charcoal of which there are examples in the British Museum. It was sometimes soaked in oil, a method which made it adhesive and permanent but left a yellow stain round the black line.

Chardin, Jean Baptiste Siméon (*b*. Paris, 2 Nov. 1699; *d*. there, 6 Dec. 1779), French painter of still life and middle-class life, the son of a master carpenter. Pupil or assistant of Cazes, Coypel and van Loo, he took early advantage of the taste for Dutch and Flemish still life prevalent in France in the early eighteenth century, and developed, from this kind of subject, paintings which were equally distinct from those of the Netherlands and from the elegance of Oudry or Monnoyer. His art, that of a realist in the 'age of artificiality' of Louis XV and Boucher, is visual testimony to the existence of a cultivated bourgeoisie, as distinct from the court as from the peasantry, and the whole of his life was placidly spent in this milieu in Paris. His early still-life paintings, e.g. 'The Skate' (Louvre), greatly admired by Largillierre (q.v.), instantly secured his admittance to the Académie,

J. B. S. CHARDIN—The House of Cards—Mellon Collection, National Gallery of Art, Washington, D.C.

of which he became the treasurer and 'tapissier', hanger of pictures in the Salon. His own art was never particularly profitable and in 1752 he received a pension from the king; he was lodged in the Louvre from 1757. In later life he took to pastel in which, as a famous Self-Portrait (Louvre) shows, he excelled La Tour (q.v.). He is a 'modern' among seventeenth-century French painters in the largeness of design and the study of light which gave both to his figures (e.g. 'La Pourvoyeuse'—Louvre) and to the vessels and foodstuffs of the bourgeois table a dignity and interest of their own. With a structural quality of design admired by Cubists and a use of broken colour which has been called Impressionist he combined a love of simple things in which the essence of his genius is to be found, and in his revelation of a profound beauty underlying an apparent simplicity his art is a parallel to that of Vermeer.

Charlet, Nicolas-Toussaint (*b.* Paris, 20 Dec. 1792; *d.* there, 29 Dec. 1845), French graphic artist, the pupil of Gros and the friend of Géricault (q.v.), whom he accompanied to London and whom he interested in lithography. He served as a youth (1814) in the National Guard, and the lithographs of his maturity, belated in martial sentiment, perpetuated the Napoleonic legend in visual terms.

Charonton, Enguerrand (*b.* Laon, active mid fifteenth century), French painter of the school of Avignon. His great work is the altarpiece of 'The Coronation of the Virgin' (Hospice of Villeneuve-les-Avignon), for which the contract survives, making both authorship and date (1453) precise. Another document of 1454 shows that he painted the 'Madonna of Mercy' (Musée Condé, Chantilly) in collaboration with Pierre Vilatte of Limoges. An outstanding master, he was at one time identified with the Master of Avignon (q.v.) though this suggestion has been discarded.

Chase, William Merritt (*b.* Williamsburg, 1 Nov. 1849; *d.* New York, 25 Oct. 1916), American painter who studied at Munich under Piloty but was later more favourably influenced by Whistler (q.v.). In New York he established a school of his own and was eminent among the American artists of his time, being president of the Society of American Artists for ten years. He worked in oil, water-colour and pastel and also produced etchings; his range of subjects included figures, landscape, still life and many portraits, those of Whistler and the painter Frank Duveneck being highly esteemed. In brilliance of execution he bore some resemblance to Sargent.

Chassériau, Théodore (*b.* Santo Domingo, 20 Sept. 1819; *d.* Paris, 8 Oct. 1856), French painter, the pupil of Ingres (q.v.), whose influence is apparent in his best work in portraiture, 'The Two Sisters', 1843 (Louvre). The rival genius of Delacroix (q.v.), however, and a visit to Algeria caused him to turn to Romantic (oriental and dramatic) themes. He did much decorative painting in a mixed classic-romantic style, notable being the decorations, 1844–8, for the Cour des Comptes, Paris, partially destroyed by fire during the Commune, but of which panels are preserved in the Louvre.

T. CHASSÉRIAU—The Two Sisters—Louvre.

'**Château de Steen**', painting by Rubens of his country house near Malines and the surrounding landscape in autumn, a companion picture to his 'Rainbow Landscape' in the Wallace Collection. Rubens acquired Steen Castle in 1635 and the picture was painted in 1636. It was presented to the National Gallery by Sir George Beaumont in 1826.

Chiaroscuro, light and shade as used in painting to represent the solidity of objects and their position and relation in a given space, and also to give an emotional effect, in terms of tone as distinguishable from colour. It developed with the art of oil-painting, which allowed of more subtlety and depth in the treatment of shadow than other media such as fresco, and as an effect of gradation (*see also* SFUMATO) plays an important part in the work of Leonardo and Correggio. It is, however, more commonly associated with the forceful and dramatic contrasts obtained by Caravaggio and painters of the seventeenth century (*see also* TENEBRISM), Rembrandt being the greatest exponent. The chiaroscuro woodcut was a form of reproduction from a number of wood blocks by which several tones of one colour were rendered in a print.

Children's Art, a spontaneous form of expression among children between the ages approximately of five and fifteen, having a distinct character as a visual product which may be compared with that of the adult 'primitive' (*see also* PREHISTORIC AND PRIMITIVE ART). Its encouragement by educationalists was the eventual and logical outcome of the influential ideas of J. H. Pestalozzi (1746–1827) and F. W. A. Froebel (1782–1852) and the stress they laid on the value of free activity, though it was not until the twentieth century that it became a generally accepted feature of the school programme. As such it is considered of importance, not as a first stage in the training of professional artists but as an outlet for the imaginative faculty. Modern art,

CHILDREN'S ART—Head (by boy of 7)—Photo: 'Sunday Pictorial'.

[134]

LI LIN—A Game of Polo (Water-colour on Silk)—Victoria and Albert Museum.

with its fresh valuation of instinct, has contributed to draw attention to the remarkable qualities of colour and design attained in paintings by young children before adolescence takes them into a new stage of conscious development. Modern artists, e.g. Henri Matisse, have studied the results, not, of course, to imitate childish effort but with the idea that a similar release of spontaneous expression is possible and desirable in the work of the adult artist.

Chinese Painting ranks among the greatest products of the world's art in its imaginative portrayal of the elemental and sublime in nature, its emphasis on the spiritual rather than material, its appeal to the imagination of the spectator in its suggestion rather than completeness of form, and its subtleties of colour and design. Its earliest examples are known only by literary references which show that it was practised long before our Christian era. The invention of the hair brush is ascribed to the third century B.C. The philosophic and religious precepts of Confucius and Lao-Tzu seem at an early date to have guided the artist in attitude and choice of subject— portraits of sages, the contemplation of mountain and water, the symbolic representation of tiger and dragon as natural and spiritual forces. Though painting was often practised not only by professional artists but by emperors, scholars and the cultured class in general, the close relation of brush painting and calligraphic writing and the skill applicable to both eliminated the western idea of the 'amateur'.

The beauty of simplified design and spacing is to be seen in the

[135]

CH'IU YING—The
Emperor Kuang Wu ford-
ing a River (Ink and Colour
on Silk, Hanging Roll)—
National Gallery of Canada.

CHAO PEI—A Clump of
Tall Bamboo—National
Museum, Stockholm. 136

CHINESE PAINTING (Probably Eighteenth Century)—Birds and Rabbits in Winter Landscape (detail)—Victoria and Albert Museum.

work of Ku K'ai-chih (fourth century), a famous painting by him in the British Museum showing all the subtlety and refinement thus resulting. During the T'ang dynasty (618–906) the influence of Buddhism and of Indian Buddhist painting was brought to China by Indian missionaries, the large flowing rhythms and the realistic modelling of the Ajanta frescoes bringing a new element into Chinese painting. In turn the work so inspired, as well as Buddhism itself, was conveyed from China to Japan, and the nature of T'ang painting in this phase is largely to be estimated from its reflection in Japanese work. (*See also* INDIAN PAINTING; JAPANESE PICTORIAL ART.) The name of Wu Tao-tzu (q.v.) is famous for mural paintings of Buddhist themes, though no authentic work by him seems to have survived the destruction of Buddhist temples in the ninth century. 'Buddha under the Mango Tree', a painting in ink and colour on paper by Ch'en Yung-chih (fl. *c.* 1023) of a seventh-century work, reflects the style of that century. 'The Death of Buddha' (British Museum), founded on one of Wu Tao-tzu's reputed masterpieces, gives some idea of his powers. The T'ang period, known as the golden age of Chinese art, divides into two main schools of painting, the northern founded by Li Szu-hsun, who excelled in landscape, the southern by Wang Wei

[137]

(q.v.), who was noted for the delicacy of his work, though none seems to have survived. A copy by Chao Meng-fu (1254–1322) of Wang Wei's view of the Wang Ch'uan is in the British Museum. The northern school is distinguished by its naturalism, the southern by its poetic character. Another famous T'ang painter was Han Kan (eighth century), who was noted for his paintings of horses which set a style much followed. The period of the Five Dynasties (907–59) produced the masters Hsu-Hsi, who excelled in flower and bird painting, and Huang Ch'uan. It was followed by a great age, that of the Sung Dynasty (960–1279), when landscape in particular was superbly developed, exquisitely interpreting the contemplative spirit of Zen Buddhism. The southern school, which delighted in the gorges of the Yangtse, is represented by Ma Yuan (q.v.) (fl. early thirteenth century), whose representations of the philosopher

MING PERIOD—Woven Picture—Victoria and Albert Museum.

contemplating nature were often copied, and Hsia Kuei (q.v.), famous
for the atmosphere and movement he imparted to his views of the
changing panorama of the Yangtse along its course. The northern
school, which favoured the scenery of the Hwang Ho, included Li
Sheng, noted for his rain and mist, and Kuo Hsi, noted for impressive
vistas. The great landscape tradition continued during the Mongol
Yüan Dynasty (1280–1368), the reinterpretation of ancient models
being always a feature of Chinese painting. The Ming Dynasty gives
copious example, though it is distinguished also by an elaborate and
decorative style of court art as in the elegant depictions of court
ladies in the setting of ornate pavilions in the work of Chiu Ying
(early sixteenth century). Shen Chou (1427–1509) well represents the
refined culture of the time in landscape. Lin Liang (fl. early fifteenth
century) is noted for superb renderings of bird life. Wen Cheng-ming
(1470–1559), noted for his brushwork, was one of the most distinguished scholars, poets and painters of the Ming era. In the Ching
Dynasty, the long and troubled period that lasted from 1644 to 1912,
Chu-Ta (q.v.) is to be signalized as one of the celebrated 'monk
painters' who retired into hermitage, devoting themselves to calligraphy and painting, Tao Chih (1630–after 1707) being another.
Chu-Ta displays the ultimate simplicity of direct brushwork. The
'Four Wangs', Wang Shih-min (1529–1680), Wang Chien (1598–
1677), Wang Hui (1632–1717) and Wang Yuan-chi (1642–1715), were
eminent in landscape; so too was Wu Li (1632–1718). Yun Shou-p'ing
(1633–90) was a painter of flowers with a delightful sense of colour.

[139]

CHINESE PAINTING (after Yen Lipên, Sung copy)—Scholars Collating Chinese Classic Texts—Museum of Fine Arts, Boston.

EMPEROR HUI TSUNG (after Chang Hsuan)—Ladies Preparing Silk—Museum of Fine Arts, Boston.

CHI PAI-SHI—Crabs (Painting on Paper)—Francis Hopp Museum of Eastern Asiatic Arts, Budapest.

HSÜ WEI—Banana Tree and Bunch of Prunus—National Museum, Stockholm.

The upheavals and trials of modern times have not caused the disappearance of the native tradition of brush drawing or impaired the innate artistic sense of the Chinese, though evidently the contacts of East and West and drastic political change have set their problems. Chi Pai-shi (*b.* 1863) is eminent among those who have carried on

CHINESE PAINTING, Fourteenth–Fifteenth Century, Style of Chao Mêng-fu—Horses and Grooms crossing a River (Ink and Colour)—Freer Gallery of Art.

LI T'ANG (attributed to)—Buffaloes and Piping Herd Boy (Water-colour on Silk)—Victoria and Albert Museum.

the great tradition into the twentieth century with no loss of vitality. Printing from wood blocks is said to have been invented in China in the sixth century A.D. and the colour print dates back to before the seventeenth century, but the Japanese, who borrowed the wood-cutting technique from the Chinese, developed it to a far greater extent and to more creative purpose.

Chinoiserie, decorative style in seventeenth- and eighteenth-century Europe fostered by trading contacts with the Far East, and the examples of Chinese lacquer, porcelain, textiles, etc., brought thence. The free adaptation of Chinese design motifs is mainly seen in ceramics, furniture, wallpaper and interior design, but in France, as in the art of Boucher, they were an ingredient in rococo decorative painting.

[142]

Chirico, Giorgio de (*b.* Volo, Greece, 1888), Italian painter who studied art at Athens and Munich (where he was influenced by the work of Max Klinger and Böcklin, q.v.). Painting in Paris between 1911 and 1915, he produced symbols and memories of classical antiquity in Greece and Italy, in which an imaginative mood was conveyed by long shadows, devices of perspective and the introduction of incongruous elements such as a locomotive or factory chimney. 'Melancholy and Mystery of a Street', 1914 (Museum of Modern Art, New York), is an example. With Carlo Carrà (q.v.) he developed, about 1917, what they called 'metaphysical painting', in which geometric forms took on a strange life and poetry. After the Second World War he turned against modern art in general, though, as the creator of a magical or dream-like world, prior to that period he ranks as a precursor of Surrealism and one of the most imaginative artists of his time.

Chodowiecki, Daniel (*b.* Danzig, 16 Oct. 1726; *d.* Berlin, 7 Feb. 1801), Polish painter and engraver, historically included in the German School and once known as the 'German Hogarth'. He became director of the Berlin Academy in 1797. He was a prolific illustrator and his studies of the eighteenth-century German middle class have much documentary value.

Christus, Petrus (*b.* Baerle, 1410; *d.* 1472–3), painter of the early Netherlandish School, active at Bruges by 1444. That he continued the van Eyck manner is evident, though it is doubted whether he was Jan van Eyck's pupil. It is not impossible that he was the 'Piero de Bruges' who worked with 'Antonello da Sicilia' for the Duke of Milan in 1456, which might suggest that Antonello da Messina (q.v.) acquired the van Eyck oil technique through him. Portraits such as those of 'A Young Man' (National Gallery) and 'A Young Woman' (Berlin) show a highly capable painter and designer if not one of the great artists.

[143]

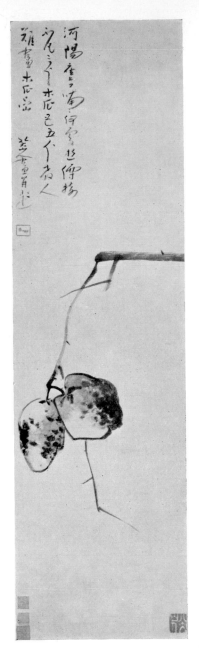

Church, Frederick E. (*b.* Hartford, Connecticut, 14 Mar. 1826; *d.* New York, 7 April 1900), American landscape painter, one of those who carried on the romantic tendencies of the Hudson River School. He took his subjects from many sources in America, north and south, and in the West Indies, painting the majesty of nature with strong effects of light and in great detail.

Chu-Ta (1626 after 1705), Chinese painter, a descendant of the House of Ming, who lived at Nanchang, Kiangsi province. Like his contemporary Tao Chi he became a Buddhist priest and after the fall of the Ming Dynasty took refuge in monastic solitude, devoting himself to calligraphy and painting. He had an extraordinary gift for creating a picture with a few free calligraphic brush-strokes.

Cima, Giovanni Battista (called **Cima da Conegliano**) *b.* Conegliano, 1459–60; *d.* there, 1517–18), Italian painter of the Venetian School, a pupil of Montagna. His work resembles that of Giovanni Bellini (q.v.), whose studio foreman he is said to have been. Paintings by him are in various churches in Venice and a number of galleries, including Milan, Munich, Dresden, the Louvre and the National Gallery. He was noted for his colour and for setting his Madonnas against a landscape background, that of the 'Virgin and Child' in the National Gallery representing the town and castle of his native place.

[144]

G. B. CIMA—Tobias and the Archangel Raphael—Accademia, Venice.

Cimabue, Giovanni (otherwise known as Cenni di Pepo) (b. Florence, 1240; d. there, c. 1302), Italian painter. Very little is known of his life, though he worked in Rome, where he may have received his training, also at Pisa and Florence. He is buried in the cathedral at Florence. The brief reference by his contemporary Dante indicates that he was famous in his own time, believed himself without equal, but was eclipsed in fame by Giotto. Vasari's account of him lacks historical confirmation, and a number of works attributed to him, such as the Rucellai altar-piece of Santa Maria Novella, Florence, are now assigned to Duccio or his school. His only certainly authentic work is the figure of St John in the absidal mosaic of Pisa Cathedral. Frescoes in the Upper Church of St Francis, Assisi (much deteriorated), are credibly attributed to him, and also the versions of 'Madonna and Child with Angels' now in the Uffizi and Louvre, Byzantine in conception but showing a far from conventional vigour of line and humanity of expression. The emotionally impressive 'Crucifix' in Santa Croce, Florence, ascribed to him, was one of the major losses

[145]

CIMABUE—Virgin and Child with Angels—Louvre.

in the calamitous floods
at the city in 1966, be-
ing damaged by oil and
water beyond repair.

Cione, Andrea di, *see*
ORCAGNA; VERROCCHIO.

Claesz, Pieter (*b.*
Steinfurt, Westphalia,
1597-8; *d.* Franckesteeg,
1661), Dutch painter
who worked at Haarlem.
He was noted for the
richness of material
quality in his still lifes.

Classical Painting,
term loosely describing
what can be gathered as
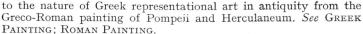
to the nature of Greek representational art in antiquity from the
Greco-Roman painting of Pompeii and Herculaneum. *See* GREEK
PAINTING; ROMAN PAINTING.

Classicism, term indicating the pursuit or attempted revival of an
ideal character in painting, in particular the conception of an ideal
type of human figure. Greek sculpture and to some extent Greco-
Roman painting were the original sources which inspired it, and the
themes of classical mythology provided a suitable type of subject.
The first great return to the antique ideal was that of the Italian
Renaissance, but the masters of that period attained a perfection of
their own in figure painting and composition which also became the
ideal of a later Classicism. Thus Poussin is to be considered a classicist
in his adherence both to antique models and to the grand manner of
Raphael. Rococo painters of the eighteenth century such as Boucher
were classical in subject-matter but not in style, and the attempt to
purify and redefine a classical style was the essence of what is known
as 'neo-classicism', a movement of the late eighteenth and early
nineteenth centuries, to which the discoveries at Pompeii and Herculaneum gave some impetus. Jacques Louis David in painting and his
great pupil Ingres in painting and drawing, and in England John
Flaxman as sculptor and draughtsman, were exponents of neo-
classicism. The style that resulted was linear, hard and would-be
sculptural, rejecting the sensuous attraction of colour, and the
classical subjects favoured by David were severe and republican
rather than the frivolities of fable. It is customary to oppose the neo-
classic to the Romantic, Ingres, e.g., to Delacroix (q.v., *see also*

[147]

RAPHAEL—Parnassus (detail)—Vatican, Rome.

ROMANTIC PAINTING), though the tendencies were not incompatible. The nineteenth century drew away from Classicism in so far as its aims were realist, Realism (q.v.) clearly denoting the departure from the 'ideal'. The legacy of Classicism is to be found in the importance attached to figure drawing by Ingres and such a later disciple as Degas and by the academies of art in teaching. An insular and late form of classic revival was that of the nineteenth century in England, in some degree due to the impression made by the Elgin Marbles, traceable in the academic art of Leighton and Poynter. In a modern sense Classic and Romantic have become convenient terms to point the contrast between the creation of determinate form and the freedom of emotional expression; a geometric abstraction, for instance, might represent the former, an expressionist exercise in colour the latter.

Claude (Gellée) (called Claude Lorrain or Lorraine) (b. Chamagne, Lorraine, 1600; d. Rome, 21 Nov. 1682), French landscape painter, one of the greatest artists of the seventeenth century. Left an orphan as a child, poor and unlettered, he is thought to have lived for a while with his brother, a woodcarver, at Freiburg, and is said to have worked in his early days as a pastry-cook. Travelling merchants, possibly relatives, took the boy to Italy where he found humble employment in artists' studios. He may have studied under an obscure view-painter, Gottfried Waals, at Naples, and at Rome was servant-assistant to Agostino Tassi, the landscape painter and former pupil

[148]

CLAUDE—Seaport: Embarkation of the Queen of Sheba—National Gallery.

CLAUDE—The Enchanted Castle—Birmingham Art Gallery.

of Paul Bril (q.v.). He made one journey, 1625, back to his native country, but at the age of twenty-seven settled in Rome, where he spent the rest of his life, painting works which were highly esteemed and in great demand among patrons resident in Rome, and visiting connoisseurs, French and English. His pictorial record of his compositions, the *Liber Veritatis* (engraved by Earlom in 1777), seems to have been as much a reference list of works that had gone abroad as a list of authentic pictures that could expose forgery. His art was to some extent based on the formulae of Elsheimer (q.v.), Bril and Tassi, and there are threads which link it with the landscape of Domenichino (q.v.), but salient facts are that Claude was a close and original student of nature and a northerner, the more deeply impressed for that reason by the ruins and ancient associations of Rome and its environs. As a painter of luminous effect, sunrise or sunset, he is unequalled, even by Turner, who wished his rival compositions to hang by the Claudes in the National Gallery. The poetic sense of wonder in a legendary land is seen in such a work as the 'Enchanted Castle', which inspired Keats, or in the great 'Seaports' of the National Gallery and Louvre. The duality as between realist and dreamer may be seen in comparison of these with the direct drawings from nature such as the 'View on the Tiber'. (This and many other remarkable drawings are in the British Museum.) Unlike his friend and *confrère* in Rome, Poussin (q.v.), he was 'classical' only in the implication of subject and not in style. To a simple and little varying scheme of composition he added picturesque irregularities of form, and indeed was a founder of that 'picturesque' tradition which, in eighteenth-century England, reproduced 'Claudes' in nature—in the landscape gardening of wealthy art-lovers' estates. He was not a figure draughtsman and variations of style seem to indicate that figures in his paintings were put in for him by other hands, though these small theatrical additions by Jan Miel and others do not detract from the splendour of effect.

J. VAN CLEVE—The Death of Mary (altar-piece)—Wallraf-Richartz Museum, Cologne.

J. CLOUET—Portrait of Francis I—Louvre.

Cleve, Joos van (Joos van der Beke) (*b. c.* 1464; *d.* Antwerp, 1540), Flemish painter, perhaps born at Cleve, who worked at Antwerp but also travelled in Italy, Germany and England. He has been identified with the 'Master of the Death of the Virgin' (q.v.) and painted religious subjects and portraits in which the trace of various masters' styles has been detected, though a main influence on his work was that of Quinten Massys (q.v.).

Clouet, Les, French portrait painters and draughtsmen of the sixteenth century, father and son. The father, **Jean** (or **Janet**) (*b.* Brussels, *c.* 1485; *d.* 1541), is assumed to have been of Flemish origin, possibly the son of the painter Jehan Cloët who was working at Brussels in 1475 and is mentioned in the account books of the Duke of Burgundy. He became painter and *valet de chambre* to Francis I in 1516. The renewal of court life in Francis's reign was accompanied by a great demand for portrait drawings in black or red chalk in which Clouet excelled, his work including 127 such portraits, mostly at the Musée Condé, Chantilly, comparable with those of Holbein, though distinct and freer in style. His son, **François** (*b.* Tours, before 1520; *d.* Paris, 22 Sept. 1572), succeeded his father in Francis I's service in 1541 and worked also under Henry II, Francis II and Charles IX. His portrait of a Parisian apothecary, Pierre Quthe, 1562 (Louvre), and that of Elizabeth of Austria, 1571, attributed to him, show the Italian influence of the time. His drawings (Musée Condé and Bibliothèque Nationale) are less robust than those of Jean, but his fame was even greater (though both were renowned), Ronsard calling François 'honneur de notre temps'. The name of a third Clouet (de Navarre) appears in records, and a number of other artists worked in a closely related style.

Codex (Lat. 'block of wood'), manuscript in the book form which first came into use at the beginning of the Christian era, as distinct from the earlier roll, and originating from the wax-covered tablets

on which the Romans wrote. A codex of two leaves was called a diptych, of three a triptych and so on, these terms persisting in the Middle Ages as a description of the hinged panels on which an altar-piece was painted. The use of vellum brought with it the art of manuscript painting and ornamentation, the earliest specimen extant of the painted codex being the Virgil of the Vatican Library (third or fourth century A.D.). The term is applied not only to early European manuscripts but to the picture-books of pre-Columbian Mexico, painted on strips of deerskin or tree-bark. *See* MEXICAN PAINTING.

Coello, Alonso Sánchez (*c.* 1532–88), Spanish portrait painter, the pupil of Anthonis Mor (q.v.). He became court painter to Philip II, of whom he painted a number of likenesses. As keeper of the royal collection he had works by Titian under his care, and utilized Titian's portrait accessories in his own painting, devoting much meticulous attention to rich detail of costume. The 'Portrait of a Young Man', probably Alessandro Farnese (National Gallery of Ireland), is a good example of his somewhat stiff distinction. He was the master of Pantoja de la Cruz (q.v.).

Coello, Claudio (*b.* Madrid, *c.* 1630; *d.* there, 20 April 1693), Spanish painter of religious and decorative works on a large scale, who became painter to Charles II. He was of Portuguese descent. His principal work was the altar-piece in the sacristy of the Escorial, the 'Transfer of the Eucharist', which introduced Charles kneeling among the nobles of his court. He was saddened at the end of his life by the preference given by the king to the Neapolitan, Luca Giordano (q.v.).

Cole, Thomas (*b.* Bolton, Lancashire, 1 Feb. 1801; *d.* Catskill, 11 Feb. 1848), American landscape painter, the principal representative of the Hudson River School (*see* AMERICAN PAINTING). Born in England, he emigrated with his family in 1819 to Ohio, whence he went to New York, settling, 1826, at the village of Catskill on the west bank of the Hudson. He was a self-taught artist but developed a skill in rendering spacious views which won great success, 'In the

Catskills' (New York Metropolitan Museum) being an example. He was able to travel to England and Italy, 1829 –1832, and returned with larger Romantic ambitions, producing a series of landscape allegories ('The Voyage of Life', 'The Course of Empire') and nostalgic Italian compositions.

Collage (Fr. 'pasting', 'sticking' or 'paper-hanging'), use of materials of any kind—pieces of newspaper, wallpaper, fabric, etc.—stuck on a canvas or other surface, usually in conjunction with a painted or drawn element of design, a device of Cubist and Dadaist artists. The purpose, as in the Cubist still life of Braque and Picasso, was not only decorative but also to provide a visual stimulant by the contrast or harmony of a real material substance with a painted surface. The Dadaists extended the idea to any assortment of incongruous objects, fortuitously producing some striking or ingenious effect, such as Kurt Schwitter's 'compositions' of bus tickets and other odds and ends. Max Ernst gave it a surrealist weirdness by fitting together incongruous cuttings from nineteenth-century wood-engravings, a process which may be compared with the photographer's 'montage'. He also invented 'frottage' (q.v.), which simply meant the addition to a design of a rubbing taken from some uneven surface and reproducing its irregularities and texture.

Commonwealth Art Museums and Galleries. The National Gallery of Canada, Ottawa, founded by the Marquess of Lorne in 1880, contains a large collection of Canadian art, many fine works of the historical European schools and a collection of growing importance of modern painting and sculpture. The Art Gallery of Toronto, established in 1913, also contains works by Canadian artists and works by British and French masters. The Beaverbrook Art Gallery, founded by Lord Beaverbrook, was opened at Fredericton, New Brunswick, in 1959. The National Art Gallery of New South Wales, Sydney, first opened in 1885, contains the most representative collection of Australian art as well as examples of modern British and European painting. The National Gallery of Victoria, first opened in 1875, has a large bequest which has been devoted to the acquisition of many important works by historical European masters, e.g. Tiepolo's 'Banquet of Cleopatra', purchased in 1933. The National Art Gallery of South Australia, Adelaide, has a large collection of Australian art. The National Gallery of New Zealand, Auckland, opened in 1888, is divided between the work of New Zealand artists and examples of modern British and continental painting. The South African National Art Gallery, Cape Town, founded in 1872 and opened in its present buildings in 1930, has a number of works by British and modern European artists. The Africana Museum, Johannesburg, founded in 1936, has an extensive collection of paintings and prints of South Africa.

Composition, intended effect of a painting seen as a whole; the various means by which its unity and coherence are achieved. Linear composition implies the basic two-dimensional plan as represented by, e.g., a diagonal, a system of radiating or curving lines, or such a simple geometrical figure as the triangle, these being implicit in well-composed pictures of an elaborately representational kind. Chiaroscuro (q.v.) is another aspect of composition, concerned with the balance of light and shade and the arrangement of objects in depth to give the effect of three dimensions. Colour composition is the application of principles of harmony, contrast and repetition.

Conder, Charles (b. London, 24 Oct. 1868; d. Virginia Water, 9 Feb. 1909), English painter and lithographer who spent some early years in Australia but returned to Europe in 1890, studying art in Paris and settling in London, 1894. He cultivated a decorative style of delicate charm, especially in water-colours on panels of white silk, painted fans of Watteauesque suggestion being typical of his art.

Coninxloo, Gillis van (b. Antwerp, 1544; d. 1607), Flemish landscape painter and engraver, the pupil of Pieter Coecke. He settled at Amsterdam and is notable not only for his influence on the development of Dutch landscape but also in having helped to inspire that of Rubens. His son, of the same name, was noted as a flower painter.

Constable, John (b. East Bergholt, Suffolk, 11 June 1776; d. Hampstead, 1 April 1837), one of the greatest landscape painters, the son of an East Anglian miller. Employed as a youth in the family mill he developed slowly as an artist, being twenty-three before he began to study at the Royal Academy Schools, and thirty-five when the 'Dedham Vale' of 1811 first proclaimed his striking originality. In this long formative period two main factors can be found: firstly the study and assimilation of what had been achieved in landscape painting by Claude, Ruisdael, Rubens, Gainsborough and Girtin (the collection of Sir George Beaumont, who encouraged him, being a great stimulus); and secondly a love of nature as represented by the unobstructed cloud panorama, the flat lands, streams, water meadows and cornfields of his native East Anglia and especially the part of the

G. VAN CONINXLOO II—Flowers in a Vase—Collection of Mrs Geoffrey Hart.

J. CONSTABLE—The Leaping Horse—Royal Academy, Diploma Collection.

Stour valley near his home now known as the 'Constable country'. His subjects were not confined to Suffolk, though when settled in London he went there nearly every year. He painted memorable works at Salisbury, Hampstead and Brighton also, but was essentially an artist of the lowlands and scenes of a modestly rural kind, and a visit to the Lake District in 1806 did not incline him to the mountain scenery delightful to the Romantic mind. The self-imposed limitation distinguishes him from his contemporary (of nearly the same age) Turner; Constable is typical of the Romantic period, in which he lived only in the Wordsworthian return to nature and the study of natural phenomena after the stresses of revolution and war.

Married in 1816 after a lengthy period of waiting, an A.R.A. in 1819 and in that year relieved of money anxieties by a timely legacy, Constable now devoted all his powers to a succession of great works, among which may be cited the 'Hay-wain' (originally 'Landscape, Noon'), painted in 1821 and exhibited in the Paris Salon of 1824, where it made a deep impression (National Gallery), the 'Leaping Horse', 1825, perhaps his masterpiece (Royal Academy), 'The Corn-field', 1827 (National Gallery), 'Hadleigh Castle', 1829 (National Gallery), 'Salisbury Cathedral from the Meadows', 1831, 'The Valley Farm', 1835 (Tate Gallery).

His finished works were preceded by large preparatory paintings in which his freshness of handling, technical freedom and audacity in

J. CONSTABLE—Weymouth Bay—National Gallery.

J. CONSTABLE—Study for 'The Hay-wain'—Victoria and Albert Museum.

the use of broken colour are more apparent. These again are to be distinguished from the small sketches made from nature which give incomparably the vividness of direct impression. His water-colours are subsidiary, mainly preparatory studies for oils, though including so dramatic an example as the 'Stonehenge' in the Victoria and Albert Museum, which has the magnificent family bequest of his work. His paintings were sympathetically reproduced in the excellent mezzotints of David Lucas. In England the immediate influence of his genius was practically nil; in France, on the other hand, it was a revelation inspiring to the landscape school of the 1830's, while Impressionism has in him its great forerunner. (Colour   )

Constructivism, art movement which developed in Russia in the early years of the Bolshevik Revolution. It was the product of Cubism and Futurism, Cubist collage (q.v.) and 'constructions' of various materials suggesting new uses for and effects to be gained from glass, metal, wire, etc., while Futurism added the theory that movement in space was a more desirable end than a static solidity. Thus the architect Vladimir Tatlin projected a monument to the Third Communist International consisting of a series of glass chambers continually revolving at different speeds. Constructivism reflected a trend of ideas, short-lived in Russia, which operated more generally in modern architecture, industrial design and plastic experiment, the last being the contribution to sculpture of the brothers Pevsner and Gabo, who worked in Russia until 1921 and subsequently in Germany and Paris. The movement contributed little or nothing to pictorial art except to affirm an abstract or non-figurative trend.

Contour, outline in a drawing or painting which suggests the modelling and character of the form it contains and also its relation to a given spatial area.

Contrapposto, Italian word signifying an opposition of movement, and referring to the rendering of the human figure in which the upper part of the body turns in one direction, the lower limbs in another. A device used by Hellenistic sculptors, it was employed by painters of the Italian Renaissance and after to give a dramatic and energetic effect.

Conversation Piece, informal portrait group showing members of a family, sometimes with their friends, with a background of their customary surroundings and belongings, usually in a domestic interior and unselfconsciously engaged in some familiar routine. The scale is generally small and appropriately intimate. Prototypes of the *genre* are to be found in seventeenth-century Dutch and Flemish art, but it was more particularly a development of eighteenth-century English portraiture, Hogarth, Devis, Zoffany and others providing many examples. English artists have always found it congenial, Sir William Nicholson's 'Mr and Mrs Sidney Webb', 1929 (London School of Economics), being a modern instance.

Cooper, Samuel (*b.* London, 1609; *d.* London, 5 May 1672), English

[158]

miniature painter who studied under his uncle, John Hoskins. He painted many celebrities of the Commonwealth and Restoration, one of his best works being his portrait of Oliver Cromwell, his miniature from the life (collection of the Duke of Buccleuch) being the 'master-sketch' of many versions. He departed from the tradition of Hilliard and Oliver in giving the miniature some of the quality of the large oil portrait, being known as a 'van Dyck in little'. His contemporaries greatly admired him and to Aubrey he was 'the prince of limners'. His brother Alexander (fl. 1630–60) was also a miniature painter who worked at Amsterdam and at the court of Queen Christina of Sweden.

Copley, John Singleton (*b.* Boston, Mass., 3 July 1737; *d.* London, 9 Dec. 1815), American painter of portraits and historical subjects, who became a portrait painter at Boston as a young man. He probably had some training from his stepfather, Peter Pelham, a painter and engraver of Boston. In the sincerity of his study of character and his fine craftsmanship he ranks as the most distinguished of the portraitists of the colonial period, his 'Mrs Thomas Boylston' (Harvard) being an impressive example. He painted George Washington in 1755 and by 1774 had produced some three hundred portraits. Encouraged to go to England by Reynolds and West, he settled in London after a visit to Italy and was elected R.A. in 1799. American critics give a somewhat gloomy view of his life in England and its effect on his art, yet the 'history pictures' to which he turned show his exceptional ability, 'The Death of Major Pierson'

J. S. COPLEY—The Death of Major Pierson—Tate Gallery.

G. COQUES—The Verbiest Family—Reproduced by Gracious Permission of Her Majesty the Queen, Buckingham Palace.

(Tate Gallery) being a masterpiece in this *genre*, while his portrait of the Royal Princesses (Buckingham Palace), painted for George III in 1785, is an excellent work. His son became Lord Chancellor, titled Baron Lyndhurst.

Coques, Gonzales (*b*. Antwerp, 1618; *d*. there, 18 April 1684), Flemish portrait and *genre* painter, the pupil of Pieter Brueghel the Younger (q.v.) and the minor painter, David Ryckaert. He had great success with paintings on a miniature scale in which he sought to adapt van Dyck's elegance, being known as the 'little van Dyck'.

Corbusier, Le (Charles-Édouard Jeanneret) (*b*. La Chaux-de-Fonds, 1887), French-Swiss architect and artist. Though noted mainly for his work and books on modern architectural design and planning, he was, together with Ozenfant, an originator of 'Purism' in painting, a form of abstract design developed from the Cubism of Gris and Léger (qq.v.), somewhat related to his ideas of architecture.

Corinth, Lovis (*b*. Tapiau, East Prussia, 21 July 1858; *d*. Zandvoort, Holland, 17 July 1925), German painter, etcher and lithographer, a leading exponent of Impressionism in Germany. He studied at Königsberg and Munich and in Paris under Bouguereau, and from 1900 worked in Berlin, being active in the Berlin Secession (*see* SECESSION). He is noted for his portraits.

[160]

Corneille de Lyon (Corneille de la Haye) (*d. c.* 1574), painter of the French School, born in the Netherlands, probably at The Hague. He became a naturalized Frenchman in 1547 and was court painter to Henry II and Charles IX, working at Lyons between 1541 and 1574. He painted small portraits, a number of such works, distinguishable from those of his contemporary François Clouet (q.v.) (and not apparently based like them on preliminary drawings), being considered as in his style, though no works are attributed to him with certainty.

Cornelisz, Cornelis (Cornelis van Haarlem) (*b.* Haarlem, 1562; *d.* there, 11 Nov. 1638), Dutch historical and portrait painter, the pupil at Haarlem of Pieter Aertzen (q.v.), studying also at Rouen and Antwerp. His 'Banquet of the Archers' Guild' (Haarlem) illustrates the type of group portraiture that became a distinctive Dutch achievement.

Cornelisz, Jakob (Cornelisz van Oostzanen) (*b.* Oostzanen, *c.* ?1477; *d.* Amsterdam, before 18 Oct. 1533), Dutch painter who worked at Amsterdam. He is one of the Dutch 'primitives', his style modelled on that of the south Netherlands but adding to it a hard precision, as in the 'Christ appearing to Mary Magdalene' (Kassel). He was the master of Jan Scorel (q.v.).

Cornelisz, Lucas (*b.* Leyden, 1495; *d. c.* 1552), Dutch subject and portrait painter trained by his father, Cornelisz Engelbrechtsz. He came to England, *c.* 1527, and was one of Henry VIII's court painters. At a later date he was employed at Ferrara.

Cornelius, Peter von (*b.* Düsseldorf, 23 Sept. 1783; *d.* Berlin, 6 Mar. 1867), German painter, a member of the Nazarener group (q.v.). He worked in his early days at Frankfurt and in 1811 joined Overbeck (q.v.) and others in Rome in their attempt to revive a monastic workshop. In 1824 he was appointed director of the Academy of

Munich, being greatly admired by Ludwig of Bavaria, and was responsible for much fresco painting in Munich and Berlin, e.g. the 'Last Judgment' (Ludwigskirche, Munich). His work was insipid and imperfect in colour, though as a teacher he was influential and had numerous pupils.

Corot, Jean Baptiste Camille (*b*. Paris, 16 July 1796; *d*. there, 22 Feb. 1875), French painter, renowned in landscape. According to the wishes of his parents, who had a fashionable dress shop in Paris, after education at the college of Rouen he worked until 1822 in a cloth warehouse, but was then given a small allowance to study painting. He spent a few months with the young and short-lived Michallon, who directed him to the study of nature, afterwards (to no recorded purpose) working under another painter, Victor Bertin. It is reasonable to suppose that he was impressed by Constable in the Salon of 1824; going to Rome the following year he showed in his first Italian landscapes a response to effects of sun and cloud that seems, as in the 'Claudian Aqueduct' (National Gallery), related to the work of the English master. Their breadth and directness of style marked a new conception of landscape in French art. His first Salon picture, 1827, was the 'Vue prise à Narni' (National Gallery of Canada), and in 1828 he returned to France, painting some of his best pictures in the following six years, and working in Paris and Normandy, at Fontainebleu, Ville d'Avray and elsewhere, the light of Italy giving place to harmonies of silvery grey. His stay at Fontainebleau places him in close relation with the Barbizon School (q.v.). A second visit to Italy,

J. B. C. COROT—Dance of the Nymphs—Louvre.

J. B. C. COROT—Interrupted Reading—Art Institute of Chicago, Potter Palmer
Collection.

J. B. C. COROT—Horseman in a Wood—National Gallery.

1834, and another in 1843 produced further masterly works, such as his 'Villa d'Este', though it was long before Corot sold a picture or obtained public recognition, despite the admiration of friends. Late in life, however, he enjoyed great success, generously sharing its rewards with such less fortunate artists as Daumier (q.v.), though the paintings most popular were not always his best. His work can be conveniently divided into three groups: the paintings and studies made directly from nature, which include landscapes painted in Italy, France, Switzerland and Holland and figures painted either in the open or in the studio; the more academic Salon pictures with some religious, mythological or literary element of subject; thirdly the 'souvenirs' of the 1860's and 1870's, quickly executed small landscapes of a vaporous charm which tended to become superficial. These, once constituting the most sought-after phase of his art, are now looked on as something of an aberration, though splendid works directly inspired by nature were produced at the same time or later. His figures, e.g. 'Interrupted Reading' (Chicago Art Institute), showed a master's power, and a late work, such as 'The Belfry of Douais', 1871 (Louvre), is of undiminished vigour. A benevolent and illustrious bachelor, 'le Père Corot' was a guiding light of nineteenth-century French landscape, of Boudin, Pissarro, Berthe Morisot (qq.v.) and in general of the Impressionists.

Correggio, Antonio Allegri da (b. Correggio, c. 1489; d. there, 5 Mar. 1534), Italian painter so called from the place of his birth, a small town near Modena. He studied as a boy in the studio of Bianchi Ferrari at Modena and at Mantua with Mantegna, though temperamentally he was less in sympathy with that master than with Leonardo, whose influence is to be seen in Correggio's subtly graduated chiaroscuro. His time was divided in the main between Parma and his native town, but there is a strong presumption that he visited

CORREGGIO—Mercury instructing Cupid before Venus—National Gallery.

Rome and that the great frescoes of Michelangelo and Raphael inspired him with a new vigour and audacity apparent in the series of frescoes he undertook at Parma. Those in the Camera di San Paolo (the chamber of the abbess) in the monastery of St Lodovico, 1518, were the earliest, but the 'Ascension of Christ' for the cupola of San Giovanni, 1520–3, and the 'Assumption of the Virgin' for the cathedral, 1524–30, which won the highest praise from Titian, show his full capacity. In his powerful and theatrically audacious grouping of a host of figures he anticipates the baroque methods of church decoration. As an oil painter of both religious and mythological subjects he perfected a rich technique, and famous examples are the 'Nativity' (Dresden), 'Ecce Homo' and 'Mercury instructing Cupid' (National Gallery), the 'Marriage of St Catherine' and 'Jupiter and Antiope' (Louvre), 'Jupiter and Io' (Vienna) and 'Danae' (Rome). In the pagan subjects especially there appears a sensuous and feminine charm and softness of modelling, another aspect of the genius which provided a model for the artists of the Counter-Reformation.

Cortona, Pietro da (*b.* Cortona, 1 Nov. 1596; *d.* Rome, 16 May 1669), Italian painter and architect called after his birthplace, his real name being Pietro Berettini. He was a main exponent of the baroque style of church and palace decoration in the extravagant form it took in the Italy of the Counter-Reformation. He studied at Cortona under a Florentine painter, Andrea Commodi, and then in Rome, where he attracted the notice of Urban VIII and enjoyed the patronage of a succession of pontiffs. Between 1620 and 1640 he produced paintings for the Marchese Sacchetti (Rome, Capitoline Gallery), frescoes for Cardinal Francesco Barberini in Santa Bibiana and other Roman churches, and his masterpiece, the allegorical ceiling painting for the Barberini Palace, 1633–9 (Rome, Galleria Nazionale), in which the illusionist effect of figures foreshortened and floating in space as seen from below was contrived with immense skill and daring. Outside Rome he worked only in Florence (decorations for the Pitti Palace, 1640–7), refusing invitations to go to France and Spain; later resuming work in Rome in the Pamfili and Barberini palaces. He collaborated with the theologian G. D. Ottonelli in a treatise on painting and sculpture, 1653, and as architect was responsible for the façade of Santa Maria in Via Lata and the church of San Martino in which he was buried.

Cosimo, Piero di, *see* PIERO.

Cossa, Francesco (*b.* Ferrara, 1435; *d.* Bologna, 1477), Italian painter of the Ferrarese School, probably the pupil of Cosimo Tura (q.v.). He worked at the court of Ferrara, and a series of frescoes representing 'The Months' for the Schifanoia Palace, 1470, constitutes one of his best-known works. A figure of Autumn (Berlin) is a distinguished work of this kind. He quitted Ferrara for Bologna, where he produced a number of church paintings, including his altarpiece, 'The Madonna Enthroned'. A painter of great ability and influence, he was the master of Lorenzo Costa (q.v.).

F. COSSA—Allegory of Autumn—Staatliche Museum, Berlin.

L. COSTA—St Urban converting St Valerian—Church of St Cecilia, Bologna.

Costa, Lorenzo (*b.* Ferrara, 1460; *d.* Mantua, 1535), Italian painter of the Ferrarese School, a pupil of Francesco Cossa (q.v.), whose work has also some relation with that of Cosimo Tura and Ercole de Roberti (qq.v.). He worked at Bologna, a celebrated early painting being his 'Madonna Enthroned with the Bentivoglio Family', 1487, in the Bentivoglio Chapel of San Giacomo Maggiore. Francesco Francia (q.v.) was his assistant and colleague at Bologna. He followed Mantegna as court painter to the Gonzagas at Mantua in 1509. His two sons, Ippolito and Girolamo, were also painters.

Cosway, Richard (*b.* Tiverton, 1742; *d.* London, 4 July 1821), English portrait painter and fashionable miniaturist of the Georgian and Regency period. He led the eighteenth-century revival of the

J. S. COTÁN—Quince, Cabbage, Melon and Cucumber—San Diego Gallery, California.

miniature, showing an exceptional lightness of touch and becoming very successful through the favour of the Prince of Wales, who greatly admired his portrait of Mrs Fitzherbert (Wallace Collection). He lived a life of lavish splendour with his wife Maria Cecilia Louisa, also a miniature painter, who lived abroad after his death and published a volume of his designs, Florence, 1826.

Cotán, Juan Sánchez (1561–1627), Spanish painter who became a Carthusian monk, trained by the still-life painter, Blas de Ledesma. He worked at Granada and produced many pictures of fruit and flowers, related to the still life of Caravaggio (q.v.) in design and lighting and anticipating the still life of Zurbarán (q.v.). His 'Quince, Cabbage, Melon and Cucumber' (San Diego, California) is one of the masterpieces of the *genre*.

Cotes, Francis (*b*. London, 1726; *d*. there, 19–20 July 1770), English painter and pastellist, the pupil of George Knapton. A minor artist, he shared in the elegance of the age of Reynolds and Gainsborough, worked in London and Bath and was a founder member of the Royal Academy. His crayon portraits were much esteemed and he is also seen to good advantage in his oil portrait of Paul Sandby

J. S. COTMAN—The Ploughed Field (Water-colour)—Temple Newsam Gallery, Leeds.

J. S. COTMAN—Greta Bridge, Yorkshire (Water-colour)—British Museum.

(Tate Gallery). His brother and pupil was the miniaturist, Samuel Cotes (1734–1818).

Cotman, John Sell (*b*. Norwich, 16 May 1782; *d*. London, 28 July 1842), English landscape painter in water-colour and oils. He studied as a youth in London, was one of Dr Monro's protégés, and exhibited at the Royal Academy, 1800–6, early water-colours made in Yorkshire, e.g. the beautiful 'Greta Bridge' (British Museum) being among the classics of the art. He returned to Norwich in 1807, worked there and at Yarmouth as drawing master, and with Crome was a leader of the 'Norwich School' (q.v.). His appointment as drawing master at King's College, London, in 1834 lightened a constant burden of material difficulties. In the simplification of design to broad, expressively silhouetted areas, he was highly original and unlike any of his contemporaries. Time spent on drawing antiquities for his patron in Norfolk, Dawson Turner, was largely wasted, and his later work is unequal, but it included excellent oil-paintings in his own distinct manner as well as some masterly drawings. Of his two painter sons, Joseph John (1814–78) and Miles Edmund (1810–58), the latter is the more distinguished for his river and sea views.

Courbet, Gustave (*b*. Ornans, 10 June 1819; *d*. La Tour de Peilz, Vaud, 31 Dec. 1877), French painter, born of a peasant family of Franche-Comté. He went to Paris in 1841, his training mainly consisting in the study and imitation of old masters in the Louvre, especially Velazquez and Rembrandt. In defiance of both Romanticism and Classicism he evolved the idea of Realism, asserting,

G. COURBET—The Artist's Studio—Louvre.

G. COURBET—Winter Scene with Deer—Musée de Lyon.

that is, that painting should consist in 'the representation of real and existing things', his aim therefore being, in his own words, to 'interpret the manners, ideas and aspect of our own time'. In this there were some social and proletarian implications, as might be gathered from his 'Stonebreakers', 1849 (Dresden, destroyed 1945), and the 'Burial at Ornans' (Louvre), with its sombre group of peasants, which caused an uproar when exhibited at the Salon of 1850. This picture and 'The Artist's Studio' (Louvre), described as an 'allegory of reality' and depicting the artist at work on a landscape watched by a nude model and a group of friends including Baudelaire and Proudhon, were refused by the jury of the Exposition Universelle of 1855. Courbet opened a rival exhibition with a catalogue containing a manifesto on Realism, and in the notoriety that followed stood out as a new force in art, acclaimed as such both in France and elsewhere in Europe. The 1860's saw his triumph; 1870, when he exhibited 'The Stormy Sea' and 'La Falaise d'Etretat', the height of his glory; but he was involved in the riots of the Commune of 1871, and though he protected the Louvre from fire was held responsible for inciting the destruction of the Vendôme column and sentenced to six months' imprisonment (occupied by painting a self-portrait and some magnificent still lifes). Special animus seems to have pursued him as a man of revolutionary ideas, for the case was reopened in 1873, his goods

were confiscated and he took refuge in Switzerland, spending the last
four years of his life near Vevey painting landscapes (numerous
versions of the Château de Chillon) and portraits. His powerful
genius found expression in portraiture; figure composition; landscape—the gorges and forests of his native Franche-Comte and superb
paintings of the Normandy coast, 'The Wave' being famous in
several versions; sensuous paintings of the nude; animal studies and
still life. In technique he was heavy-handed and opened no new
prospect, but a massive genius is always apparent in his work and the
Realism which was his watchword was inspiring to Manet and the
young Impressionists. He is one of France's great artists.

Courtauld Institute Gallery, London, gallery of the Courtauld Institute of Art, opened to the public in 1958. It comprises the collection of old masters of the late Lord Lee of Fareham, the collection
of modern paintings made by Roger Fry, the old master drawings
(3,500 in total) bequeathed by Sir Robert Witt to the Courtauld
Institute, and the great collection of modern French masters formed
by the late Samuel Courtauld. The Gambier–Parry collection of early
Italian paintings, ceramics and ivories was an important bequest in
1967.

Cousin, Jean (*b.* Sens, *c.* 1490; *d.* Paris, 1560 or 1561), French painter
of the Fontainebleau School. He began as a glass painter but is mainly
of note as having produced the first important French painting of the

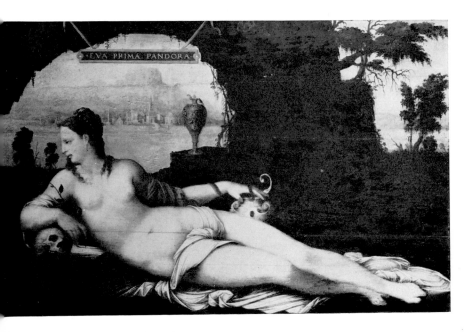

J. COUSIN—Eva prima Pandora—Louvre.

nude, his 'Eva prima Pandora' (Louvre), a Mannerist work influenced by Titian and Giorgione. His son, Jean Cousin the Younger (*c*. 1520–*c*. 1592), was an artist of varied talents, being also a glass painter and goldsmith, miniaturist, sculptor and engraver. He painted in oils a 'Last Judgment' (Louvre) with a multitude of nude figures.

Couture, Thomas (*b*. Senlis, 21 Dec. 1815; *d*. Villiers-le-Bel, 31 Mar. 1879), French painter, a pupil of Gros (q.v.), noted mainly for his academic (and politely orgiastic) 'Romans of the Decadence', 1847 (Louvre). He was also an able portrait painter and celebrated in the 1850's as a teacher, Manet (q.v.) being among his pupils. He abandoned art in later life, retiring into obscurity.

Cox, David (*b*. Deritend, nr Birmingham, 29 April 1783; *d*. Harbourne, 7 June 1859) English landscape painter. After a varied experience in painting the lids of snuff-boxes and also scenery for the provincial theatre, he had some lessons in water-colour from John Varley (q.v.) and became a drawing master in London and at Hereford. In later years he painted much in North Wales and his inn sign for the Royal Oak, Bettws-y-Coed, is famous. He is noted for water-colours in which broken touches and atmospheric effect give a distant anticipation of Impressionism. He took to oils late in life, adapting his water-colour technique. '**A Windy Day**' (Tate Gallery) well shows his special gift. His treatises on painting are the more conventional recipes of the drawing master.

Coxcie (**Coxcyen**), **Michiel van** (*b*. Malines, 1499; *d*. Antwerp, 10 Mar. 1592), Flemish painter and engraver of religious subjects. He was the pupil of van Orley (q.v.) but after his visit to Rome based his style on that of Raphael. He worked at Brussels and Antwerp, where his 'St Sebastian' and 'Triumph of Christ' are in the Musée Royal, and copied the van Eyck 'Adoration of the Lamb' for Philip II.

Coypel, name of a French painter family. **Noël** (*b*. Paris, 25 Dec. 1628; *d*. there, 24 Dec. 1707) was the founder of the dynasty. He was employed, 1655, on the decoration of the Louvre, became a member of the Académie, 1659, and director of the French Academy at Rome, 1672, afterwards executing further decorative paintings in Paris (Tuileries and vault of the Invalides). His son, **Antoine** (*b*, Paris, 11 April 1661; *d*. there, 7 Jan. 1722), studied under Noël at Rome and was much influenced by baroque art, decorating in this manner ceilings of the Palais Royal and of the chapel of Versailles. He became principal painter to the king, 1715. Like his father he executed numerous designs for Gobelins tapestries. Another son of Noël, **Noël Nicolas** (*b*. Paris, 17 Nov. 1690; *d*. there, 14 Nov. 1734), was a minor subject painter. The son of Antoine, **Charles-Antoine** (*b*. Paris, 11 July 1694; *d*. there, 14 June 1752), like his father was painter to the king, and was also director of the Académie and illustrator of *Don Quixote* and works by Molière.

Cozens, Alexander (*b. c*. 1717; *d*. London, 23 April 1786), English painter, born in Russia, son of a shipbuilder employed by Peter the Great. He was sent to Italy to study art, settled in England and

J. R. COZENS—Between Chamounix and Martigny (Water-colour)—The J. Leslie Wright Collection.

became drawing master at Eton and to children of George III. He devised a system of evolving a composition from more or less accidental blots (on lines originally suggested by Leonardo) which caused him to be described as 'blotmaster to the town'. It is expounded in his pamphlet (published 1785) 'New Method for Assisting the Invention in the Composition of Landscape'.

Cozens, John Robert (*b.* London, 1752; *d. c.* 1797–9), one of the most poetic of English water-colourists, the son and pupil of his father, Alexander. He accompanied Richard Payne Knight, 1776, and William Beckford, 1782–3, on the Grand Tour as professional draughtsman, going via Switzerland to Italy. Paintings of Swiss mountain scenery, possibly owing something to the Swiss water-colourist Ducros, and of the couutry round Rome, where he stayed, 1778–9, were romantic in vision rather than topographical, spacious in effect and harmoniously conceived in a limited range of tones. There is a splendid collection in the British Museum. He became insane in 1794 and was cared for by Dr Monro, the patron of art, Cozens's drawings in his collection being a major influence on the young Girtin and Turner, employed by Monro in copying them.

Craig, Edward Gordon (*b.* Stevenage, 16 Jan. 1872; *d.* Venice, 18 July 1966), stage designer and graphic artist. The son of the architect E. W. Godwin and Ellen Terry, he had early connections with the stage and was also taught wood-engraving by William Nicholson (q.v.). He produced in all more than five hundred wood engravings, designs for scenes and costumes or book decorations and had an

[175]

international influence on theatrical production. His *Hamlet*, 1930, was a main work of book decoration.

Cranach the Elder, Lucas (*b.* Kronach, Franconia, 4(?) Oct. 1472; *d.* Weimar, 16 Oct. 1553), German painter and engraver who adopted the name of his birthplace, being originally Lucas Maler (or Muller). He is supposed the pupil of his father, Hans, went to Vienna about 1500 and from 1505 was court painter to three successive Electors of Saxony at Wittenberg, of which he was twice burgomaster. Frederick the Wise granted him the crest of winged serpent with which he marked his work. He accompanied the Elector Johann Friedrich during his captivity at Augsburg and Innsbruck, 1550–2; returned to Wittenberg in 1552 and then retired to Weimar. A friend of Melanchthon and Luther, he reflects in his art the cross-currents of his time, his religious subjects giving place to portraits of the Lutheran circle and to the mythology or allegory popular with Renaissance princes. The nude figures of his allegories are distinct and original in style and charm. His engravings on wood and copper are also distinguished but rare. He had a busy workshop in which he was assisted by his two sons, Hans (*d.* 1537) and Lucas the Younger (*d.* 1586).

Crawhall, Joseph (*b.* Morpeth, Northumberland, 1861; *d.* London, 1913), English painter noted for his water-colours of animals and birds in which he showed an unusual capacity for rendering essentials with simplified brushstroke. He worked for a time in Glasgow and a number of his best works are in the Burrell Collection at Glasgow. 'The Dove' (Tate Gallery) well illustrates his style.

Crayer (Craeyer), Gaspar de (*b.* Antwerp, 1 April 1584; *d.* Ghent, 1669), Flemish painter of religious and allegorical subjects and portraits. He was greatly influenced by Rubens and painted many church altar-pieces, among them 'The Assumption' (Ghent Cathedral). He went to Madrid as painter to the court but settled afterwards at Ghent.

'Creation of Adam', by Michelangelo, perhaps the greatest of the compositions into which the ceiling of the Sistine Chapel, painted 1508–12, is divided, fourth of the series in which he interprets the Creation as described in the Book of Genesis.

Credi, Lorenzo di (*b.* Florence, *c.* 1458; *d.* there, 12 Jan. 1537), Italian painter of the Florentine School, the son of a goldsmith and a fellow pupil with Leonardo da Vinci under Verrocchio, whose portrait he painted (Uffizi). He remained Verrocchio's assistant until the latter's death in 1498. His work reflects the influence of the young Leonardo but shows no great originality. He burnt some of his paintings in Savonarola's bonfire of 'vanities', 1497, though he was little affected by the pagan direction of Renaissance art and is mainly known by decorous religious paintings in which his fondness for painting children appears. They include the Nativity (Florence, Accademia), the 'Madonna and Child' (Louvre), considered by Vasari his masterpiece, and Madonnas in the National Gallery and elsewhere.

[176]

L. CRANACH—Jealousy—National Gallery.

Crespi, Giovanni Battista (*b.* Cerano, *c.* 1557; *d.* Milan, 1633), also called Il Cerano, Italian painter, sculptor and architect, a gifted and versatile artist of the Lombard School. He studied in Milan, Rome and Venice and from 1620 was director of the painting school in the Accademia Ambrosiana, Milan. Guercino (q.v.) was his pupil.

Crespi, Giuseppe Maria (*b.* Bologna, 1665; *d.* there, 1747), Italian painter of religious subjects, portraits and *genre*, called 'Lo Spagnuolo' from his love of finery. He studied at Bologna under Canuti and Cignani and formed his style on the Carracci, Guercino, Barocci and Correggio, though later declaring his attachment to Pietro da Cortona. His characteristic dusky tones had their appeal for the Venetian, Piazzetta. He also produced caricatures and etchings after Rembrandt and Salvator. Among his principal works are the 'Massacre of the Innocents' (Bologna), the series of 'Seven Sacraments' (Dresden) and 'Aeneas, the Sibyl and Charon' (Vienna). His three sons were also painters.

Crivelli, Carlo (*b.* Venice, active 1457; *d.* 1493), Italian painter of the Venetian School, trained in the school of the Vivarini (q.v.) at Murano, but also showing the influence of Squarcione (q.v.) and the Paduan School. He seems to have left Venice under a cloud after 1457 and thereafter worked mainly at Ascoli Piceno. He was knighted by Ferdinand II of Naples in 1490, after that date adding to his signature, 'Carolus Crivellus Venetus', the title 'Miles'. His strongly characterized art goes back to the Byzantine tradition of Murano in its passion for a richly ornamented surface, this being combined with a linear sense of form and a mannered and fanciful treatment of detail. The National Gallery has the finest collection of his work, including the richly embellished 'Demidoff' altar-piece and the magnificent 'Annunciation', 1486. In addition to its formal splendour the latter includes a famous detail, the little girl peeping round a doorway, depicted with sympathetic humour. Retrograde, in the sense that he did not participate in the Venetian movement towards breadth of treatment in form and colour, Crivelli, if not one of the greatest Venetians, is one of the most fascinating in his strange and personal achievement.

Crome, John (*b.* Norwich, 22 Dec. 1768; *d.* there, 22 April 1821), one of the great masters of English landscape, who, except for brief visits elsewhere, spent his whole life in his native city. The son of a journeyman weaver and in youth a doctor's errand-boy and then apprentice to a coach painter, he was largely self-taught but studied with profit Dutch and other paintings in a local collection. He seems to have learned mainly from Hobbema, Gainsborough, Morland and as regards luminous effect from Richard Wilson. Earning a living as a drawing master at Norwich, in 1803 he founded with others the Norwich Society of Artists, thus becoming the main strength of the remarkable provincial phenomenon the 'Norwich School' (q.v.), to which Cotman also added lustre. Cotman inspired him to produce some beautiful water-colours and he also made a number of etchings, but his main work is in oil-paintings, broadly treated and with true

[178]

C. CRIVELLI—The Annunciation—National Gallery.

J. CROME—Moonrise on the Marshes of the Yare—National Gallery.

grandeur of design. His masterpieces include the 'Boy keeping Sheep' (Victoria and Albert Museum); 'Mousehold Heath' ('painted for air and space') and 'The Poringland Oak' (National Gallery); and 'The Slate Quarries' and 'Moonlight on the Yare' (Tate Gallery): all products of his later life. As 'Old Crome' he is distinguished from his son, John Bernay Crome (1794–1842), who also worked at Norwich as painter and art master and specialized in effects of moonlight.

Cross, Henri-Edmond (*b.* Douai, 20 May 1856; *d.* Saint-Clair, 16 May 1910), French painter associated with Seurat and Signac (qq.v.) in 'Divisionist' or 'Pointillist' painting. 'Cross' is the translation he adopted of his real name, Delacroix (which no doubt would have invited invidious comparison with the great artist of that name). He settled in the south of France and painted with a brilliance of colour which had some influence on the 'Fauves'.

Cruikshank, George (*b.* London, 27 Sept. 1792; *d.* there, 1 Feb. 1878), English caricaturist and illustrator, the son of Isaac Cruikshank (*c.* 1756–1811). Following his father he began with political and social caricatures in the Gillray and Rowlandson style, but evolved a grotesque and humorous manner of his own in sketches of Victorian London life and in book illustration. Notable productions are his etchings, 1823–6, for Grimms' fairy-tales and the spirited melodrama of those for Dickens's *Oliver Twist* and Harrison Ainsworth's *Old St Paul's*. His brother Robert (1789–1856) was also a caricaturist and a miniature painter. They collaborated, 1821, in illustrating the late-Georgian humours of Pierce Egan's *Life in London*.

[180]

J. CROME—Slate Quarries—Tate Gallery.

Cruz, Pantoja de la, *see* PANTOJA.

Cubism, most influential of modern movements in art as a new 'way of seeing'. Its source is to be found in the efforts of Cézanne to give painting a solid basis of construction, as exemplified by his famous remark that 'everything in nature is based on the sphere, the cone and the cylinder'. Though he did not mention the cube, the implication that geometrical figures underlay all natural forms and were the essential reality in any representation of them was clear enough and was pursued by the joint inventors of Cubism, Georges Braque and Pablo Picasso. The name itself was originally the coinage of adverse criticism. Matisse is said to have referred somewhat contemptuously to the 'cubes' in a picture by Braque in 1908, when talking to the critic Louis Vauxcelles, and the latter used and popularized the name in further criticism. Cubism may be divided into three phases: first a germinating period of about 1906–9 during which Braque gave an increasing emphasis to the structural character Cézanne had indicated and Picasso proceeded on parallel lines, though with wider reference to comparable essentials of form derived from the study of African and primitive Iberian sculpture. There followed the decisive period of 'analytical' Cubism, *c.* 1909–12, in which by means of a scaffolding of geometric planes the artists broke through surface appearance and

[181]

PICASSO—Girl with Mandoline.

gave an 'analysis' of form seen in various aspects simultaneously and structurally reconstituted. The work of Braque and Picasso in this phase is closely related and virtually an austere monochrome. A third phase, 1912 and onwards, was that of 'synthetic' Cubism, more two-dimensional and decorative in character, arbitrarily combining objects in various aspects and reintroducing definite colour. The Cubist still life, making use in this way of familiar things—a plate of fruit, café table and newspaper, mandoline, etc.—was a typical product, also marked by the use of collage (q.v.). The movement attracted many adherents, among them Juan Gris, Fernand Léger, Marcel Duchamp, Jacques Villon, Henri Laurens, Robert Delaunay, Albert Gleizes, Jean Metzinger, Louis Marcoussis, Francis Picabia, Gino Severini and others. The first group exhibition was held at the Salon des Indépendants in 1910. Theoretic statements were those of Gleizes and Metzinger in *Du Cubisme*, 1912, and Guillaume Apollinaire in *The Cubist Painters*, 1913. The stimulating effect of Cubism is seen in various subsequent developments: the *style mécanique* and interest in machine forms of Léger and the Futurists; Russian Constructivism; and in the rise of abstract art, more especially in the geometric form of abstraction. Braque has been the most consistent practitioner of Cubism.

Currier and Ives prints, famous series of hand-coloured lithographs produced in New York by Nathaniel Currier (1813–88) and J. Merritt Ives (1824–95) in partnership. Currier was a lithographer who produced his first topical print in 1835 and took Ives as partner in 1850, the prints having their joint imprint after 1857. Topical events, racing, hunting, yachting, Mississippi steamboats, Red Indians and so on provided endless subjects, a number of specialists being employed. Without pretensions as works of art, they are a rich mine of social history.

A. CUYP—Cattle and Figures: The Large Dort—National Gallery.

A. CUYP—A Road near a River—Dulwich College Picture Gallery.

Curry, John Steuart (*b*. Kansas, 1897; *d*. 1946), American painter, one of the 'regionalists' of the 1930's. He studied at the Art Institute of Chicago and for a year in Paris, afterwards devoting himself to pictures of life in his own state of Kansas, choosing such dramatic or emotional themes as the advance of a tornado or a country baptism. His work stresses illustrative rather than aesthetic interest.

Cuyp, Aelbert (*b*. Dordrecht, Oct. 1620; *d*. there, 15 Nov. 1691), Dutch landscape painter, the son of the portrait painter, Jakob Gerritz Cuyp (1594–1651–2), with whom he first studied painting. A landscapist of great distinction, he painted sea and river views, meadows with cattle and (imagined) mountainous country, being especially noted for the glowing effects of sunlight which earned him the description of the 'Dutch Claude'. English connoisseurs especially delighted in his pictures; the Dulwich Gallery has more Cuyps than any other and the National Gallery an ample representation, including the typical 'Large' and 'Small' Dort.

D

Dada, defiant outburst of poets and painters which began at Zürich in 1916 as a protest against the war. It took the form of bitter mockery of all established institutions (including 'art'), its title (meaning 'hobby-horse'), being a word chosen at random from the dictionary, indicating its irrational and nihilistic character. The poet Tristan Tzara, the sculptor Hans (Jean) Arp, Francis Picabia and Marcel Duchamp were among the original promoters of scandalous shows and efforts to shock the public by irrational behaviour. These were renewed in the aftermath of the First World War by Dada exhibitions and publications in France and Germany. An eccentric exhibition at Cologne in 1920, where hatchets were provided for the audience to attack the objects of 'anti-art' on the walls, was closed by the police. At a similar manifestation in Paris, Duchamp produced a colour reproduction of the Mona Lisa to which he had added a moustache and beard. From the Dadaist anarchy, however, emerged the imaginative aims of Surrealism (q.v.). The collages of Kurt Schwitters and Max Ernst are illustrations of the transition from Dadaist to Surrealist expression.

Daddi, Bernardo (active *c.* 1320–50), Italian painter of the Florentine School, probably a pupil of Giotto and founder of the Guild of St Luke in Florence in 1339. Versions of the 'Madonna and Child' (Florence, Accademia and Uffizi) show him leaning towards the charm of colour and delicacy of line of the Sienese, as represented by Ambrogio Lorenzetti (q.v.). Frescoes of the lives of St Stephen and St Lawrence in Santa Croce, Florence, are attributed to him.

Dali, Salvador (*b.* Figueras, 1904), Spanish painter and propagandist of the irrational in art. He reacted against the training of the Madrid Academy and settled in Paris, joining the Surrealist opposition to a modern art aesthetically and formally conceived. He flouted Cubism (q.v.) with an expressed admiration for the Pre-Raphaelites and 'art nouveau' (qq.v.), painting thinly and in minute detail and borrowing from the symbolism and analysis of dreams with often gruesome and sinister suggestion. He settled in New York in 1939, creating a sensation with fantastic window displays and other forms of advertisement. With Luis Bunuel he was responsible for two Surrealist films, *Le Chien Andalou* and *L'Âge d'Or*. He took later to religious subjects, as in the 'Christ of St John of the Cross', 1951 (Glasgow), 'Last Supper' (Washington, National Gallery) and 'St James in Glory' (New Brunswick, Beaverbrook Gallery). These attracted much popular attention but were regarded more suspiciously by modern critics than earlier products of a so-called 'paranoiac' fantasy such as

[185]

S. DALI—Christ of St John of the Cross—Glasgow Art Gallery.

the limp watches of 'The Persistence of Memory' (New York, Museum of Modern Art).

Dalmau, Luis (active 1428–60), Spanish painter of Catalan origin. He worked for Alphonso V of Aragon, on whose behalf he went to Bruges in 1431. Either there or in Spain he assimilated the van Eyck style of composition and treatment of detail, though he did not adopt the Netherlandish oil method. His single masterpiece, the magnificent 'Virgin and the Councillors', 1445 (Barcelona), is painted in tempera. Though closely following Netherlandish style in symmetrical arrangement, architectural setting and landscape distance, in portraiture and total effect it has its own distinct Spanish character.

Danby, Francis (*b.* nr Wexford, 16 Nov. 1793; *d.* Exmouth, 9 Feb. 1861), Irish painter who studied in Dublin and worked in Bristol and London, living abroad, 1830–42, but exhibiting regularly at the Royal Academy (A.R.A., 1825). In Romantic and imaginative landscape and subject pictures, e.g. 'The Deluge' (Tate Gallery), he may be compared with John Martin and Washington Allston (qq.v.).

Da Ponte, *see* BASSANO.

Daubigny, Charles-François (*b.* Paris, 15 Feb. 1817; *d.* there, 19 Feb. 1878), French landscape painter, the pupil of his father, also a landscape painter, and later of Delaroche (q.v.). After a period of hack work, painting box tops and clock faces and producing commercial illustrations, he turned to landscape etching and then to painting in the spirit of the painters of Barbizon, though he added to their study of nature the practice of executing complete pictures of

C.-F. DAUBIGNY—St. Paul's from the Surrey Side—Tate Gallery.

H. DAUMIER—The Third Class Carriage—Metropolitan Museum of Art, New York, The H. O. Havemeyer Collection.

considerable size in the open air. He gained success in the Salons of the 1850's, his 'Bords de l'Oise' (Bordeaux) being especially popular, and then constructed a houseboat studio in which he travelled along the Oise and the Seine, painting their quiet river reaches. He visited London in 1866 and again 1870–1, 'St Paul's from the Surrey Side' (Tate Gallery) being a product of his visit, and in later life painted in Holland also. His best pictures are those of French river country and rural scenes with no especial features of picturesqueness or grandeur, excellent in their grasp of essential form.

Daumier, Honoré (*b*. Marseilles, 26 Feb. 1808; *d*. Valmondois, 10 Feb. 1879), French graphic artist, caricaturist and painter, the son of a picture framer. He went to Paris in youth and worked as professional lithographer and satirical draughtsman. Joining the staff of *La Caricature* in 1831, he became noted for his attacks on the July Monarchy, and his caricature of Louis Philippe as Gargantua swallowing the pence of the poor led to his imprisonment for six months in 1833. Later, as contributor to *Charivari*, he widened his range to give a satirical picture of bourgeois society in general. A masterpiece of political satire is his *Ventre législatif*, 1834, with its fantastic array of ministers; of serious comment his lithograph of massacred civilians, 'La rue Transnonain', also 1834. The law and

[188]

GERARD DAVID—The Judgment of King Cambyses, Left Panel: The Arrest of the Perjured
Judge—Musée Communal, Bruges.

lawyers incited him to brilliantly vitriolic sketches, as also the
pomposities, absurdities and meannesses of middle-class life. In
caricature he showed something of the sculptor's vision, and modelled
little clay figures which he adapted in his lithographs, retaining
sculptural contrast of light and shade. When he was about forty,
however, he turned to painting, perhaps on the advice of his painter
friends of the Barbizon School (q.v.), and in this art achieved greatness in a dramatic simplification and concentration on tone. A
realist in subject (if we except the Don Quixote theme, which had a
special fascination for him), he painted scenes of everyday life and
was drawn towards the theatre and to railway travel in particular, his
several versions of the 'Third Class Carriage' showing at once his
feeling for the group and for the isolation of the individual within it.
He had studied Rembrandt in the Louvre but he has a closer affinity
in style with the later paintings of Goya. The affinity with Goya,
indeed, may also be found in his graphic work. Daumier gradually
lost his sight and died almost blind in the little house his friend Corot
provided for him at Valmondois, Seine-et-Oise. He was not un-
appreciated as a painter by his contemporaries, but it has since been
more fully recognized that he was one of the most original masters of
his age.

David, Gerard (*b*. Oudewater, *c*. 1460; *d*. Bruges, 13 Aug. 1523), last
great painter of the early Netherlandish School at Bruges, in succession to Memlinc (q.v.). Born in Holland at a village near Gouda,
he arrived in Bruges in 1482, married, in 1501, Cornelia Cnoop,
daughter of the dean of the Goldsmiths' Guild and a miniaturist, and
apart from a short stay at Antwerp, *c*. 1515, when he was admitted to
the Painters' Guild, spent his working life in that decaying but still
wealthy city. Tranquil and highly detailed, his art takes elements
from van Eyck, van der Weyden and Memlinc (qq.v.), late works
suggesting also the influence of Quinten Massys (q.v.). Famous paintings are the panels ordered by the magistrates of Bruges for the Hall
of Justice depicting the arrest and punishment of the corrupt judge,
Sisamnes (Bruges, Musée Communal), and the 'Baptism of Christ',
also at Bruges. Some miniatures are attributed to him.

David, Jacques Louis (*b*. Paris, 30 Aug. 1748; *d*. Brussels, 29 Dec.
1825), French painter who came of a bourgeois family long established in Paris, a kinsman of Boucher (q.v.), who gave him some
instruction. He studied also with Vien (q.v.), gained the Prix de Rome
after several attempts in 1774, and joined Vien in Rome, where he
spent six years, copying the antique, steeped in the neo-classicism of
which his master was one of the devotees, and developing the style
that aspired to what Diderot called 'the great and severe taste of
antiquity' for which he is famous. Among several early paintings of
classic themes, the 'Oath of the Horatii', 1785 (Louvre) (q.v.), stands
out as an equation between art and politics, its example of stern republican virtue or fanaticism being intended or accepted as a call to
contemporary sacrifice of all private interest in the cause of revolution. At a stroke David might be said to have abolished the rococo art

L. DAVID—Madame Sériziat—Louvre.

J. L. DAVID—Mme Récamier—Louvre.

of the Old Regime with all its frivolous gaiety and to have forged a propaganda weapon for the French Revolution, in which he played a zealous role as a representative of Paris in the Convention and a member of the Committee of Public Safety. A disciplinarian and man of system, he recalls, despite the changed epoch, the dictatorship of Le Brun (q.v.) in the age of Louis XIV. He abolished the Académie (and invented an academic system of his own), reorganized the Louvre as a public gallery, planned the revolutionary fêtes, designed costumes for the deputies and ministers, and brought all the arts and crafts into line. His painting 'The Death of Marat' (Brussels) of the 'Year Two' is a masterpiece of this period in which emotion triumphs over self-imposed austerity: here one can see why Géricault should have called David the 'regenerator of our school'. To get a true picture of David as an artist it is necessary to see his Classicism as a phase. Imprisoned after the fall of Robespierre, he painted on his release some exquisite portraits in which there is the beauty of the French tradition, that of his sister-in-law, Mme Sériziat, 1795 (Louvre), being perhaps the most delightful example, though his 'Mme Julie Récamier', 1800 (Louvre), is more famous. Subsequently, as a painter to Napoleon, he exchanged Republican austerity for the imperial richness of the 'Sacre de l'Empereur', 1804 (Louvre), and in such a work as 'Napoleon on Mont St Bernard' heralds the tempestuous spirit of Romanticism. Exiled to Brussels as a regicide after the

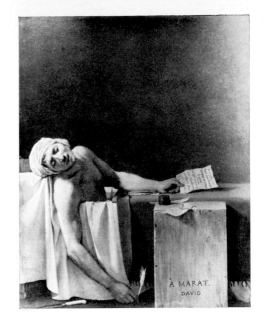

return of the Bourbons, he continued to wield great influence on artists. Despite the freezing effect of theory on some of his paintings he must be accounted one of the giants of French art. He had a multitude of pupils, among them Gros, Gérard, Girodet and, most famous of all, Ingres (qq.v.).

Davies, Arthur Bowen (*b.* Utica, New York, 26 Sept. 1862; *d.* 1928), American painter of idyllic landscapes with figures. After studying at the Art Institute of Chicago he visited Europe in 1893, absorbing many influences, that of Puvis de Chavannes (q.v.) being noticeable. Eclectic and open-minded, he was one of the main organizers of the Armory Show of 1913 which confronted America with the modern movements in European art. In later life he designed tapestry, woven in France at the Gobelins.

'**Death of General Wolfe**', painting by Benjamin West (q.v.), 1772 (Ottawa), showing the death of the conqueror of Quebec in 1759 at the scene of victory. The picture is of note as the first to introduce historical accuracy of costume and circumstance in a period when heroic action and events were usually conceived in antique terms and in the conventional guise of 'history painting' (q.v.).

'**Death of Marat**', painting by Jacques Louis David (q.v.), now at Brussels, executed in 1793 soon after Marat had been stabbed in his bath by Charlotte Corday. The dead leader is depicted holding in his hand the message in which Charlotte Corday had sought an interview. The picture, dramatic in its austere simplicity, is inscribed A MARAT/DAVID/L'AN DEUX.

Decadence in art implies a certain artificiality and preciousness in style and a preference for exotic, far-fetched or morbid subject-matter. Historically it refers to a nineteenth-century phase of European art and literature (*see also* ART FOR ART'S SAKE) and also to the Symbolist movement of the *fin de siècle*. Huysmans's novel *A*

Rebours, the lithographs of Odilon Redon (as therein described) and the drawings of Aubrey Beardsley give examples.

Decamps, Alexandre Gabriel (*b.* Paris, 3 Mar. 1803; *d.* Fontaine-bleau, 2 Aug. 1860), French painter and lithographer. An 'orientalist' somewhat earlier than Delacroix (q.v.), he visited Constantinople and Asia Minor and painted many scenes of Arab life which were popular with the French public after the occupation of Algiers in 1830. One of Lord Hertford's favourite painters, he is well represented in the Wallace Collection at Hertford House.

Decorative. A painting is said to be decorative when it has been designed to fit a particular space and to harmonize with a particular scheme of interior decoration and the style of other objects composing it. Thus rococo painting, such as that of Boucher, in its harmonious and intended relation with a Louis Quinze interior, is decorative. The

E. DEGAS—The Ballet Scene from ' Robert le Diable '—Victoria and Albert Museum.

E. DEGAS—La Répétition—Glasgow Art Gallery and Museum.

term is extended to certain conventions of style, e.g. the flat colour and simplified forms of some mural painters.

Degas (originally **De Gas**), **Hilaire Germain Edgar** (*b*. Paris, 19 June 1834; *d*. there, 26 Sept. 1917), French painter and graphic artist who came of a well-to-do family, his father being a banker. He entered the École des Beaux-Arts in 1855 and in that year was introduced to the aged Ingres (q.v.), of whom, in his regard for draughtsmanship, he was a lifelong follower. Between 1855 and 1858 he travelled in Italy making a careful study of the early Renaissance masters. He first attempted figure compositions on conventional lines, as in the several versions of his 'Young Spartans', but after 1865 gave up 'history' and devoted himself to scenes of contemporary life and portraiture. Racecourse scenes were followed in the 1870's by the superb paintings of the theatre and especially of the ballet, viewed in rehearsal, from the wings or from the auditorium, for which he is celebrated. A visit to his brothers at New Orleans (where his mother's family had settled after the Revolution) produced an interesting departure in his view of the Cotton Exchange, 1873 (Musée de Pau). In this decade he also exhibited with the Impressionists, having associated with Monet, Renoir and Sisley (qq.v.) in their meetings at the Café Guerbois before the Franco-Prussian War (in which he served in a battery). While he is often termed an Impressionist he was in many ways quite distinct from the group. He had no great interest in landscape or in painting direct from nature. The representation of objects by areas of divided colour and without outline offended the draughtsman in him, while he believed in a carefully planned form of composition to which the Impressionist method was alien. If he gave a momentary 'impression' like that of a dancer in movement it was not only by observation but by deliberately planned devices of composition. It is one of his merits to have introduced into art a new resource of arrangement departing from the conventional symmetry and balance of the past, in this making skilful use of the suggestions afforded by the Japanese print and even the photograph. Degas delighted in and experimented with many media, oil, water-colour, pastel, etching, monotype, aquatint, though it was in pastel that he produced his most brilliant effects of colour. From middle age onwards he tended increasingly to concentrate on the study of woman, adding to his dancers, in the 1880's, remarkable pastels and drawings of the 'femme au tub'. Failing sight turned him to sculpture, which he called a 'blind man's art', and his small bronzes of dancers or horses are of great beauty. Somewhat isolated, Degas had no direct following in France, though through his English pupil, Sickert (q.v.), he may be said to have benefited English art.

Deineka, Alexander Alexandrovich (*b*. Moscow, 1899), Russian painter of contemporary subjects, designer and illustrator. He studied in the Kharkov Art School and the Moscow Art and Technical Workshops, 1921–5. A notable work was his 'Defence of Petrograd', 1928 (Central House of the Soviet Army, Moscow). He has since developed along the lines of Soviet 'socialist realism'.

'Déjeuner sur l'Herbe, Le', the 'Picnic', painted by Manet in 1863 and now in the Louvre. Representing a bathing party of artists and their models, the latter unclothed and the men fully dressed, it gave a modern interpretation of Giorgione's 'Concert Champêtre', but was hotly assailed as being improper and was rejected at the Paris Salon. It became the main object of attack and defence at the Salon des Refusés of 1863, where it was exhibited under the title 'Le Bain' (it was given its present title in the Manet exhibition of 1867). Although painted in the studio and not in the open it probably helped to turn younger painters of the time to open-air subjects, but its main influence was as a symbol of artistic freedom which brought together the rebellious nucleus of Impressionism. Claude Monet painted a picture of the same title.

Delacroix, Ferdinand Victor Eugène (*b*. Charenton, 26 April 1798; *d*. Paris, 13 Aug. 1863), French painter, one of the great forces of nineteenth-century art. His father, who had been foreign minister under the Directory (a post in which he was superseded by Talleyrand), died when he was seven, his mother when he was sixteen, and though well educated the young Delacroix was left dependant on his own efforts. Helped by an uncle, he studied art under Guérin, meeting in his studio Géricault (q.v.), whose 'Raft of the *Medusa*', 1819, was one of his great early experiences. His own first Salon success, 'The Barque of Dante', 1822 (Louvre), while showing his devotion to Rubens, was already intensely individual and full of that 'fever' which he considered the truly creative atmosphere of art. It was followed, 1824, by his masterpiece, 'The Massacre at Scio' (theme inspired by the Greek struggle for independence). The contrast between martial figures and suffering civilians was derived from Gros's 'Plague Victims at Jaffa'; the colour technique owed something to Constable's 'Hay-wain', which Delacroix saw at the Salon and which led him to some repainting; though again the result was magnificently individual. 'Greece expiring on the ruins of Missolonghi', 1827 (Bordeaux), and 'Liberty leading the People, 28th July 1830' (q.v.), were further products of genius and a freedom-loving spirit that may well be called Romantic. It was at this time that the term Romanticism first came into use in France and Delacroix was hailed as leader of the movement, though he himself regarded such terms with deep mistrust. Yet his visit to England in 1825 (prompted by his friendship with Bonington (q.v.), and the example of Géricault) certainly involved him in the Romantic subject-matter of poetry and the theatre. Byron's tragedy inspired the gorgeous 'Sardanapalus', 1827 (Louvre); a performance of *Faust* in London, the 'Faust'

E. MANET—Le Déjeuner sur l'Herbe—Louvre.

E. DELACROIX—Baron Schwiter—National Gallery.

lithographs of 1828; and he even pictured himself as Hamlet. While an admirer of classic order, as in Racine or Mozart, nevertheless he sought all means of extending the emotional experience and sensation given by painting. In this respect a new phase began when in 1832 he visited Spain and Morocco. The colour and costume of North Africa excited him afresh; a result was the superb richness of the 'Women of Algiers', 1834 (Louvre). It may be considered good or bad fortune that between 1833 and 1856 Delacroix, through the influence of Thiers, had the opportunity denied so many great nineteenth-century artists of decorating buildings on a vast scale: the Chamber of Deputies in the Palais Bourbon, the Senate Library in the Luxembourg, the ceiling of the Galerie d'Apollon, Louvre, the Chapel of the Saints Anges in the Church of St Sulpice. Except in the Louvre, the best of these works, the execution was entrusted to assistants and their imaginative power was neutralized by dull colour and inferior workmanship. His temperament was more suited to the individualistic picture, and his studies (produced in the intervals of decorative labour) of exotic or oriental life, of the ferocity and energy of wild animals, or of the richness of flowers such as he painted at his country house at Champrosay seem more truly expressive. A man of cultivated intelligence and remarkable character (so well described by Baudelaire), he has left in his *Journals* both shrewd comments on his contemporaries and an impassioned testimony to his own love of all the arts.

Delaroche, Hippolyte (known as **Paul**) (*b.* Paris, 17 July 1797; *d.* there, 4 Nov. 1856), French painter of historical subjects, a pupil of Gros (q.v.). He represents a popular and inferior variant of the Romanticism so nobly exemplified by his great contemporary Delacroix (q.v.), in scenes of English history, pictured with the help

R. DELAUNAY—The City of Paris—Musée d'Art Moderne, Paris.

of Scott and Shakespeare and depending on their anecdotal or senti-
mental interest of subject. One of his best-known works is 'Les
Enfants d'Édouard' (the Princes in the Tower), 1830 (Louvre).

Delaunay, Robert (*b.* Paris, 12 April 1885; *d.* Montpellier, 25 Oct.
1941), French painter, apprenticed to a theatrical designer at an
early age, who took to painting *c.* 1905. He was influenced both by
Cézanne and by the colour theories of Chevreul, and *c.* 1910 entered a
Cubist phase during which he painted a striking series of pictures
using the Eiffel Tower as a theme. He became progressively more
abstract and his entirely non-representational 'Circular Forms' in
pure colour had an influence on Klee and Kandinsky. His art was
described as 'Orphist' (essentially musical) by Guillaume Apollinaire.
He carried out a huge decorative scheme (ten large reliefs in colour
and a vast 'Rhythm') for the Palace of Air and Railway Pavilion of
the Paris Exposition of 1937, and with other artists, including his
wife, the Russian artist Sonia Terk, decorated the sculpture hall at
the Salon des Tuileries in 1938.

De Loutherbourg, Philip James (*b.* Strasbourg, 1740; *d.* London,
1812), painter and scenic designer of Polish origin and cosmopolitan
experience, who worked in England. The son of a miniature painter,
he studied in Paris and became a member of the Académie in 1762.
After travel in Switzerland, Germany and Italy he settled in England
in 1771, became R.A. in 1781 and exhibited at the Academy, 1772–
1812. He was noted for his battle-pieces, landscapes and inventive
stage sets.

[199]

Delvaux, Paul (*b.* 1897), Belgian painter who may be called Sur-realist in having devised a 'dream world' in which figures, nude and in modern dress, recline or move impassively in gardens or among classical temples.

Denis, Maurice (*b.* Granville, 25 Nov. 1870; *d.* 1943), French painter, engraver and writer. He studied at the École des Beaux-Arts and became a moving spirit of the 'Nabi' group (q.v.) in the 1890's. His 'Hommage à Cézanne', 1901, depicts members of the group admiring a Cézanne still life. His published *Théories* contained the statement by which perhaps he is mainly remembered: 'A picture—before being a war-horse, a nude woman or any subject whatever—is essentially a plane surface covered with colours in a certain order.' He turned to wall-paintings in a simplified decorative manner which are of only minor interest.

'Departure for Cythera', 'Fête galante. L'Embarquement pour l'Île de Cythère', diploma painting of Watteau on his admission to the Académie Royale in 1717 and one of his most poetic compositions, now in the Louvre. A less famous version is at Berlin. Watteau was specifically admitted to the Académie as a painter of *fêtes galantes*, assemblies of courtiers in some fanciful open-air setting, originally suggested to him by the entertainments given by his patron, the wealthy banker and connoisseur Antoine Crozat, at Montmorency.

A. WATTEAU—Departure for Cythera—Louvre.

A. DERAIN—Barges on the Thames—Temple Newsam Gallery, Leeds.

Here the fashionably dressed company advance towards the gilded and rococo barge that is to bear them to the Temple of Aphrodite.

Derain, André (*b*. Chatou, 17 June 1880; *d*. Chambourcy, 8 Sept. 1954), French painter of the School of Paris. He studied art at the Académie Carrière, where he met Matisse, working with him and Vlaminck, his close friend, at Collioure and contributing to the 'Fauve' exhibition of 1905. His paintings of the Thames, 1905–6, brilliant in Fauvish reds and blues, are a notable product of this period. From 1908, however, he was attracted towards Cubism (q.v.), though he was never a thorough-going revolutionary, solid construction in figure, landscape and still life being his aim. Subsequently various changes in style seemed to lead back to tradition, though at no time did his work lack quality. He produced many stage designs as well as paintings, from the sets for Diaghilev's *La Boutique fantasque*, 1919, to those for Rossini's *Le Barbier de Seville*, 1953.

Desiderio ('**Monsu**') (active early seventeenth century), painter of the Neapolitan School, now identified with François Didier Nomé. He produced paintings of architecture with small figures in a distinctive style and these have gained modern attention by their romantic

DESIDERIO—Imaginary City

strangeness of atmosphere. There are examples in the National Gallery and Southampton Art Gallery and others are in Budapest and Vienna.

Design (Lat. *designare*, to mark out), drawing or plan which serves as a guide to a finished work of art; alternatively the general conception of a work of art in relation to its intended purpose, almost but not quite the same as its composition. In modern usage it refers less frequently to the fine arts than to the use of materials or production of objects for some utilitarian end.

De Stijl, influential modern art movement, originating in the journal of that title, founded in 1917, by a group of Dutch artists. The movement has also been called 'neo-Plasticism', from a pamphlet thus entitled, promulgated by the artists in Paris in 1920. Its leaders were the architect and painter Theo van Doesburg (1883–1931), the painter Piet Mondrian (q.v.) and the architect J. J. P. Oud. Their aim was a system bringing all the visual arts together in consistent fashion; painting, sculpture, architecture and the various arts of design as represented by furniture, typography, etc. They applied a general simplification, based on rectangular shapes and, in painting, primary colour. Tending to a logical extreme of mathematical abstraction, it is most strikingly represented in painting by

[202]

the work of Mondrian though its influence was mainly felt in architecture and industrial design. It affected the outlook of such leaders in modern design as Walter Gropius and Le Corbusier, by its comprehensiveness and radical simplicity and stimulated the direction of study at the Bauhaus (q.v.).

De Wint, Peter (*b*. Stone, 21 Jan. 1784; *d*. London, 30 June 1849), landscape painter of Dutch-American descent born in Staffordshire, where his father, a doctor (born in New York), had his practice. He was apprenticed to the engraver John Raphael Smith, but was directed towards water-colour by the advice of John Varley and the example of Girtin, whose work he admired in Dr Monro's collection. From 1806 onwards water-colour was his chief means of expression and the country round Lincoln (the home of his wife) his main theme, his best work being executed with broad washes summarizing natural forms.

Diaz de la Peña (Narcisse Virgilio) (*b*. Bordeaux, 21 Aug. 1808; *d*. Menton, 18 Nov. 1876), painter of the Barbizon School (q.v.), born in France of Spanish expatriate parents. He was left an orphan and lost a leg in childhood, working in his early days in a china factory. He first exhibited in the Salon in 1831 and from 1840 onwards was associated with Barbizon, painting with Romantic feeling and in dusky tones many admirable views of glades and ponds in the forest of Fontainebleau, though sometimes introducing, like Corot, an

DIAZ DE LA PEÑA—Common with Stormy Sunset—National Gallery.

irrelevant addition of mythological figures. 'Sous Bois', 1855 (Louvre), is one of his best forest paintings.

Diptych, term originally applied to the Roman 'codex' or 'book' of two leaves or tablets fastened together; in modern times to a painted or ornamented altar-piece, usually movable, consisting of two hinged panels.

'Disputà (del Sacramento)', title given to the wall-painting by Raphael in the Stanza della Segnatura of the Vatican. This, however, does not represent (as the title might suggest) theological argument or debate concerning the doctrine of transubstantiation but presents the majesty and splendour of Christianity. The composition is in two halves, linked by the host on the altar, the upper representing Christ enthroned with the Madonna and the Baptist, the figure of God being seen above and saints and angels on either side. Below is an assembly of the devout, the Fathers of the Church being grouped on either side of the altar, St Gregory and St Jerome to the left, St Augustine and St Ambrose to the right. Popes and theologians are ranged round them and Raphael also introduced the portraits of Fra Angelico, Dante and Savonarola.

Distemper (Fr. *détrempe*, It. *tempera*), one of the earliest painting media, known in Egypt and ancient Mesopotamia and used by the Greeks in interior decoration, a mixture of powdered colour with water and some glutinous substance. In this definition it comes under the same general heading as tempera (q.v.), but is to be distinguished from egg tempera in being mixed with size or gum and given opacity by whitening, and also in being less permanent and unsuited to fine work. It was used in Renaissance Italy for decorative painting on a large scale where swiftness and ease of execution rather than permanence were main considerations, e.g. for cartoons in colour for mural paintings or tapestry. Raphael's cartoons, the most famous examples, have defied the impermanence of the medium. In modern times it has been used for theatrical scene-painting, but the word now mainly denotes house-painting as distinct from the tempera of the picture painter.

Divisionism, extension of the Impressionist method of translating light and shade into colour, practised by the Neo-Impressionists Seurat and Signac. It consisted in the use of the primary or spectrum colours in complementary relationships as a mosaic of dots or patches fusing into various tones when seen at a distance but giving a heightened brilliance and vibration of atmospheric effect. The method was also known as 'Chromo-luminarism' and is still commonly referred to as 'Pointillism' (Fr. *pointiller*, to dot or stipple), though Divisionism was the term preferred by its exponents. *See also* NEO-IMPRESSIONISM.

Dix, Otto (*b*. Unterhausen, 1891), German painter and etcher, who expressed the social criticism of 'die Neue Sachlichkeit' (q.v.) after the First World War. In his series of etchings, 'War', 1924, he conveys the same sense of disgust and horror as such writers of the time

W. DOBSON—Endymion
Porter—Tate Gallery.

as Remarque and Bar-
busse. In painting he
portrayed character in
a harsh and satirical
fashion. He may be
compared with Grosz
and Beckmann (qq.v.).

Dobson, William (*b.*
London, 1610; *d.* there,
Oct. 1646), English por-
trait painter, perhaps
the pupil of the Ger-
man decorative painter
Francis Cleyn. He
became attached to the
court in the period
immediately preceding the Civil War, introduced, it is said, by van
Dyck, acquaintance with the Venetian pictures in the collection of
Charles I possibly contributing to the richness of his colour and style.
His known works belong to the period 1642–6, when he worked at the
royalist headquarters at Oxford, producing portraits of great vigour
and character of noblemen and cavalier officers. He died in poverty
after the royalist collapse. His 'Endymion Porter', *c.* 1643–5 (National Gallery), is a famous example of English art, owing little to
van Dyck.

Doesburg, Theo van (*b.* Utrecht, 1883; *d.* Davos, 1931), Dutch
architectural painter-designer, who promoted the de Stijl movement
(q.v.) as a means of co-ordinating and relating painting, architecture
and the decorative and useful arts. He is important as a zealous
propagandist of a consistently modern attitude to all forms of design
and from this point of view may be compared with Le Corbusier.

Dolci (Dolce), Carlo (Carlino) (*b.* Florence, 25 May 1616; *d.* there,
17 Jan. 1686), Italian painter, one of the last representatives of a
local Florentine school, a pupil of Jacopo Vignali. He painted portraits of the imperial family at the emperor's court and a number of
religious subjects, e.g. 'St Andrew praying before the Crucifixion'
(Pitti), 'St Cecilia' (Dresden) and 'St Veronica' (Dulwich), in which
pathos approaches sentimentality.

Domenichino (Domenico Zampieri) (*b.* Bologna, 27 Oct. 1581; *d.*
Naples, 6 April 1641), Italian painter of the Bolognese School, pupil
of Calvaert and the Carracci (qq.v.). A friend of Albani (q.v.), he
visited with him Parma, Modena and Reggio to study Correggio and
Parmigiano, later joining Albani at Rome. The classical art-theorist,

[205]

Cardinal Agucchi, was his first patron and employed him in his palace. He was the assistant of Annibale Carracci in the decoration of the Farnese Palace, painting 'The Death of Adonis' from his own designs, and also painted frescoes for Cardinals Borghese and Aldobrandini. Among his best frescoes were those for the Basilian Abbey of Grottaferrata, and his oil-painting, the 'Last Communion of St Jerome', was considered by Poussin the best in Rome next to Raphael's 'Transfiguration'. Like Annibale Carracci, he contributed to the development of 'classical' landscape. After working in Rome and Bologna he went to Naples in 1630 to decorate the Cappella del Tesoro in the cathedral, though the jealous and sinister factions of Neapolitan art conspired to persecute him and drive him away. He was forced to leave but returned to the struggle and died at Naples (it was suspected of poison). One of his principal works at Rome was the choir and pendentives of St Andrea della Valle, including his 'Four Evangelists', 1624–8, the dome being entrusted to his rival and enemy Lanfranco (q.v.). Good examples of his landscape are in the National Gallery, and Constable regarded his 'Landscape with a Fortified Building' (formerly at Bridgewater House and now in a private collection) as 'of the highest order'.

Domenico Veneziano (b. early fifteenth century; d. Florence, 15 May 1461), Italian painter, presumed to be of Venetian origin, though affiliated with the Florentine School. He worked on the decorations of the Portinari Chapel in Santa Maria Novella, Florence, 1439–44, and is said to have used an oil medium. He died several years after the death of Andrea del Castagno (q.v.), whom Vasari accused of having murdered him. His principal remaining works are the 'Madonna and Saints' (Uffizi) and the much damaged 'Madonna Enthroned' (National Gallery). In the scientific and geometrical

DOMENICO VENEZIANO —Portrait of a Young Woman — Staatliche Museum, Berlin.

planning of his compositions he seems to have indicated the direction his pupil, Piero della Francesca (q.v.), was to follow.

Dongen, Kees van (*b.* Delfshaven, 26 Jan. 1877; *d.* Monte Carlo, May 1968), Dutch painter who went to Paris to study art at the age of twenty. He exhibited with the 'Fauves' in 1905 and also with the German 'Die Brücke' group (q.v.), developing a highly simplified style of Post-Impressionism. Such exploits as painting with lipstick the portrait of an actress gave his work a certain *succès de scandale* and he was a favoured painter of international society in the 1920's, his pictures expressing something of the character of the period.

Doré, Gustave (*b.* Strasbourg, 6 Jan. 1832; *d.* Paris, 23 Jan. 1883), French painter and illustrator. At sixteen he was drawing for the *Journal pour Rire* and later produced many series of illustrations for books (wash drawings for the most part, translated into wood-engraving by professional engravers), including Balzac's *Contes Drôlatiques*, Dante's *Divina Commedia*, Milton's *Paradise Lost*, Tennyson's *Idylls*, La Fontaine's *Fables*, Rabelais's *Gargantua and Pantagruel*, Cervantes's *Don Quixote* and the Bible. They showed a strikingly grotesque and fantastic character of a kind which made him highly popular. Some of his best work resulted from a visit to Victorian London and is contained in Blanchard Jerrold's *London*. Ambitious to excel in 'high art', he produced huge religious paintings, aesthetic failures but a sensational success when shown at the Doré Gallery in London in the 1870's. As a sculptor he is remembered by his statue of Alexandre Dumas the elder in Paris.

Dossi, Dosso and **Battista,** Italian painter brothers, pupils of

Lorenzo Costa (q.v.), who worked in Venice for some time and also at Mantua, but mainly at Ferrara and Modena. Their real name was Luteri. Battista, the younger brother (*d. c.* 1548), was the landscape painter while Giovanni (Dosso) (*b. c.* 1479; *d.* 27 Aug. 1542) painted the figures, in which his association with Giorgione and Titian leaves its trace. They excelled in fanciful composition, a somewhat romantic background often being enveloped in a strange coppery light. The painters were the friends of Ariosto, who mentions them in *Orlando Furioso*, from which they took subjects. Many of their paintings are at Ferrara, where they were employed by Alfonso I, a number also at Dresden. Versions of 'Circe' (Rome, Borghese; Washington, National Gallery) and 'Muse inspiring a Court Poet' (National Gallery) are among principal works.

Dou, Gerard (*b.* Leyden, 7 April 1613; buried there, 9 Feb. 1675, Dutch *genre* and portrait painter. He became one of the young Rembrandt's first pupils at Leyden in 1628. His 'Rembrandt in his Studio' (Cook Collection) having documentary interest in this respect. At first he imitated his master's light and shade but later developed a highly finished manner of his own, sometimes criticized as overminute, but showing delicacy and observation of nature. 'The Woman with the Dropsy' (Louvre) is accounted his masterpiece.

Douris (early fifth century B.C.), Greek vase painter of the Attic School, an exponent of the red-figured style. He excelled in decorating drinking-cups. A celebrated work of pathetic beauty is the 'Eos receiving the Body of her dead Son, Memnos' (Louvre).

DOSSO DOSSI—Nymph and Faun—Pitti Gallery, Florence.

Dove, Arthur G. (*b.* Canandaigua, New York, 1880; *d.* 1946), American painter, one of the pioneers of abstract art in the United States. He studied in France and Italy and began to develop the use of collage and of large and simple forms about 1912.

Drawing, the art of representing in line forms seen or imagined. It can be carried out in many mediums, chalk, pencil, pen or brush or by various means of graphic reproduction, line engraving, etching, wood engraving and lithography (see under corresponding headings). It has been practised at all times and is an element in all pictorial art though in respect to its purpose it may be considered under two main headings:

(1) As a preliminary stage in the creation of a work of art, picture, fresco or sculpture. The great wealth of European old master drawings is due to the need for careful studies of composition, figures, drapery and other details to be included in a finished work; such guidance being particularly necessary in fresco (q.v.), where the whole work had to be completely preconceived and also where a number of pupils were employed who would follow the master's graphic indications.

(2) As a finished work of art in itself, the water-colour drawing being an example. Some old masters produced finished drawings to show their patrons what the completed picture would be like, the portrait drawings of Holbein give an example. The nature of drawing makes it especially suitable for certain types of work which are an end in themselves, e.g. topography and caricature.

Apart from these functions artists have always valued drawing as a personal exercise and intimate means of expression.

[209]

L. VAN LEYDEN—Allegorical Figures seated on a Globe. (Pen and Ink)—British Museum.

B. DI LESE (GOZZOLI) — Head of a Youth (Chalk)—Royal Collection, Windsor Castle.

S. DALI—Cavalier of Death (Ink Drawing)—Museum of Modern Art, New York.

GUERCINO—Venus and Cupid (Pen and Wash)—Courtauld Gallery, London.

H. FRAGONARD — Confidences (Sepia) —
Rotterdam, Boymans Museum.

T. GAINSBOROUGH—Study of a Lady (Black
and White Chalk) British Museum.

A. CANALETTO—London Bridge (Pen and Wash)—British Museum.

A. DEL SARTO—Study of Two Figures (Red Chalk)—British Museum.

P. CEZANNE.—Portrait of Mme Cézanne (Pencil)—Rotterdam, Boymans Museum.

DOMENICHINO—Boy climbing a Wall (Chalk Drawing)—Photo, Royal Academy.

Dresden Gallery, art collection the foundations of which were laid by Augustus I in the sixteenth century and by Francis III, Duke of Modena, who purchased Raphael's 'Sistine Madonna' from the Benedictines of San Sisto. The 'Sistine Madonna' is the great treasure of the collection, returned by the U.S.S.R. to the gallery in 1955 with other pictures. The gallery is rich in works by Italian, Dutch and old German masters, and its masterpieces include Vermeer's 'Young Courtesan' and Giorgione's 'Sleeping Venus', supposed to have been left unfinished and completed by Titian.

Drypoint, mode of engraving in which lines are scratched on the surface of a copper plate with a steel point. The slight ridge ('burr') of copper furrowed out by the point and remaining on the surface of the plate holds the ink when the plate is printed and adds a soft richness to the line. The burr quickly wears down so that only a limited number of impressions can be taken. It is often used in conjunction with etching (q.v.). Dürer and Rembrandt made drypoints, though examples are few before the nineteenth century. The revival of the method in Britain by David Wilkie and Andrew Geddes (qq.v.) is of some note.

Dubuffet, Jean (*b.* Le Havre, 1901), French painter and experimentalist in painting media, sculptural relief and collage. He began to paint in 1918 but gave it up in 1925 to become a wine merchant. Since 1944, when he resumed painting and held his first one-man show, he has been distinguished for his cultivation of 'l'Art Brut' (primitive, non-professional and child art). He founded a society to collect examples of it and obtains in his own work striking effects by the use of a variety of materials—tar, white lead, cement, plaster, pebbles, industrial paints and lacquers coalescing into primitive imagery.

J. DUBUFFET—Bedouin and Palms—Photo, Tooth Gallery.

[213]

DUCCIO—The Angel of the Resurrection—Cathedral Museum, Siena.

Duccio di Buoninsegna (active 1278; *d.* Siena, Aug. 1319), Italian painter of the Sienese School, its first great representative. He is frequently mentioned in the records of Siena, fines for debt and offences against authority suggesting an extravagant and unconventional character. The one unquestioned work by him is the great altarpiece, the 'Maestà', carried to the cathedral from his studio, 19th June 1311, amid general acclaim and to the sound of bells, trumpets and drums (now in the Siena Cathedral Museum). It consists on one side of the Virgin with a host of angels and saints, with seven small paintings on the predella, and on the reverse a series of episodes from the life of Christ. Most of these are still at Siena but small paintings from the altar-piece, removed at some unknown time, are in galleries at Berlin, London (National Gallery) and Washington. The 'Rucellai Madonna' painted for Santa Maria Novella, Florence, 1285 (Uffizi), long attributed to Cimabue (q.v.), is almost certainly his. Other works attributed to him are the 'Virgin Enthroned with three kneeling

[214]

Franciscans' (Siena, Pinacoteca), triptychs in the National Gallery and Buckingham Palace, 'Virgin and Angels' (Perugia, also at Bern) and 'St John Preaching' (Budapest). His art is distinct from that of his contemporaries Cimabue and Giotto, definitely Byzantine in style, though it is important to note that it is related not to the stereotyped icons of Greek monkish painters but to the refined products of Byzantine revival at the imperial court of Constantinople from the eleventh century, as exemplified in exquisite manuscript illuminations. The use of gold in background and detail, an elegant quality of line, a beautiful use of colour for the sake of its own harmonies (and not as with Giotto an ancillary to form) are characteristic. His art is also to be distinguished from that of Sienese successors, Simone Martini and the Lorenzetti (qq.v.), in which a Gothic element is infused.

Duchamp, Marcel (*b*. Blainville, 1887; *d*. Paris, 1 Oct. 1968). French painter, brother of the sculptor Raymond Duchamp-Villon and the painter Jacques Villon. He was first influenced by Cézanne and the

Cubists but Futurism incited him to fantastic invention. Successive stages of motion are represented in his 'Nude descending a Staircase' (Philadelphia Museum of Art), 1912. In cultivating an 'anti-art' attitude, making use of the oddities of machine forms and a prankish enthusiasm for 'found objects' he was one of the protagonists of Dadaism. He settled in New York.

Dufresne, Charles (*b*. Millemont, 23 Nov. 1876; *d*.La Seyne,1938),French painter and decorative artist, whose work combines Romantic

MARCEL DUCHAMP— Nude descending a Staircase No. 2, 1912—Philadelphia Museum of Art.

[215]

C. DUFRESNE—The
Toilet—Lefevre Gallery.

and Cubist elements. He began to paint about 1906, being first influenced by both Delacroix and the Fauves and later by the Cubists. Two years in Algeria, 1910–12, greatly affected his attitude to subject matter. He favoured exotic landscapes and scenes of the chase, applying a modern technique to these themes. Works by him are in the Musée d'Art Moderne, Paris, and in the galleries of Amsterdam, Stockholm, Belgium and the U.S.A.

Dufy, Raoul (*b.* Le Havre, 3 June 1877; *d.* Forcalquier, 23 Mar. 1953), French painter noted for his calligraphic and witty style. He studied at the École des Beaux-Arts in Paris and in 1905 was won over to Fauve colour by Matisse's picture 'Luxe, Calme, Volupté'. He was also influenced in his early work by Cézanne, but from about 1912 developed his characteristic manner, light and sketchy in both oil and water-colour and well adapted to a gay rendering of such favoured scenes as regattas, race meetings or theatre interiors. From 1911 he did much decorative designing for printed silks and tapestries. His decorative work included a huge mural for the Electricity Pavilion at the Paris Exposition of 1937. He won the International Prize for paintings at the Venice Biennale of 1952.

Dujardin, Karel (*b.* Amsterdam, 1622; *d.* Venice, 20 Nov. 1678), Dutch painter of landscape, portrait and *genre*, the pupil of Berchem (q.v.), whom he resembles in Italianate landscape. His work, however, is varied in inspiration; as a young man in Rome he painted 'Bambocciante' pictures of local life; *c.* 1654–5 the influence of Paulus Potter turned him to animal studies; later he reverted to Italian themes under the influence of Adriaen van de Velde. He died on his second visit to Italy.

Dunoyer de Segonzac, André (*b.* Boussy-Saint-Antoine, 6 July 1884), French painter and graphic artist. He studied, 1901–6, at the École des Beaux-Arts, the Académie Julian and 'La Palette' and

R. DUFY—Sea Front at Nice—Collection of Marcus Wickham-Boynton, Esq.

produced his first landscapes at St Tropez in 1908. Subsequently he developed a style of his own in landscapes, still lifes and paintings of the nude, vigorously simplified and restrained in colour. Water-colour is a means of expression he found especially congenial, attaining by an elaborate technique something of the depth of oil. His brilliant gifts as a draughtsman can be appreciated in his many book illustrations, among them the etchings to *La Treille Muscate* of Colette, his neighbour at St Tropez, and the superb series for the *Georgics* of Virgil, 1947. Segonzac was elected an honorary member of the Royal Academy in 1947.

Dupré, Jules (*b.* Nantes, 5 April 1811; *d.* L'Isle-Adam, 6 Oct. 1889), French painter, the son of a porcelain manufacturer. He became the friend of Diaz (q.v.) and one of the leading spirits of the Barbizon School (q.v.), deriving benefit from both Constable (he visited England) and the Dutch seventeenth-century landscape painters. He travelled widely in France but is mainly noted for his paintings of the forest of Fontainebleau and of sea and storm, of which 'The Headland' (Glasgow) is an impressive example.

Dürer, Albrecht (*b.* Nuremberg, 21 May 1471; *d.* there, 6 April

[217]

J. DUPRÉ—The Headland—Glasgow Art Gallery.

1528), German painter and graphic artist, the outstanding figure of
the Renaissance in northern Europe. He was the third of the fifteen
children of a Hungarian goldsmith who had settled and married at
Nuremberg, first worked under his father and from 1486 to 1490
studied painting under Michael Wolgemut (q.v.). A beautiful silverpoint drawing (Albertina) is a self-portrait at the age of thirteen
already characteristic of his genius. To complete his training he
worked as an engraver in Basel and Colmar, seeking instruction in
the studio of Martin Schongauer (q.v.) (whom he greatly admired),
though after Schongauer's death in 1491. In Nuremberg, 1494, he
married Agnes Frey, the daughter of a musician and man of wealth,
and in the autumn of that year went to Italy for the first time, one
result of the journey being a splendid series of landscape studies in
water-colour. He visited Italy again, 1505–7, staying in Venice, and
these journeys were of first importance in his career. Not only was he
impressed by Mantegna, Pollaiuolo and the Bellinis; his curiosity
was aroused as to the science of Renaissance artists and his sense of
an ideal beauty as distinct from his early detailed realism was
awakened. He was employed by the Emperor Maximilian, from whom
he received an allowance, and after Maximilian's death made his only
other journey of note—to the Netherlands in 1520 to win the

[218]

A. DÜRER—The Hare (Pen and Water-colour)— Albertina, Vienna.

patronage of the Emperor Charles V. He then saw and admired the treasures of Aztec art and craftsmanship which had been brought back from the New World and was also received in Antwerp, Brussels and Bruges with every mark of respect. In the art of Dürer there is a balance between—and sometimes a conflict of —the Gothic spirit and northern craftsmanship and the broad intellectual outlook of the Renaissance. The fifteen large woodcuts of the Apocalypse which appeared in book form in 1498 with German and Latin text were Gothic masterpieces, grim and crowded, while at the same time wonderfully imaginative. The 'Life of the Virgin', which belongs to the period of his second Italian journey, has a new breadth and sense of space in composition which recalls Bellini. His genius was essentially linear and his copper engravings, woodcuts and drawings include his most famous and moving works. The 'Fortune', 1500, 'Adam and Eve', 1504, the 'Great Horse' and 'Little Horse', 1505 (studies of equine proportion), the great 'Melancolia', 1514, in which he seems a northern Leonardo brooding over the endless and unsatisfied quest for knowledge, and the 'Knight, Death and the Devil', 1513, are masterpieces of line engraving. The 'Great Passion', 1498–1510, and 'Little Passion', 1509–11, are notable woodcut series. His portrait drawings and studies of animals and plants, e.g. 'The Hare' and the 'Tuft of Grass' (Albertina), are superb. Painting was never to the same extent his *métier*, though the self-portraits of 1493 (Louvre), 1498 (Prado) and 1504 (Munich) have an impressive place in his work, and the 'Adam and Eve' of the Prado is a beautiful product of his Italian studies. His paintings include a number of altar-pieces, among his best religious works being the 'Adoration of the Trinity', 1511 (Vienna), the 'Adoration of the Magi', 1504 (Uffizi) and the 'Four Apostles', 1526 (Munich). His final works were his three books, on measurement and perspective, 1525, the fortification and construction of towns, 1527, and human proportion, 1528. Inexhaustible in invention, minute in observation, impeccable in craft, he was also remarkable in intellect and his art, it was said by Melanchthon, represented only a fraction of his personal greatness of mind.

[219]

A. DÜRER—Self-portrait, 1498—Prado.

Dutch Art Museums. The principal art collection of Holland is the Rijksmuseum (q.v.), Amsterdam. Modern Dutch painting is represented in the Stedelijk Museum, Amsterdam. The Mauritshuis at The Hague, once the residence of Count John Maurice of Nassau, a public gallery since 1821, is a fine collection of Dutch paintings, including Vermeer's 'View of Delft'. The Boymans Museum, Rotterdam, contains the work of both old and modern masters. The Haarlem Museum Gallery is mainly devoted to the work of Frans Hals and the Kröller-Müller Gallery, Otterlo, to that of Vincent van Gogh.

Dutch Painting, in its beginnings scarcely separable from the art of the southern Netherlands, became a great and distinct national school when the Dutch gained independence in the seventeenth century. The early Netherlandish masters of the northern provinces in the fifteenth and sixteenth centuries include Cornelisz van Oostzanen, Geertgen Tot St Jans, Jan Mostaert, Cornelis Engelbrechtsz, Lucas van Leyden and Jan van Scorel. Scorel's pupil Anthonis Mor was a portrait painter of international fame and clientele, and in the late sixteenth and early seventeenth centuries some Dutch painters showed the effect of Italian Mannerism and the work of Caravaggio, the School of Utrecht, of which Abraham Blomaert and Gerard Honthorst were typical, being noted for this Italianate tendency. Other Italianizers were Pieter Lastman and H. Terbruggen, while Pieter van Laer and Jan Both worked much in Italy. At the same time, however, the growth of a native realism is to be seen in W. Buytewech's paintings of modes and manners and the landscapes of Hercules Seghers, and there quickly follows the great expansion of a realistic and entirely Dutch art. Rembrandt was a supreme master in every field, with many pupils, including Ferdinand Bol, Jan Lievens, van der Eeckhout, Gerard Dou, Nicholas Maes and S. van Hoogstraten.

C. ENGELBRECHTSZ—
Christ taking leave of his Mother—Rijksmuseum, Amsterdam.

S. VAN RUISDAEL—Scene on the Ice—Collection of Mr & Mrs E. Assheton Bennett.

W. DUYSTER—A Guard Room—Collection of Sir Harold Wernher, Bt.

M. SORGH—A Lady at the Virginals—
ection of Mrs Geoffrey Hart.

J. C. VAN OOSTZANEN— Salome with the Head
of John the Baptist—Rijksmuseum, Amsterdam.

TERBRUGGEN—Man playing Bagpipes—
molean Museum, Oxford.

J. VAN DER VELDE—Still Life with Strawberries
—Ashmolean Museum, Oxford.

The Dutch, however, tended to specialize. The portrait painters include Mierevelt, van Ravesteyn, van der Helst and, outstandingly, Frans Hals; landscape masters, van Goyen, van der Neer, Jan Wynants, van Everdingen, Berchem, Cuyp, Koninck, Ruisdael, Hobbema, Wouwerman and Saftleven; painters of seascape, van de Cappelle, van de Velde, Bakhuyzen; of town views, Gerrit Berckheyde, E. de Witte and P. Saenredam; of animals, Paulus Potter, J. Asselijn, Jan Weenix and Hondecoeter; of flowers and still life, Kalf, Heda, van Beyeren, de Heem, Huysum, Ruysch; of social life, Metsu, Ter Borch, Jan Steen, Maes, Dirck Hals, Ostade, Jan Molenaer. Amsterdam was a main centre but Haarlem, Leyden and Delft were centres also. The School of Delft is represented by Carel Fabritius, Pieter de Hooch and, above all, by the great genius of Vermeer. In the nineteenth century there was a revival of painting; of *genre* with Josef Israels and of landscape with Jongkind, the brothers Maris, and Mauve. From this *milieu* came the extraordinary genius of Vincent van Gogh. Modern Dutch painting reflects the conjoined influence of architectural and abstract design in the de Stijl movement, Piet Mondrian being internationally known. Abstract Expression also has recent adherents.

Dyce, William (*b*. Aberdeen, 19 Sept. 1806; *d*. London, 14 Feb. 1864), Scottish painter, trained in Edinburgh, London and Rome,

W. DYCE—Pegwell Bay, Kent—Tate Gallery.

where, 1825–7, he met the German 'Nazarener' (q.v.). Their influence and that of early Florentine masters caused him to pursue an earnest and precisely detailed style of painting in which he was a precursor of the Pre-Raphaelites. His 'Titian's First Essay in Colouring', 1859, and 'Pegwell Bay', 1861, well show the affinity. He also painted Arthurian frescoes in the House of Lords and was made R.A. in 1848.

Dyck, Sir Anthony van (Antoon van) (b. Antwerp, 22 Mar. 1599; d. London, 9 Dec. 1641), Flemish painter and great master of portraiture and baroque composition, the son of a silk merchant. As a boy the pupil of Hendrik van Balen, he developed quickly and at the age of nineteen was one of the talented assistants Rubens gathered round him, becoming in two years his most favoured and brilliant pupil, closely related to him in style. Introduced to the court of James I by the Earl of Arundel, he stayed in England a year, then in 1621 set off for Italy, visiting a number of cities and being especially impressed by the great Venetians, Titian above all. The Italian period, 1621–7, is marked by his portraits, which gained in dignity from his Venetian studies, those he produced at Genoa (e.g. the 'Marchese Cattaneo'—National Gallery) being notable; while baroque religious painting also widened his range of style and composition. He returned to Antwerp as the rival of Rubens, having his own flourishing studio, and between 1628 and 1632 reached a peak of development. To this period belong his 'Iconography', the superb set of etchings of distinguished contemporaries, and religious works in a personal version of baroque unlike that of Rubens, 'The Ecstasy of St Augustine' (Church of St Augustine, Antwerp), being a fine example. Again invited to England in 1632 by Charles I, who knighted him and arranged his marriage with Mary, daughter of Sir Patrick Ruthven, he began that remarkable record of the royal family and English

SIR A. VAN DYCK—
Queen Henrietta Maria—
Reproduced by Gracious
Permission of Her Majesty
the Queen.

SIR A. VAN DYCK—King Charles I—Louvre.

SIR A. VAN DYCK—The Ecstasy of St Augustine—Church of St Augustine, Antwerp.

aristocracy which in refinement of style and colour and dignity of composition left its profound impress on subsequent portraiture in England. The portrait of Charles I, now in the Louvre, and the many memorable works still in the Royal Collection are a distinct creation, and despite the large extent to which van Dyck employed studio assistants, never fall into superficiality. The effect of environment may be noted in his landscape studies (British Museum), which anticipate Constable in conveying the atmosphere of the English countryside. He died at Blackfriars, aged forty-two, when the regime of which he has left the best defence was approaching its end.

E

Eakins, Thomas (*b*. Philadelphia, 25 July 1844; *d*. there, 25 June 1916), American painter of *genre* and portraits. He studied at the Pennsylvania Academy of Fine Arts and in Paris at the École des Beaux-Arts under Gérôme and Bonnat, whose academic realism left its traces on his style. He settled at Philadelphia, painting its people, home life and outdoor sports, while his scientific interests are reflected in 'The Gross Clinic', depicting a surgical operation. An independent realist, too unconventional to be appreciated in his own day, he has historical importance in the development of American art, and he now ranks as one of its most powerful representatives.

Earl, Ralph (*b*. Leicester, Massachusetts, 11 May 1751; *d*. Bolton, Connecticut, 16 Aug. 1801), American historical and portrait painter, one of the self-taught and itinerant artists of the colonial and early republican periods. His battle scenes of Lexington, engraved by Amos Doolittle, are said to have been the first historical pictures by an

T. EAKINS—Turning Stake Boat—The Cleaveland Museum of Art, Hinman B. Hurlbut Collection.

American. He went to
London after the War
of Independence, studied
with Benjamin West
(q.v.) and painted a
number of portraits,
returning to America in
1786. He made portraits
of many distinguished
Americans and his works
include a painting of
Niagara Falls.

**Early Christian Paint-
ing,** wall - paintings,
mosaics and manu-
scripts produced in the
early centuries of the
Christian era, prior to
the development of the
Romanesque and later
Byzantine styles. *See
also* BYZANTINE PAINTING. Most of the earliest paintings are found in
the catacombs of Rome, second to fourth centuries A.D. These continue
the style of classical painting as represented at Pompeii in a simpler
and less elegant form, converting a number of its motifs to symbolic
use. The architectural backgrounds of Pompeian decoration long
remained a feature of Byzantine wall-paintings and manuscripts.
Representations of the Virgin appear by the third or fourth centuries.
Jesus in early representations appears youthful and beardless. The
removal of the seat of empire from Rome to the old Hellenistic city
of Byzantium by Constantine and the adoption of Christianity as the
official religion had the effect of bringing art above ground, while at
the same time it created somewhat different trends in the western and
eastern districts of the Empire. Mosaic (q.v.), the material of ancient
pavements, was now converted to pictorial use on wall and ceiling,
examples of the fourth and fifth centuries being those of Santa Maria
Maggiore and Santa Constanza at Rome. The mosaics of Ravenna are
wonderful examples (fifth to sixth centuries A.D.). From the eighth
century and in the period of Charlemagne as Emperor of the West
the art of the western and eastern Christian worlds became increasingly distinct. While images were banned in the Iconoclastic
period of Byzantine art, in the Carolingian dominions they were
encouraged and early Christian and classical models were copied.

The Carolingian period is especially notable for its impressive manuscript painting. A separate development of great interest in the late seventh and early eighth centuries was that of Celtic illumination. *See* BOOK OF KELLS; ILLUMINATED MANUSCRIPTS; LINDISFARNE GOSPELS. After A.D. 1000 Christian art in the west developed the magisterial character of the Romanesque style (q.v.).

Eastlake, Sir Charles Lock (*b.* Plymouth, 17 Nov. 1793; *d.* Pisa, 24 Dec. 1865), English painter and official, the pupil of B. R. Haydon (q.v.). He worked in Rome, 1817–30, and was later P.R.A., 1850, subsequently becoming Director of the National Gallery, 1855–65. He is of less note as a painter than for his treatise *Materials for the History of Oil Painting*.

Eclecticism, practice or theory in art, as in philosophy, of selecting and adopting various styles with a view to combining them in a composite system. The maxim with which Tintoretto is credited, 'the colour of Titian and the drawing of Michelangelo', serves as an instance. 'Eclectic' was the term often used in the past to describe the School of Bologna in the sixteenth century (*see* CARRACCI), though modern criticism deprecates this application in so far as it obscured the originality of the Bolognese artists and suggested merely a sterile academicism.

Eeckhout, Gerbrandt van den (*b.* Amsterdam, 19 Aug. 1621; buried

SIR CHARLES EASTLAKE—The Colosseum from the Esquiline Hill—Tate Gallery.

EGYPTIAN PAINTING, New Kingdom—Detail of Fresco, The Royal Couple—Ashmolean Museum, Oxford.

there, 29 Sept. 1674), Dutch painter of religious subjects, *genre* and portraits, one of Rembrandt's later pupils and most consistent followers. Rich colour and rhetorical use of gesture characterize his biblical subjects, among which are 'Tobit' (Brunswick), 'The Woman taken in Adultery' (Rijksmuseum), 'Simeon in the Temple' (Dresden) and 'Christ among the Doctors' (Munich). The *genre* paintings of this versatile artist recall Ter Borch.

Egyptian Painting has its earliest examples in the animals, etc., painted in white slip on red vases in the prehistoric period which dates back to *c.* 5000 B.C. Some relation seems to have existed between prehistoric Egypt and the north African settlements of Neolithic people who arrived at the pastoral stage between 6000 and 2000 B.C. and have left a remarkable series of rock paintings in the Saharan regions, though this is still a matter for research. *See also* PRE- HISTORIC AND PRIMITIVE PAINTING. The art of Egypt, however, was transformed under the dynasties of the Old Kingdom from about 4000 B.C., and its characteristic style underwent few major changes until about 300 B.C., when the Hellenistic influences of the Ptolemaic period had their effect. Like sculpture, Egyptian painting was gov- erned by strong conventions, firm outlines being filled in with flat bright colour and the faces, legs and feet being habitually rendered in profile with shoulders and arms in frontal view. Its main applica- tion was mural, on the exterior and interior walls of temples and palaces and in tombs. The low relief with which the walls of a public

EGYPTIAN PAINTING—Fowling Scene from Tomb at Thebes—British Museum.

building were decorated, gaining a sharp outline in the brilliant sunlight and representing the gods or the victories of a Pharaoh, was
filled in with bright colour giving the effect of fresco. On the wall
surface of the tombs hollowed out of rock, painting only was used. In
spite of rigid conventions imposed by a priestly and autocratic caste,
the idea of a continuance of life in the hereafter led to the depiction
of the Egyptian mode of life and made the tomb paintings varied and
informative in subject-matter. They include such scenes as banqueting, harvesting, boatbuilding and fowling in the marshes of the
Delta. The keenness of the artists' observation is shown in their portrayal of foreigners or captives, Semitic, Asiatic and negroid. Painting
reached its highest point in the period of the New Kingdom between
2000 and 1000 B.C., being then full of lively incident and even showing
some touches of comedy. Famous examples in the British Museum
show a fowling scene (from a tomb at Thebes, c. 1400 B.C.) and an
entertainment with musicians and dancers (c. 1500 B.C.). The reign of
Akhnaton brought to painting as to sculpture a new freedom and
naturalism of treatment. Painters were employed not only on mural
decoration but in illustrating papyri, e.g. with the religious symbolism

[233]

of the Book of the Dead, though during the New Kingdom examples of comic illustration for fables or popular themes are found. The extinction of the native art as a result of foreign settlement and conquest is signalized by the Greco-Roman portraits of mummy cases (*see* ROMAN PAINTING). The disappearance also of the ancient religion is signalized by the growth of an Egyptian (Coptic) Christian Church in the period between the official recognition of Christianity and the Moslem Conquest, fourth to seventh centuries A.D. Coptic painting was a result—a crude amalgam of styles retaining something of the old sense of decoration but much influenced by Byzantine models.

Elsheimer, Adam (*b.* Frankfurt-on-Main, 18 Mar. 1578; *d.* Rome, 11 Dec. 1610), German painter who studied at Frankfurt under a minor landscape artist, Philip Uffenbach, leaving the city about 1598 to work at Munich and in Venice with Johann Rottenhammer (q.v.). In 1600 he settled in Rome, where he was known as 'Adamo Tedesco', and began to produce small pictures, painted, like Rottenhammer's, on copper, which had a great influence on the development of seventeenth-century landscape. Landscape played a principal part in these works, ostensibly biblical or mythological in subject, and in its treatment Elsheimer seems to have drawn suggestions from a variety of sources, Tintoretto, the Carracci, Caravaggio and the Flemish painter Paul Bril. He is noted for the effective contrast between different sources of light in the same picture, e.g. the firelight, torchlight and moonlight in his 'Flight into Egypt' (Munich; replica in Louvre), which may well have inspired Rembrandt's 'Flight into Egypt' (Dublin). Effects of this kind delighted and influenced Rubens, who bought works by him. He also made a study of the country round Rome and his sketches in the Campagna foreshadow the 'classical' landscape with ruins that Claude was to perfect.

Empire Style, neo-classicism as applied to furniture and interior decoration in the Napoleonic age. David's portrait of Mme Récamier provides a famous instance of the use of this *décor* in painting.

Enamel, vitreous glaze or glazes fused on the surface of metallic objects and used decoratively with an effect analogous to that of mosaic and stained glass painting or even as a form of picture. It has an ancient tradition. Examples of cloisonné enamel fused in cells formed by thin metal strips bent to the outline of a pattern and soldered to a metal base have been found in a Mycenaean tomb in Cyprus of the thirteenth century B.C. The champlevé technique—enamel fused in troughs cut out in the metal baseplate—was used by Celtic craftsmen of the pre-Christian era. Enamels were made in the northern provinces of the Roman Empire and reappear in the sixth century A.D. in Anglo-Saxon England. A great revival of cloisonné enamel began in Constantinople in the tenth century A.D.; a great masterpiece of this Byzantine enamel is the Pala d'Oro in St Mark's, Venice. During the Middle Ages the demand for church ornament, decorated reliquaries, crosses, etc., encouraged a number of technical developments. The Rhine and Meuse valleys, Limoges in France and

A. ELSHEIMER—The Shipwreck of St Paul—National Gallery.

north Spain were centres of a new style of champlevé enamel from the twelfth century. In the fifteenth century, in north Italy and at Limoges, *painted enamels* were first made, applied by brush, spatula or point over a design scratched in outline on the baseplate. Masters of this form of art were Nardon and Jean Penicaud, Pierre Raymond and Leonard Limousin. A later development in the seventeenth century was the miniature painted enamel in which the colours were applied after the enamel was fired and fused, as practised by the Toutin family in Paris. Stubbs in England produced enamel paintings.

Encaustic Painting, ancient method of painting with heated wax, used by the Greeks and Romans on both walls and panels. Wax colours, liquefied by heat, were applied with either a spatula or a brush. No classical Greek examples remain, but a number of portrait panels on mummy cases discovered in Egypt and ranging in date from the first to third century A.D. show impressively the mastery and distinction of style obtained by Greco-Roman painters in the medium and bear witness also to its durability. Experimental attempts have been made to follow ancient practice, but broadly speaking the method is obsolete. A wax emulsion has been used by some modern artists in wall-painting, but this is distinct from the 'burning-in' process which the word encaustic conveys.

[235]

Engraving, primarily the art of drawing on a substance by means of an incised line and in this sense of great antiquity, prehistoric art giving examples of pictorial engraving on rock, bone or ivory, while gems have been engraved from early times. Technically, however, and in present usage the word generally refers to the incision of a design on a metal plate or wood block for the purpose of taking reproductions from it on paper. Before the invention of photographic means of reproduction it was a way of recognizably interpreting paintings, drawings, statuary, etc., in prints for popular distribution and in this aspect was an imitative craft. At all times, however, it has been practised by artists as a method of original expression and thus as a form of art. It has two main forms, *relief*, in which the design to be printed is left on the surface, the unwanted part of the material used being cut away, as in the woodcut, lino-cut or wood-engraving, and *intaglio*, where the lines cut or bitten into metal plate constitute the impression, being filled with ink in printing and transferred to paper under considerable pressure, as in line engraving and etching. To these may be added the special form of surface print obtained by lithography. *See* separate articles on AQUATINT; DRYPOINT; ETCHING; LINE ENGRAVING; LITHOGRAPHY; MEZZOTINT; STIPPLE ENGRAVING; WOODCUT; WOOD ENGRAVING.

Ensor, James (*b.* Ostend, 13 April 1860; *d.* there, 19 Nov. 1949). Belgian painter, son of an English father and a Flemish mother, a British subject until 1930, when he became a Belgian (and also a baron), He studied at the academy in Brussels and first painted dark landscapes and seascapes, but in the 1880's quickly developed a richness of colour and a macabre quality of imagination in which he has been compared with his Flemish forerunners Brueghel and Bosch. (He has been

J. ENSOR—Self-portrait with Masks—Photo, Marlborough Fine Art.

claimed also as a forerunner of Surrealism.) He worked quietly at Ostend in a studio over a shop which sold seaside gift oddities, 'happily confined', in his own words, to 'the solitary realm where the mask rules'. Between 1880 and 1900 his creative range of subject and style was fully established, appearing in tormented and tragic religious themes and in his grotesque world of masks and animated skeletons. Early works such as his 'Christ's Entry into Brussels' were treated with contempt, but in 1908 Emile Verhaeren first recognized his gifts and the exhibition at the Palais des Beaux-Arts in Brussels in 1929 may be said to have 'made' the (by then aged) painter's reputation. In addition to paintings he produced a large number of drawings and etchings. The most eminent of modern Belgian painters, he is adequately represented in the national collections at Antwerp and Brussels.

Ernst, Max (*b.* Brühl, nr Cologne, 2 April 1891), German Surrealist. A student of philosophy in his early days, he turned to art in 1913 and brought Dadaism (q.v.) to Cologne in 1919, organizing a sensational exhibition which was closed by the police. In 1920 he moved to Paris, where he was associated with André Breton and Paul Eluard in the

MAX ERNST—Sombre Forest and Bird—Arts Council Photograph.

REMBRANDT—Christ Healing the Sick (Etching)—Victoria and Albert Museum, Crown Copyright.

foundation of Surrealism (q.v.). Characteristic products were fantastic works in which the Cubist 'collage' was employed to ironic or macabre effect, an instance being his 'novel' *La Femme 100 Têtes* of 1929. He escaped from a concentration camp in France, 1940, and stayed in the United States until 1950, when he returned to France. He was awarded the Grand Prix of Painting at the Venice Biennale of 1954.

Escorial, El (The Escurial), sixteenth-century building erected by Philip II thirty-one miles north-west of Madrid, comprising palace, monastery, library and a splendid collection of paintings by Spanish and Italian masters and tapestries.

Etching, art of engraving by biting into a metal plate with acid. The plate is covered with a wax ground, through which the artist draws with a metal point ('etching needle'), removing the wax ground but not scratching the plate in the lines he opens. The ground is usually smoked over a flame so that the lines show plainly. The plate, the back of which is varnished for protection, is then immersed in an acid bath, dilute nitric acid or hydrochloric acid and potassium chlorate ('Dutch bath') being mordants commonly used. By 'stopping out' at intervals, i.e. by varnishing over lines sufficiently bitten, gradations of line from light to dark can be obtained. In printing, the ink left in the bitten lines is transferred to the paper by considerable

PETRVS BREVGEL
ANTVERPIÆ PICTOR RVRALIVM ACTIONVM.

A. VAN DYCK—Portrait of P. Brueghel (Etching)—Victoria and Albert Museum, Crown Copyright.

G. B. PIRANESI—Etching from the 'Carceri' series—Victoria and Albert Museum, Crown Copyright.

J. McN. WHISTLER—Black Lion Wharf (Etching)—Victoria and Albert Museum, Crown Copyright.

pressure. Some artists add an adventitious element of tone by leaving a certain amount of ink on the surface as well as in the lines. Variants of the process are aquatint (q.v.) and soft-ground etching. In the latter tallow is mixed with the ground and the design is firmly traced on it through a sheet of paper with a pencil, thus producing from the bitten plate a grained effect like that of a pencil or crayon drawing.

Many great painters and draughtsmen have used the process to creative effect. The earliest dated etching is by Urs Graf, 1513. Dürer was a pioneer also with his 'The Cannon', etched on iron. Van Dyck's portrait etchings of his contemporaries (completed in line engraving by assistants, 1626–32) are masterpieces of etched line. Rembrandt in his three hundred plates showed himself the greatest of etchers in variety of style, range and depth of expression, in portraits, landscape and subjects taken either from scripture or from daily life. Other notable painter-etchers of the Netherlands were Hercules Seghers, Ostade, Teniers, Paulus Potter and Berchem (qq.v.). Callot, Claude, Watteau, Boucher and Fragonard (qq.v.) are among the great French practitioners, and in Italy Tiepolo, with his delicate 'Capricci', Piranesi and Canaletto (qq.v.). Hogarth used etching as well as line-engraving; Rowlandson and Gillray etched in outline, their prints being completed by hand-colouring. Cruikshank's etched illustrations to Dickens's novels are also of note. Crome, Girtin, Cotman and Turner (who etched the outlines for his mezzo-tinted *Liber Studiorum*) give landscape examples in England, and in France etching was revived by Théodore Rousseau, Daubigny, Corot, Millet and Méryon. Whistler in his London and Venice series was unsurpassed. In more recent times the art has been extensively practised in England, Walter Sickert, Sir D. Y. Cameron, Sir Frank Brangwyn and Sir Muirhead Bone being distinguished. The most outstanding modern etchings have been produced in France, Chagall,

[241]

ETRUSCAN PAINTING—Ceremonial Burning of the Dead: set of panels from Cerveteri—Louvre.

Derain, Matisse, Picasso, Rouault and Segonzac all having executed remarkable etched works. *See also* DRYPOINT; STIPPLE ENGRAVING.

Etruscan Painting, art of the ancient Italian people who occupied the district of Etruria, between the rivers Arno and Tiber on the south-west side of the Apennines and between the cities of Rome and Florence. Their origin is uncertain but they probably came from Asia Minor *c.* 1000 B.C., and they were noted in the sixth century B.C. as a sea power. This was the period in which their art flourished. It was strongly influenced by Greek art of the transitional period from archaism to classic, the Greek influence being explained by the presence in Italy of Greek colonists and craftsmen and by the maritime relations of Etruria and Athens. Painting took the form of fresco or paintings on terra-cotta slabs affixed to the wall in the subterranean tombs at Tarquinia, Chiusi, Orvieto, Vulci, Cerveteri and elsewhere. The subjects of this funerary art were banquets, dancing, athletic contests, hunting and other scenes of actual life; though the underworld and its demons become prominent in subject-matter after the fifth century. A sombre and a materialistic character, related in spirit to the art of Rome rather than that of Greece, have been discerned in Etruscan art. The conquest and absorption of Etruria by Rome in the fourth century B.C. merged the Greco-Etruscan art into that of the victorious city.

Etty, William (*b.* York, 10 Mar. 1787; *d.* there, 13 Nov. 1849), English figure painter, pupil of Sir Thomas Lawrence (q.v.) for a year, after seven years in the employ of a printer. He made a reputation by

W. ETTY—The Bather—Tate Gallery.

A. VAN EVERDINGEN—Landscape with Water Mill—National Gallery.

fanciful subject pictures in the Romantic taste and was made R.A. in 1828, but continued to attend the life class at the Academy with a humble desire to reach perfection, and his studies of the nude on canvas or millboard are now the most valued part of his work. His colour was inspired by Rubens and the Venetians, a visit to Venice being influential in his development. He also painted some able portraits and in later life retired to York. The York Art Gallery has a large collection of his paintings.

Euphronios (sixth–fifth centuries B.C.), Greek vase painter of the Attic School, one of those who introduced the red-figured style, a new form of figure drawing, more advanced in anatomy and foreshortening. The bowl showing Herakles and Antaeos wrestling (Louvre) signed by him is a notable example.

Euston Road School, name applied to a group of English painters associated with the 'School of Drawing and Painting', founded in 1937 in London by (Sir) William Coldstream (*b.* 1908), Victor Pasmore (*b.* 1908), Claude Rogers (*b.* 1907) and Graham Bell (1910–43). These painters worked alongside their students in the school and encouraged them to 'keep their eyes on what they saw', without being preoccupied by theory or the dominant influence of the School of Paris. The enterprise flourished until the outbreak of war in 1939, and apart from its educational aspect, came to stand for a kind of realism which has a well-defined place in English art of the the mid-twentieth century, its essence being the belief that everyday life is by no means exhausted as the material for art.

Everdingen, Allart van (*b.* Alkmaar, baptized 18 June 1621; *d.* Amsterdam, buried 8 Nov. 1675), Dutch landscape painter and etcher who studied under Roelandt Savery, travelled in Norway and Sweden and is noted for having introduced into Dutch art the romantic ruggedness of Scandinavian scenery, as in his 'Norwegian Waterfall' (Berlin) and his 'Swedish Landscape' (Boymans Museum, Rotterdam), inspiring Ruisdael to paint similar subjects. There are 121 of his drawings, some in water-colour, in the British Museum.

Exekias (sixth century B.C.), leading vase painter of the Attic School in the archaic black-figured style. A notable example is an amphora from Vulci, Etruria (Vatican), depicting Kastor and Polydeukes and signed by the painter.

Expressionism, form of art which endeavours to express the inner life of the artist or to project a personal emotion into what he represents, by means of some distortion of form or emphasis of colour. Representation thus becomes symbolic of personal experience,

H. VAN EYCK—The Three Marys at the Sepulchre—Boymans Museum, Rotterdam.

H. VAN EYCK (?)—The Last Judgment—Metropolitan Museum of Art, New York.

physical, intellectual or spiritual, and Expressionism implies some unusual exaltation or some disturbance or disquiet of mind which the artist feels it needful to signalize. Historically a classic example is the work of Matthias Grünewald, as in his Isenheim altar-piece, though the painting of El Greco might be said to answer to the definition. Largely, however, it is a modern phenomenon of northern Europe, often indicating a lack of adjustment between artist and society, the Norwegian Edvard Munch and Vincent van Gogh being regarded as the main exemplars. The melancholy of the one, the tragic violence of the other, were especially influential in Germany, where Expressionism became a well-defined movement in the early twentieth century, as represented by the two famous groups, 'Die Brücke' and 'Der Blaue Reiter' (qq.v.). Artists such as Emil Nolde and Oskar Kokoschka (qq.v.) were Expressionist in vehemence. Robert Wiene's *The Cabinet of Dr Caligari*,

JAN VAN EYCK—The Madonna of Canon van der Paele—Musée Communal, Bruges.

1919, applied the distortions of Expressionist painting to the film, with remarkable effect. Outside Germany an Expressionist sense of anguish or tragedy is conveyed by Rouault and Soutine (qq.v.). In equating a spiritual condition with abstract art Kandinsky (q.v.) gave the tendency a new direction, reflected in the present-day pursuit of 'Abstract Expressionism'.

Eyck, Hubert (Hubrecht) van (*b*. probably Maaseyck or the Maas, ? *c*. 1379; *d*. 1426), early Netherlandish painter of whom little is known for certain. He worked at Bruges and Ghent, being several times mentioned in the records of Ghent. He is presumed to have worked with his brother, Jan van Eyck (q.v.), as a miniaturist, miniatures in the 'Hours of Turin' (a manuscript destroyed in 1903) having been attributed to them. Traditionally the famous 'Adoration of the Lamb' (Ghent Cathedral) represents the art of both, the Latin inscription on this polyptych, seemingly placed there by Jan van Eyck, paying tribute to Hubert as a painter second to none and indicating that the work was finished in 1432 by Jan after Hubert's death. It is on the evidence of style only, however, that Hubert's share in this work can be assessed or any other (such as the 'Three Marys at the Sepulchre'—Boymans Museum) can be attributed to him. While expert opinion has differed greatly, the Ghent

[247]

J. VAN EYCK—Portrait of the Artist's Wife—Musée Communal, Bruges.

altar-piece as a conception has no parallel in the works executed by Jan van Eyck alone. Their sister, Margaret, supposedly a miniaturist, is an even more shadowy figure than Hubert.

Eyck, Jan van (*b.* probably Maaseyck, *c.* 1390; *d.* Bruges, June or July 1441), early Netherlandish painter, brother of Hubert van Eyck (q.v.), and traditionally regarded as his collaborator in the Ghent masterpiece 'The Adoration of the Lamb'. One of the great European masters, he is, unlike his brother, a clearly defined historical figure, the products of whose single genius are distinct and unquestioned. He worked as a miniaturist for the Duke of Bavaria, 1422–5, and in 1425 entered the service of Philip the Good, Duke of Burgundy, as court painter and 'varlet de chambre', on his behalf visiting Spain and Portugal. He settled at Bruges *c.* 1430, still working for the duke, but employed also by the wealthy burgesses of Bruges and the visitors to this international seat of trade. A succession of signed and dated masterpieces shows his profound ability in portraiture, his magical sense of detail and an appreciation of perspective that goes beyond the efforts of Italian contemporaries. They include the 'Madonna of the Chancellor Rolin', *c.* 1425–6 (Louvre), the 'Portrait of "Timotheus"', 1432, the 'Man with a Turban', 1433, and the matchless 'Marriage of Giovanni Arnolfini and Giovanna Cenami', 1434 (q.v.), of the National Gallery, the 'Madonna of Canon van der Paele', 1434 (Bruges), the 'Madonna of the Fountain', 1439 (Antwerp), and the 'Portrait of the Artist's Wife', 1439 (Bruges). He (and, it may be, his brother) improved on the (already existing) technique of oil painting, perhaps by the use of a clarified medium and varnish, though the brilliance of colour and perfection of enamel-like surface attained by Jan must be attributed also to his superbly skilled and methodical handling of paint. He may be said to have founded a school in the broadest sense, not by an immediate following of pupils and assistants but in establishing the essential character which art in the southern Netherlands retained until the sixteenth century. (Colour, *see* list.)

F

Fabritius, Carel (*b.* Amsterdam, 1622; *d.* Delft, 1654), Dutch painter, a pupil of Rembrandt at Amsterdam, who settled at Delft and was killed in the Delft explosion of 1654, a number of his works (which are now rare) perishing with him. Those which survive show an original genius and unusual capacity for experiment, as in his 'View of Delft' (National Gallery). Other remarkable paintings are his 'Self-Portrait' (National Gallery) and the famous 'The Goldfinch' (The Hague, Mauritshuis), painted in the year of his death. He may well have inspired Vermeer. His brother, Barent Fabritius (1624–73), was also a pupil of Rembrandt, a painter of religious subjects and portraits but of less note.

Falca, Pietro, *see* LONGHI.

Fantin-Latour, Ignace Henri Jean Théodore (*b.* Grenoble, 14 Jan. 1836; *d.* Bure, 25 Aug. 1904), French portrait and still-life painter, pupil of his father and influenced by Courbet. In group painting he achieved a remarkable document in his 'Hommage à Delacroix', 1864 (Louvre), which includes portraits of Manet, Whistler, Baudelaire and the critic Duranty. At Whistler's suggestion he visited England and perhaps was influenced by the meticulous detail of the Pre-Raphaelites, though

C. FABRITIUS—The Goldfinch — The HAGUE, Mauritshuis.

FANTIN-LATOUR—L'Atelier des Batignolles—Louvre.

the sincerely executed still lifes and flower-pieces by which he is best
known err if anything towards photographic realism. He produced
also some allegorical fancies, often carried out in lithography, but it
is by virtue of his still life that he has stood the test of time.

Farington, Joseph (*b*. Leigh, Lancs, 21 Nov. 1747; *d*. 30 Dec. 1821),
English topographical draughtsman, a pupil of Richard Wilson (q.v.),
and R.A., 1785. He exercised great influence in the Academy. Of
minor interest for his views of the English Lake District, he was the
author of a copious diary, of great value for its account of the art
world of his time, publication of a large part of which began in 1920.

Fauve (Fr. 'wild beast'), movement in art which originated in
Paris in the opening years of the twentieth century as a reaction
against Impressionism. The name is derived from a slighting reference
by the art critic Louis Vauxcelles to the works, hung as a group
together in the Salon d'Automne of 1905, of Matisse, Marquet,
Derain, Vlaminck, Friesz, Rouault and others. Vauxcelles described
this gallery as a *cage aux fauves*, and Fauvism is now the accepted
term for the efforts of these artists to liberate colour from a merely
descriptive function and give it an emotional value of its own. In this
they were variously influenced by Cézanne, Gauguin, van Gogh and
Seurat, though Seurat was criticized by Matisse for having split up

P. A. FEDOTOV—The Little Widow—District Land Museum, Ivanov.

colour in such a way as to lose its value (*see* DIVISIONISM). Gauguin's large areas of decorative colour were admired by both Matisse and Derain; the expressive violence of van Gogh appealed especially to Vlaminck. The group held together loosely for no more than three years, its members following decidedly individual paths, but it had some following in France, Georges Braque and Raoul Dufy being among those who passed through a Fauvist phase, and considerable influence on artists in Germany and Russia, e.g. Kirchner, Kandinsky, Jawlensky. Cubism (q.v.) replaced the movement as a centre of interest and dynamic influence by 1909, yet the basic theory of Fauvism has profoundly affected the whole modern attitude to colour.

Fedotov, Pavel Andreyevich (*b.* Moscow, 22 June 1815; *d.* 14 Nov. 1852), Russian *genre* and portrait painter. He entered the army as a young man, and while a Guards officer painted as an amateur. He retired in 1843 and devoted himself to painting. His work has something of the spirit of Gogol and the manner of English *genre* painting, as in his excellent 'A Poor Aristocrat's Breakfast' (Moscow, Tretyakov Gallery) and 'The Little Widow' here reproduced.

Feininger, Lyonel (*b.* New York, 17 July 1871; *d.* there, 13 Jan. 1956), American painter of German parentage. He went to Germany when sixteen to study music but decided to become a painter, studying in Hamburg and Berlin, 1906–8, and in Paris, 1913. From Cubism (q.v.) he developed a personal style, shown in geometrically conceived interpretations of old German cities and of seashore. He took part in the German 'Blaue Reiter' movement (q.v.) and was a teacher at the advanced school of design, the Bauhaus (q.v.), in Weimar and Dessau, 1919–33. Nazism and its attitude to art caused him to return to New York in 1937.

Feke, Robert (*b.* Oyster Bay, Long Island, *c.* 1706–10; *d.* ? Barbados after 1750), American portrait painter of whose life little is known, said to have been a sea captain. He worked in Philadelphia and Boston and produced striking portraits, e.g. his 'General Waldo' (Bawdoin College Museum), in which imperfect training is offset by an early eighteenth-century distinction of style.

Ferrara under the House of Este contributed greatly to the Renaissance in Italy and was noted for its fifteenth-century school of painting. Its painters included Bono da Ferrara, Lorenzo Costa, Ercole de Roberti, Francesco Cossa, Cosimo Tura, Boccaccino, Mazzoli, followed by Dosso Dossi and Garofalo in the early sixteenth century. Ferrarese painting was related in to that of Padua and Venice.

Ferrari, Bianchi, *see under* BIANCHI.

Ferrari, Gaudenzio (*b.* Valduggia, nr Novara, *c.* 1484; *d.* Milan, 31 Jan. 1546), Italian painter of the Lombard School, a follower of Leonardo in style. He is noted for skilfully placing his figures in uncommon attitudes. His works include a 'Crucifixion' (Varallo), fresco with twenty-six life-size figures; twenty-one scenes from the life of Christ, also at Varallo; frescoes at Soronno; 'Martyrdom of St Catherine' (Milan, Brera); and 'Pietà' (Turin).

Fête Champêtre, description of the type of picture which introduces a party of town folk or other figures not normally a part of country life into a rural setting. Giorgione's 'Concert Champêtre' in the Louvre comes under this heading, and the *fête galante* of Watteau and Lancret is its special eighteenth-century form. Manet's 'Le Déjeuner sur l'Herbe' (q.v.) is a famous later variant of the theme.

Feti (Fetti), Domenico (*b.* Rome, 1589; *d.* Venice, 1624), Italian painter, pupil of Lodovico Cigoli in Rome. He worked for Cardinal

BIANCHI FERRARI—An Idyll—Wallace Collection.

D. FETI—St Jerome (?) holding a Skull—Royal Collection, Hampton Court.

Ferdinando Gonzaga, who became Duke of Mantua, and was made court painter at Mantua. After 1622 he lived in Venice. His early work was in the manner of Caravaggio but he was an admirer also of Adam Elsheimer, the early Rubens, and Venetian painting. Small pictures, many illustrative of the Parables, are typical.

Feuerbach, Anselm (*b.* Speyer, 12 Sept. 1829; *d.* Venice, 4 Jan. 1880), German painter of classical subjects who studied at Düsseldorf, Munich, Antwerp, and in Paris under Couture. He worked in Rome, 1856–73. In his treatment of such subjects as 'Orpheus and Eurydice' he may be compared with Watts and Leighton in England.

Fielding, English family of artists, best known of whom is the water-colourist, Anthony Vandyke Copley Fielding (*b.* Halifax, 1787; *d.* Hove, 3 Mar. 1855), a pupil of John Varley (q.v.). He was one of the English exhibitors at the Salon of 1824. His brother, Thales Fielding, a landscape painter and drawing master, was a friend of Delacroix.

'Fighting Téméraire, The', painting by Turner, exhibited at the Royal Academy of 1838 with the addition to the title of the explanatory phrase 'tugged to her last berth to be broken up'. The *Téméraire*, an English warship named after a captured French ship, took part in the Battle of Trafalgar, and was handled with a spirit that caused it afterwards to be known as the 'fighting *Téméraire*'. Turner depicts her as she was towed from Sheerness to Rotherhithe in 1838, making a dramatic contrast between the steam tug and the man-of-war. The famous work was long considered his last great production.

Figurative, in art the representational element in a work, in contrast to the non-figurative, i.e. non-representational, character of painting without initial reference to form in nature.

[253]

J. BRUEGHEL—A Vase of Flowers—Ashmolean Museum, Oxford.

Flaxman, John (*b.* York, 6 July 1755; *d.* London, 7 Dec. 1826), English sculptor and draughtsman, the son of a plaster-cast maker. In pictorial art he is noted for his outline drawings for the *Iliad*, *Odyssey*, Dante and Aeschylus, produced during his stay in Italy, 1787–94. Reflecting the austere neo-classicism of his sculpture, they were also not unrelated to the work of his friends Stothard and Blake (who engraved his outlines to Hesiod in 1817). His 'purified' line made a great impression on the cosmopolitan artists of Rome, Ingres among them. The Ionides Collection at the Victoria and Albert Museum contains 173 of his designs and studies in pen and pencil.

Flemish Painting begins with a wonderful flowering of late medieval or Gothic art in the fifteenth century. Contributing to this were the Burgundian school of rich manuscript illumination and the development of painting in the Rhineland, while the rise of prosperous commercial cities such as Bruges provided wealthy patronage for both religious painting and portraiture. Though often called Flemish the first great phase was representative of the Netherlands north and south, not yet divided. It includes Hubert and Jan van Eyck, Justus van Ghent, Hans Memlinc, Rogier van der Weyden, Robert Campin, Petrus Christus, Dirck Bouts, Geertgen tot Sint Jans, Jan Provost,

A. HONDIUS—A Hawking Party—Fitzwilliam Museum, Cambridge.

C. DE VOS—A Little Girl with a Bell—Collection of the Marquess of Zetland.

MASTER OF THE GROOTE ADORATION—A Scene from the Life of a Bishop Saint—Courtauld Gallery, Fareham Collection.

D. VAN ALSLOOT—The Ommeganck; Isabella's Triumph—Victoria and Albert Museum.

C. PETERS—Still Life with Fruit and Flowers—Ashmolean Museum, Oxford.

Hugo van der Goes and Gerard David. In Jerome Bosch and Pieter Brueghel the Elder a vein of fantasy and (in the latter) an interest in peasant life appear. A second group called 'Romanists' appears in the sixteenth century, Quinten Massys, Marinus van Reymerswaele, Joachim Patenier, Jan Gossart (Mabuse) and Bernard van Orley representing the penetration of Italian and Renaissance influence. The second and more specifically Flemish great period is that of the seventeenth century, when the southern Netherlands under Spanish rule saw the rise of the great Rubens, with whom are associated van Dyck, Jordaens, Jan Brueghel, Snyders and the portrayers of peasant life Brouwer and Teniers. After a long eclipse Flemish, in the form of Belgian, painting found a revival in the nineteenth and twentieth centuries with such painters as James Ensor, René Magritte and Hans Permeke.

Florence, great centre of Italian painting from the thirteenth to the sixteenth centuries, its greatness in art coinciding with its rise as a powerful city-state and being fostered by the art-loving princes of the Medici family. The Florentine School took up the threads of ancient classical tradition and advanced also consistently on that path of intellectual and scientific endeavour which led to the supreme achievement of the Renaissance. Its first great master was Giotto, who overshadows the somewhat nebulous Cimabue. He had a number

R. CAMPIN (attributed to)—St Veronica—Fitzwilliam Museum, Cambridge.

of pupils and followers in the fourteenth century, including Bernardo Daddi, Taddeo and Agnolo Daddi, Maso di Banco (Giottino) and Andrea Orcagna. The fifteenth century, which gives its long roll of illustrious names, is marked by the continued development of dramatic and narrative fresco, and by research into perspective and anatomy. Painters of this period are Masaccio, Masolino, Lorenzo Monaco, Fra Angelico, Paolo Uccello, Andrea del Castagno, Domenico Veneziano, Fra Filippo Lippi, Benozzo Gozzoli, Alesso Baldovinetti, Pesellino, Verrocchio, Antonio Pollaiuolo, Botticelli, Jacopo Sellaio, Cosimo Rosselli, Ghirlandaio, Filippino Lippi, Lorenzo di Credi, Piero di Cosimo and Raffaelino del Garbo. The summit of Florentine art was reached at the beginning of the sixteenth century in the genius of Leonardo da Vinci and of Michelangelo. Other Florentines of this period are Fra Bartolommeo, Mariotto Albertinelli, Andrea del Sarto and Bronzino. In the sixteenth century Florence was eclipsed by Venice and Rome and its greatness in art then came to an end.

Floris, Frans (de Vriendt) (*b.* Antwerp, *c.* 1516; *d.* there 1 Oct. 1570), Flemish painter of religious and mythological subjects and portraits. He was a pupil of Lambert Lombard (q.v.) and travelled to Rome with his brother, the architect and sculptor Cornelis Floris, becoming an ardent follower of Michelangelo. His large and successful family workshop at Antwerp later helped to popularize the Italian Mannerist style in the Netherlands.

Folk Art, art produced by the people for the people in rural communities or those at an early stage of development as distinct from the

[259]

F. FLORIS—The Falconer—
Hertzog Anton Ulrick
Museum, Brunswick.

PRIMATICCIO—Apelles
painting Campaspe at the
behest of Alexander (set
in stucco sculpture)—The
Royal Staircase, Fontainebleau.

urban, professional product. The traditional peasant arts and crafts of European countries producing characteristic local styles of patterned textiles, dress, carved and painted furniture, etc., give an example and are now usually described as 'folk art' rather than 'peasant art'. A pictorial instance is provided by the portraits and other paintings produced by sign or coach painters or untrained amateurs in colonial America and the early years of the United States.

Fontainebleau, School of, term applied to the painters and decorative artists employed by Francis I of France (1515–47), in emulation of the Italian princes, to decorate the royal residences and in particular the palace of Fontainebleau. To this end he invited a number of skilled artists from Italy, Il Rosso, Primaticcio and Niccolò dell' Abbate (qq.v.), introducing a Mannerist style marked by a graceful elongation of the figure. Painting and stucco decoration were harmoniously combined. Jean Cousin the elder (q.v.) is a French painter of some note who shows the influence of the Italian immigrants. Antoine Caron (c. 1515–c. 1593), a native of Beauvais, may also be mentioned. Flourishing from about 1530 to 1560, this (first) School of Fontainebleau was followed towards the end of the sixteenth century by a short revival of less note but known as the second school, influenced both by Flemish art and by the School of Bologna. Jacob Bunel (1551–1614), Toussaint Dubreuil (1561–1602) and Martin de Fréminet (1567–1619) are minor artists representative of this phase.

Fontana, Prospero (b. Bologna, 1512; d. 1597), Italian painter, belonging to the Mannerist period of the Bolognese School. He conducted a school of art at Bologna, where Lodovico and Agostino Carracci (q.v.) were pupils. His best-known work is the 'Adoration of the Magi' in the church of Santa Maria delle Grazie at Bologna.

VINCENZO FOPPA—
Virgin and Child—Berenson
Collection, Florence.

J. L. FORAIN—The Law Courts—Tate Gallery.

Foppa, Vincenzo (*b*. Brescia, 1427–30; *d*. there, 1515–16), Italian painter of the Lombard School. He borrowed in his work from a number of sources, more particularly Bellini and the Paduans, painting at Pavia, Genoa and Milan (for the Sforza family). Frescoes by him are in the Brera at Milan. Though a minor artist he contributed to make Milan an active centre of art. Ambrogio Borgogne (q.v.) was his pupil.

Forain, Jean Louis (*b*. Rheims, 23 Oct 1852; *d*. Paris, 11 July 1931), French painter and graphic artist, a pupil of Gérôme. He depicted the social life of his time in works which combine something of Daumier's satirical view with the observation of Degas. His illustrative talent is characteristically apparent in his etchings and lithographs.

Foreshortening, application of perspective to a single figure or form, representing its shortened appearance when not perpendicular to the line of sight, heightening three-dimensional effect and often giving dramatic emphasis.

Fortuny y Carbó, Mariano José Bernardo (*b*. Reus, Catalonia, 1838; *d*. Rome, 1874), Spanish painter and etcher. He studied at the Academy of Barcelona and in Rome, and during the Spanish war in

[262]

Morocco followed the army to Africa, making many studies of local life. He had much success in a *genre* comparable with that of his French contemporary Meissonier (q.v.), the combination of anecdote and historical costume and setting.

Found Object, the *objet trouvé* of the Surrealists, some natural form, e.g. the root of a tree or a worn stone, which has taken on by chance a curiosity of shape appealing to the imagination or suggesting the deliberate fantasy of art. The 'ready-made' of this kind (to use an alternative Surrealist term), sometimes jestingly discovered, had a certain serious influence in directing painters from the scenic aspect of landscape to fresh repertoires of form implicit in aspects of nature previously ignored.

Fouquet (Foucquet), Jean (*b.* Tours, *c.* 1415, *d.* there, *c.* 1480), French painter and illuminator of manuscripts. He worked for Charles VII and Louis XI and with him the School of the Loire and art in fifteenth-century France reached its height. He was possibly trained in Paris and was an accomplished master when he visited Italy, *c.* 1445, having already painted his famous portrait of Charles VII (Louvre). His art was admired in Rome, where he painted the portrait of Pope Eugene IV and evidently studied Italian Renaissance art with profit. He produced exquisite miniatures, notably those for a Book of Hours for his patron, Étienne Chevalier, Charles VII's treasurer (Chantilly, Musée Condé), a Boccaccio (Munich) and historical compilations, Jewish and French (Bibliothèque Nationale); but on a larger scale he showed a grandeur and firmness of design (with something of the quality of Gothic sculpture) as well as appreciation of human character, which are magnificently displayed in the 'Deposition', *c.* 1466, of the Church of Nouans. Another masterpiece was the diptych, formerly in the cathedral of Melun, now divided into two parts, representing Étienne Chevalier and St Stephen (Berlin) and the Virgin and Child (Antwerp), the Virgin of the latter being probably an idealized portrait of the mistress of Charles VII, Agnes Sorel (of whose will Chevalier was an executor). National character is already mature in the work of this great artist, whose influence on his contemporaries may be gauged, for example, by the anonymous 'L'Homme au Verre de Vin' of the Louvre.

Fragonard, Jean Honoré (*b.* Grasse, 5 April 1732; *d.* Paris, 22 Aug. 1806), French painter and draughtsman, the supreme virtuoso of eighteenth-century French art. He was the son of a mercer, and studied art (for six months) with Chardin and then with Boucher (qq.v.). Winning the Prix de Rome in 1752, he spent three years in Paris under Carle van Loo before travelling to Italy, where he stayed, 1756–61, being much impressed by the art of Tiepolo. A successful and immensely productive career was virtually ended by the Revolution. During the last fifteen years of his life, divided between Grasse and Paris, though befriended by David (q.v.), he ceased to paint, as if in the revolutionary epoch his art had become an anachronism. Yet it would be a mistake (though one still made) to look on him merely

J. FOUQUET—Virgin and Child—Musée des Beaux-Arts, Antwerp.

J. H. FRAGONARD—The Schoolmistress—Wallace Collection.

as the provider of frivolous pictorial amusement for the Old Regime. He was a serious student of the masters, and while borrowing from an astonishing number and variety of sources, not only from the rococo of Boucher, but from Rembrandt and Hals, from Tiepolo and Solimena, he used them to entirely individual purpose, if with Protean changes of attitude. His range was extraordinary; he could successfully design a composition in the grand manner, as in his 'Corrhesus and Callirhoe', 1765 (Louvre), and paint the most exquisite of *scènes galantes* in 'Les Heureux Hazards de l'Escarpolette' ('The Swing') (Wallace Collection), poetic landscapes, as in the mysterious gardens he evolved from those of the Villa d'Este, and playful yet still beautifully executed *genre* pieces such as 'L'Éducation fait Tout', *c.* 1780 (São Paulo), in which, after his marriage and the birth of his children, he showed his appreciation of the charm of childhood. He was a master of every technique, oil, pastel, miniature, *gouache*, etching, wash or crayon drawing. His five hundred paintings and thousands of drawings reveal a personality far transcending that of Boucher, and his vein of fantasy had its anticipation, as in his 'Fontaine d'Amour', of the spirit of Romanticism. His son, Alexandre Evariste (1780–1850), a decorative painter, and his sister-in-law, Marguerite Gérard, were his pupils.

Francesca, Piero della, *see* PIERO.

J. H. FRAGONARD—The Swing—Wallace Collection.

Francesco di Giorgio (*b*. Siena, 1439; *d*. 1501–1502), Italian painter of the Sienese School, also sculptor, architect and engineer. He worked mainly at Siena, though also at Naples and elsewhere in Italy, and had a studio for a time with his brother-in-law, Nerocchio, but seems to have given up painting prior to entering the service of the Duke of Urbino in 1477. Two altar-pieces by him are at Siena and his few works have the Sienese charm and delicacy of line and colour.

Francia (Francesco Raibolini) (*b*. Bologna, *c*. 1450; *d*. there, 5 Jan. 1517), Italian painter, originally a goldsmith and engraver of dies for medals (becoming mint-master at Bologna), who took up painting in middle age when he made the acquaintance of Mantegna. He was much influenced by Perugino and Raphael as well as Lorenzo Costa with whom he worked, though the eclectic style thus induced had no strong character. Religious paintings by him are in the galleries of Bologna, London (National Gallery), Munich and Rome (Borghese), and frescoes in the church of St Cecilia, Bologna.

Franciabigio (Francesco di Cristofani Bigi) (*b*. Florence, 1482; *d*. there, 24 Jan. 1525), Italian painter of the Florentine School, who studied under Albertinelli and Piero di Cosimo, afterwards collaborating with his friend, Andrea del Sarto (qq.v.). They worked together in fresco at the church of the Annunziata, Florence, 1512, and in decorating the Medici palace at Poggio a Caiano, but Franciabigio is mainly esteemed for portraits such as that of a Young Man (National Gallery) which have distinct character.

[267]

F. FRANCIA—Madonna and Angels with the Dead Christ—National Gallery.

FRANCIABIGIO—Portrait of a Young Man—
Staatliche Museum, Berlin.

MASTER FRANCKE—The Scourging of
(Altar-piece of the Chapel of the Farers to En
—Kunsthalle, Hamburg.

F. FRANCKEN (The Younger)—Genre Scene—Kunsthistorisches Museum, Vienna.

Francke, Master (active Hamburg, early fifteenth century), German painter, leading master of the Hanseatic north. He is noted for his 'Altar of the Seafarers to England', painted for the Johanniskirche, Hamburg (now in the Hamburg Kunsthalle), which includes two panels devoted to St Thomas à Becket. His style was personal and full of narrative vigour.

Francken, name of a Flemish family of painters at Antwerp from the sixteenth to early eighteenth centuries. The most notable of them are **Frans the Elder** (1542–1616), pupil of Frans Floris (q.v.) and an Italianate painter of religious subjects, and **Frans the Younger** (1581–1642), painter of interiors and *genre* who studied under his father.

French Art Museums include in Paris pre-eminently the Louvre (q.v.), Musée de l'Impressionisme (q.v.) and Musée d'Art Moderne (q.v.). The Musée Guimet and Musée Cernuschi are devoted to oriental art. The Bibliothèque Nationale has a collection of manuscripts and engravings of great importance. The work of famous French artists is often well represented in their own locality, e.g. Ingres at Montauban and Toulouse-Lautrec at Albi.

G. DE LA TOUR—The New-born Child—Musée de Rennes.

French Painting is already striking in the fourteenth century in the form of the Franco-Flemish school of manuscript illumination (*see* ILLUMINATED MANUSCRIPTS). The fifteenth century sees the growth of regional schools, in Provence (Nicolas Froment), Burgundy and the north (Simon Marmion), and in the Loire country (Jean Fouquet, Jean Bourdichon, the Maître de Moulins, Jean Perréal). The desire of Francis I to create a centralized art and to rival Italy led to his introducing Italian painters into France, and from this followed the development of the School of Fontainebleau (q.v.). In the sixteenth century the art of the court portrait and portrait miniature also flourished with Corneille de Lyon, Jean and François Clouet and others. In the seventeenth century French painting is rich in genius and output, with such great individuals as Claude Lorraine, Nicolas Poussin, Georges de La Tour and Louis Le Nain. In addition there are a large number of painters of decorative and religious works, such as Simon Vouet, Sebastien Bourdon, Eustache Le Sueur and Philippe de Champaigne. This direction of effort in the second half of the seventeenth century was controlled by Charles Le Brun, under whom all artistic production was organized. Other painters of the time were Coypel, Monnoyer, Mignard and Parrocel. In the Rome of Claude

L. LE NAIN—The Forge—Louvre.

SCHOOL OF TOURS,
c. 1450—Man with a Glass of
Wine—Louvre.

and Poussin, Gaspard
Dughet and Jean de
Boullogne are also to
be noted. A ceremonial
form of portraiture was
due to Nicolas Largil-
lierre and Hyacinthe
Rigaud. The eighteenth
century saw a change
of mood from the
grandiose decoration of
the Louis XIV style to
the lightness and charm
of rococo (q.v.). The
genius of Watteau marks
the change, also evident
in his followers Pater
and Lancret. A graceful
development of this style
is found in the work of
Boucher and Fragonard,
though its artificiality decays in the painting of Greuze. In contrast
with the art of court circles, the great Chardin painted inimitable
scenes of domestic bourgeois life. In still life he took up and gave new
values to the *genre* practised by François Oudry and Jean Baptiste
Desportes and inspired by Netherlandish models. Eighteenth-century
portraiture is represented by the pastellist, Maurice Quentin de La
Tour, and by the elegance of Nattier, Perroneau, the Drouais, father
and son, and Mme Vigée Lebrun. Louis Michel van Loo was court
painter to Philip V of Spain.

The end of the eighteenth century saw a reaction against rococo
and a return to 'the antique' (*see* CLASSICISM) advocated by Vien and
vigorously prosecuted by his pupil Jacques Louis David. As a return
to the past, however, it had a Romantic element (*see* ROMANTICISM).
This appears in the work of Girodet-Trioson, Pierre Prud'hon and
Baron Gros. Romanticism is strikingly demonstrated in the works
of Géricault and Delacroix, though Ingres remained a determined
upholder of Classicism. In landscape the beginnings of a new era come
with Corot and the painters of Barbizon (*see* BARBIZON SCHOOL).
Realism (q.v.) was the keynote of the great development of French
art in the nineteenth century, with Daumier, Millet, Courbet and
Manet marking its advance, and was the essence of the landscape of
the time and a basic factor in the growth of the great Impressionist

[272]

SCHOOL OF TOURS,
c. 1496—Portrait, presumed
of Second Son of Charles
VII—Louvre.

School (*see* IMPRESSION-
ISM). Heralded by such
painters as Daubigny
and Boudin, it reached
its fruition with Monet,
Pissarro, Sisley, Renoir
and Berthe Morisot.
The Impressionist use of
colour suggested various
new departures: the
Neo-Impressionism or
Divisionism of Seurat
and Signac, and the
forms of Post-Impres-
sionism represented by
Cézanne, Gauguin and
van Gogh. Their art is
the matrix of a succes-
sion of brilliant phases
of art from the 1890's
onwards, beginning with
Symbolism (q.v.) and
the Nabi movement
(q.v.), the Fauvism of
Matisse and others (*see* FAUVISM), the work of Braque and Picasso (*see*
CUBISM) and all the modern phenomena comprised in the term School
of Paris (q.v.). Art all over the world has felt the stimulus of Paris as
an international centre in the modern age.

Fresco Painting, process of mural painting on plaster which is still
fresh (It. *fresco*) or wet. The plaster is applied to a brick or stone wall
in several coatings, the first (*arriccio*), half an inch thick to the whole
wall at once; the two finer coatings (*intonaco*) only to that portion of
the wall which it is intended to paint in any one day so that it may
not be dry before receiving the pigments. In drying, a crystal surface
of carbonate of lime forms over the plaster, and it is essential that the
pigments should be there ready to receive this coating, which is pro-
tective to them and gives them clearness. When the plasterer has
covered the portion of the wall to be painted, the painter super-
imposes his cartoon and pricks off the outlines with an instrument of
wood or bone or makes an impression of it by pouncing. The cartoon
is then removed and the colours are applied, becoming incorporated
with the substance of the plaster, and if the process is properly carried

out being as lasting as the plaster itself. As the joins of each section of plaster remain perceptible, it is possible to calculate the number of days occupied by the whole work. The colours, principally earths or minerals, which best resist the chemical action of the lime, are ground and mixed with pure water and applied thinly and transparently, rather darker than the desired effect because they become paler in drying. From its nature fresco must be executed rapidly and its effects produced by single touches of the brush. It follows that the painter must be skilled enough to work with the utmost decision and certainty and also that the whole work must be previously planned with great thoroughness. Hence the necessity of the full-sized cartoon and the many detailed studies the old masters were in the habit of making. *Buon fresco*, the true method, is distinguished from *fresco secco* (something of a contradiction in terms), painted on dry plaster. The result of the latter method was far less durable, though *fresco secco* was sometimes employed to add final touches to work carried out in true fresco. Fresco was practised in ancient times, examples coming from Egypt and also from Pompeii and Herculaneum, but is mainly associated with the history of Italian art. Climate and the style of architecture, which provided large areas of wall space, were equally favourable to its development in Italy, where its progress is represented by such masters as Giotto, Masaccio, Ghirlandaio, Piero della Francesca, Raphael and Michelangelo. In modern times it has largely fallen into disuse. It was revived with fair technical success by Cornelius and other nineteenth-century German artists in the attempt (otherwise unsuccessful) to recapture the mood of Italian religious art. The attempt to introduce fresco into England in the ambitious enterprise of decorating the Houses of Parliament by this means failed for more than one reason; partly because the method was foreign to the artists chosen and partly also because fresco could not survive unimpaired by the large quantities of sulphurous acid gas in the atmosphere. The English Pre-Raphaelites, it may be noted, arrived empirically at an imitation of fresco in the oil easel picture, painting thinly on a white ground before the latter was quite dry. A form of fresco has been practised in modern Mexico by such painters as Rivera and Orozco. *See also* MURAL PAINTING.

Friedrich, Caspar David (*b.* Greifswald, 1774; *d.* Dresden, 1840), German painter who studied art at Copenhagen and Dresden, the most notable representative of the German Romantic school in landscape. His pictures were inspired by (though never directly painted from) his native Pomerania, its coasts and Baltic shipping; and also by the mountains and forests of the Riesengebirge in which he wandered. Mysterious effects of moonlight watched by contemplative figures, phantom sailing-ships and lonely mountain views are his themes, in which there is a strong subjective element. Hamburg, Dresden and other German galleries contain most of his work, for a long period little known outside Germany.

Friesz, Othon (*b.* Le Havre, 6 Feb. 1879; *d.* Paris, 11 Jan. 1949), French Post-Impressionist painter, son of a sea-captain. He first studied art at

[274]

C. D. FRIEDRICH—The Edge of the Cliff—Winterthur Art Museum.

OTHON FRIESZ—Port of Toulon—Photo: Marlborough Fine Art.

Le Havre and at the École des Beaux-Arts in Paris, together with his friend and fellow townsman, Raoul Dufy (q.v.). Like Dufy he was attracted towards the brilliant colour of Matisse and the 'Fauve' group, but his later work, not unaffected by the emphasis of van Gogh, showed a tendency to stress expressive contour. He painted in North Africa and on the Mediterranean coast, as well as in Paris (where he started a teaching school), and a number of marine paintings resulted from his frequent visits to Toulon, La Rochelle and Honfleur. In addition to easel pictures he painted notable frescoes at the Palais de Chaillot, Paris.

Frith, William Powell (*b.* Aldfield, nr Ripon, 9 Jan 1819; *d.* London, 2 Nov. 1909), English painter of subject pictures. He studied at the Royal Academy Schools and became R.A. in 1853. His reputation depends on the three remarkable pictures in which he turned from literary and historical illustration to contemporary life, 'Ramsgate Sands', 1854 (Royal Collection), 'Derby Day', 1858 (Tate Gallery), and the 'Railway Station', 1864 (Royal Holloway College). Of lasting interest as period 'documents', they are carefully

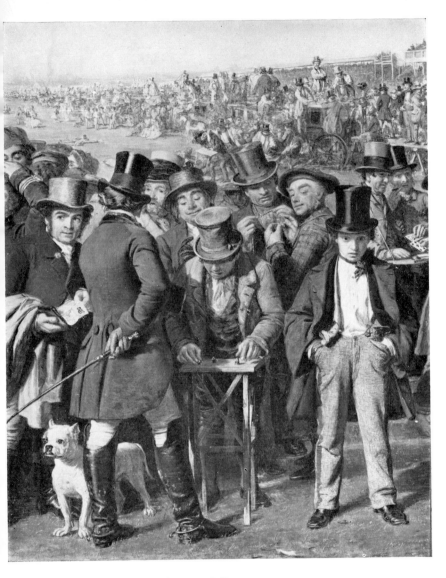

W. P. FRITH—Derby Day (detail)—Tate Gallery.

conceived in grouping and detail is handled with a painterly skill that even Whistler had to admire.

Froment, Nicolas (*b*. Uzès, ?1435; *d*. Avignon, 1484), French painter of the School of Avignon. He travelled to Italy and there painted in 1461, for a Florentine monastery, the excellent if harshly realistic 'Raising of Lazarus' now in the Uffizi. A later work by which he is known, the 'Burning Bush' (cathedral of Aix-en-Provence), painted for King René of Anjou, is of lesser value, mainly illustrating in its complex detail the difficult fusion of Italian Renaissance and Gothic elements.

Fromentin, Eugène (*b*. Saint Maurice, nr La Rochelle, 24 Oct. 1820; *d*. there, 25 Aug. 1876), French painter and writer, the son of a well-to-do physician. A follower of Delacroix (q.v.) in painting and choice of subject, he became known as the 'African master', working and travelling much in North Africa. He is, however, remembered as an author rather than a painter, by his exposition of Dutch and Flemish painting in his *Maîtres d'autrefois*, 1876, as well as his novel, *Dominique*, and his descriptions of the Sahara.

Frottage, rubbing obtained by pencilling on a sheet of paper laid over some broken, textured or ornamented surface. The rubbing from a church brass is a familiar example, but the French word *frottage* is applied specifically to the same process as used by present-day Surrealist or abstract painters seeking for novel and striking effect, Max Ernst being a notable practitioner. Stuck on a canvas or other surface it is a form of collage (q.v.).

Fry, Roger Eliot (*b*. London, 14 Dec. 1866; *d*. there, 9 Sept. 1934), English art critic and painter, influential in propagating a strictly aesthetic appraisal of works of art in a series of essays and lectures, notable publications being his *Vision and Design*, 1920, *Transformations*, 1927, and *Last Lectures* (posthumously published 1939). He first introduced Post-Impressionist painting to Britain in the celebrated exhibition of 1911. His studies of Cézanne and of African sculpture suggested new directions of thought to many English followers. Primarily a writer and scholar, he was Curator of Painting at the Metropolitan Museum, New York. 1905–10.

Fuseli, Henry (**Johann Heinrich Füssli**) (*b*. Zürich, 7 Feb. 1741; *d*. Putney, 16 April, 1825), painter of Romantic and literary subjects, son of a Swiss portrait painter and connoisseur. After a youthful revolt against authority he emigrated to England in 1764, and was encouraged by Reynolds to become a painter and study in Italy. The period spent there, 1770–8, made him a devotee of Michelangelo, though his own work depends for its interest on so different an element as the Romantic love of horror and fantasy. 'The Nightmare', of which he painted several versions, the first in 1781, made him famous, and the contributions to Boydell's 'Shakespeare Gallery' which followed gave further scope to his imagination, especially in the 'moments of terror' of *Macbeth* and in picturing the fairy world of *A Midsummer Night's Dream*, the sensation produced by the subject

H. FUSELI—The Nightmare—Kunsthaus, Zürich.

J. FYT—Still Life with Boar's Head—Kunsthistoriches Museum, Vienna.

rather than beauty of paint being his main concern. Paintings and drawings of elongated female figures with exaggerated head-dresses in which there is a strain of erotic fancy form another aspect of his work. Witty, learned and an able writer, he appears in his later years, when Keeper of the Royal Academy, as the eccentric figure vividly described by Haydon. He was the friend of Blake, and some likenesses of design, though not of aim, point to their mutual respect.

Futurism, Italian art movement organized by the poet Filippo Tomasso Marinetti in 1909, a glorification of machinery, science, speed and militant activity. It began with Marinetti's manifesto issued in Paris in 1909, which in rhetorical language denounced the effect of the art of the past and acclaimed a new art expressive of the twentieth century—*le Futurisme.* A drastic programme of change and revolt in visual art, music and literature was drawn up, laying stress on the need to express dynamic force and motion. Artists associated with Futurism were Umberto Boccioni, Carlo Carrà (q.v.), Luigi Russolo, Giacomo Balla and Gino Severini (q.v.). Theoretically in opposition to the Cubism (q.v.) of France, they made use of its geometric forms and the device of reconstituting objects as if seen from different points of view simultaneously. Exhibitions and demonstrations were staged between 1910 and 1913 in Paris, London, Berlin and Russia, but the First World War brought the movement to an end. Boccioni was killed in 1916, and other artist members of the group took to less adventurous forms of painting.

Fyt, Jan (*b.* Antwerp, Mar. 1611; *d.* there, 11 Sept. 1661), Flemish painter and etcher of animals, still life and portraits. He was the pupil of Frans Snyders (q.v.) and worked in his native city after some travel in France and Italy. He etched some plates of animal and landscape subjects.

G

Gaddi, Italian family of artists. Gaddo (*b.* Florence, *c.* 1260; *d.* 1332) was a painter and mosaic worker, a friend of Cimabue (q.v.), whose influence has been perceived in the 'Coronation of the Virgin with Saints and Angels', a mosaic in the cathedral at Florence attributed to Gaddo. Other works assigned to him are the mosaics in Santa Maria Maggiore and those of the choir of the old St Peter's, Rome. His son, **Taddeo** (*b.* Florence, *c.* 1300; *d.* 1366), was a pupil of Giotto and is considered one of his most important followers. His paintings include the frescoes 'Virgin and Child between Four Prophets' and other scenes from the life of the Virgin in the Baroncelli Chapel in Santa Croce at Florence, 1332, as well as works at Pisa, Pistoia and in various galleries. The son of Taddeo, **Agnolo** (active 1369; *d.* 1396), perhaps trained by his father, was placed on the latter's death in the care of Jacopo del Casentino and Giovanni da Milano. In 1369 he worked in the Vatican, probably with his brother Giovanni. Frescoes in Santa Croce depicting the legend of the Cross, and in the cathedral of Prato, 1392–5, representing the legends

A. GADDI—Virgin Enthroned—Galleria Antica e Moderna, Florence.

T. GADDI—Presentation in the Temple—Accademia, Florence.

of the Virgin and the Sacred Girdle, are attributed to him. He died while working on an altar-piece for San Miniato. He employed a number of assistants and Cennino Cennini was among his pupils, embodying the methods of the followers of Giotto in his famous treatise.

Gainsborough, Thomas (*b*. Sudbury, May 1727; *d*. London, 2 Aug. 1788), English painter, eminent equally in portrait and landscape, the son of a woollen manufacturer in Suffolk. He went at an early age to London, studying under the French engraver Gravelot and perhaps benefiting by acquaintance with Francis Hayman (q.v.). He returned to Suffolk when nineteen—married to a girl who brought him a moderate income—and worked as a painter, first at Sudbury, then at Ipswich, until 1753. It is evident that in this period the Dutch paintings he copied and restored greatly helped to form his view of landscape; that the 'conversation piece' as practised by Hogarth, Devis and Hayman suggested his open-air portrait groups, and no doubt a faint echo of French pastoral came to him by way of Gravelot; but already his own originality and 'Englishness' are clearly apparent. The 'Cornard Wood', 1748? 'View of Dedham', 'Painter's Daughters Chasing a Butterfly' (all National Gallery) and 'Mr and Mrs Andrews' are examples. Something of his early freshness disappeared after his removal to Bath, centre of fashion, where he stayed, 1760–74, busy mainly with portrait commissions. The van Dycks he saw at Wilton and other great houses suggested refinements of style and silvery colour. His 'Blue Boy' (San Marino, California) (q.v.) is in every way an homage to van Dyck. The landscapes he painted for his own pleasure took on an imaginary look; beautiful in rhythmic movement, the 'Harvest Wagon' (Birmingham) already has this Utopian character. A foundation member of the Royal Academy and elected to its Council in 1774, Gainsborough moved in that year to Schomberg House in London, becoming the principal rival of Sir Joshua Reynolds in portraiture. Complaining often of the enforced labour of face painting, he never failed to give of his best to portraits, and such late works as the portrait of his wife (Courtauld Institute) and 'The

[284]

T. GAINSBOROUGH—The Morning Walk—National Gallery.

T. GAINSBOROUGH—Wood Scene, Cornard, Suffolk—National Gallery.

Morning Walk' (National Gallery) respectively show his sense of character and the great elegance of style he had developed, while in landscape, influenced by Rubens rather than, as in his youth, by Ruisdael, he produced, for example, the splendid massing and play of light of 'The Market Cart' of 1786 (National Gallery). Hundreds of drawings, often in a mixture of media, show his continued pursuit of landscape for its own sake. A constant tendency to experiment produced the remarkable 'fancy pictures' or imaginative compositions of his late years, the 'Diana and Actaeon' (Royal Collection), unfinished when he died, being an example. It is not irrelevant to the study of Gainsborough as an artist to recall that he loved music and was something of a musician; the sense of rhythm and the sensitive fluent touches of his colour are indeed musical. His method of painting—what Reynolds called 'those odd scratches and marks . . . this chaos which by a kind of magic at a certain distance assumes form'—is full of temperament and life.

Gallait, Louis (*b.* Tournai, 1810; *d.* 1887), Belgian painter who studied art at Tournai. He was one of those who revived historical painting in Belgium, his huge 'Abdication of Charles V' being an example.

Gallego, Fernando (active 1466–1507), Spanish painter working in

[286]

F. GALLEGO—The Crowning with Thorns—El Greco Museum, Toledo.

J. BOSCH—The 'Garden of Delights' Triptych—Prado.

Castile in the late fifteenth century. He was active at Zamora, where he painted the altar-piece of St Ildefonso in the cathedral, and at Salamanca, where he is last mentioned. He painted in oils in the Flemish manner then dominant in Spain, recalling van der Weyden (q.v.) in particular, though in colour and the types he depicted he is distinct. His works are signed 'Fernad Galecus'. His 'Christ in Majesty' is a fine altar-piece now in the Prado. Possibly a relative and sometimes confused with him is Francisco Gallego or Gallegos, active about the same time, whose 'Triumph of the Christian Religion', also in the Prado, further exemplifies the Flemish influence.

'Garden of Delights, The', large triptych by Jerome Bosch (q.v.), the most fantastic of all products of the imagination, formerly in the monastery of the Escorial but hanging in the Prado, Madrid, since 1935. When closed the triptych represents in *grisaille* the globe of earth at the stage of the Creation when land and sea appear. On the left wing of the coloured panels when open is a representation of paradise with strange types of flora and fauna, inspired, it is supposed, by travellers' tales of newly discovered America; on the right is a weird vision of hell. The centre panel is the 'Garden of (Terrestrial) Delights' by which the whole work is known, symbolizing, according

to the Spanish chronicler of the late sixteenth century, 'vain delights and transitory joys'. The strawberry signifying sensuality is a frequent symbol, though many astonishing combinations of organic and inorganic form defy explanation.

Garofalo (Benvenuto Tisio) (*b.* Ferrara, 1481; *d.* there, 6 Sept. 1559), Italian painter, last representative of the Ferrarese School, a minor artist in an eclectic style much influenced by Raphael, whom he met in Rome in 1509.

GAROFALO—Massacre of the Innocents—Ferrara, Pinacoteca.

P. GAUGUIN—Te Rerioa—Courtauld Institute Gallery, London.

He worked for some time with Dosso Dossi (q.v.). Works by him are in churches at Ferrara, and the National Gallery has a number of examples.

Gauguin, Paul (*b.* Paris, 8 June 1848; *d.* Atuana, Marquesas Islands, 8 May 1903), French Post-Impressionist painter, with Cézanne and Vincent van Gogh one of the great formative influences on modern art. The son of a journalist and a mother of Spanish-Peruvian origin, he was taken as a child to Peru and after the death of his father and his mother's return to France entered the merchant service. After the war of 1870 he took to business in a stockbroker's office in Paris, where he did well, and in 1873 married a young Danish woman. He began to paint in his spare time, being influenced by Pissarro and the Impressionists, and in 1883, aged thirty-five, gave up family and financial career to devote himself to painting. In 1886, seeking solitude, he went to Pont-Aven in Brittany, and in 1888 he made his brief and calamitous stay at Arles with van Gogh, after which he went back to Brittany. At Pouldu he was now the centre of a group and produced some of his best works, but in 1891 he set sail for Tahiti and from 1895 lived permanently in the South Seas, in poverty, ill health and isolation but leaving beautiful pictures of 'a riot of light and vegetation' and a gentle Polynesian people. Simplified design and an emotional use of colour distinguish the works of his Brittany

[289]

P. GAUGUIN—Portrait of the Artist's Mother—Staatsgalerie, Stuttgart.

period, his 'The Yellow Christ' and 'Jacob wrestling with the Angel' (Glasgow) being notable. In Tahiti and the Marquesas his already distinctive style took on a more exotic colour. 'The White Horse' (Louvre), the 'Riders on the Shore' (Niarchos Collection) and many Tahitian figure groups show his feeling for a primal simplicity of design combined with colour of 'unsurpassed liberty'. Gauguin has touched the modern imagination as an escapist from a sophisticated civilization, but the new life he gave to colour was his legacy to modern painting. Letters, journals and the fragment of autobiography *Noa-Noa* vividly record impressions. (Colour.)

Gaulli (Baciccio), Giovanni Battista (*b.* Genoa, 1639; *d.* 1709), Italian painter, one of the most eminent 'machinists' of baroque decoration. He studied at Genoa and in Rome. The work of Rubens and Correggio, and association with Bernini, helped to form his style. He decorated many Roman churches with dazzling flamboyance, his principal work being the ceiling of the church of the Gesù, 1668–83.

Gavarni, Paul (*b.* Paris, 1801; *d.* there 24 Nov. 1866), French caricaturist and illustrator, whose real name was Hippolyte Chevalier. Like Daumier (q.v.) he worked for *Le Charivari*. He visited London in 1849, and his sombre drawings of the life of the poor were published in *L'Illustration*.

Geddes, Andrew (*b.* Edinburgh, 5 April 1783; *d.* London, 5 May 1844), Scottish painter and etcher. He studied art in London at the Royal Academy Schools and from 1810 worked in Edinburgh as a portrait painter, also in London (A.R.A., 1832). A friend of Wilkie (q.v.), he shares with him the credit for a revival of etching.

Geertgen tot Sint Jans (*b.* Leyden, *c.* 1465; *d.* ? Haarlem, 1495), Dutch painter who seems to have worked at Haarlem. His name means 'Little Gerard of the Brethren of St John' (at Haarlem), and a painting of Haarlem Cathedral still to be found there is attributed to him. He is presumed to have been the pupil of Albert van Ouwater

G. TOT SINT JANS—The
Nativity—National Gallery

GENRE PAINTING—
Three Boors Drinking—
detail of the painting in
the National Gallery,
London by A. Brouwer,
on loan from Sir Edmund
Bacon.

(q.v.). Two altar-piece panels at Vienna, 'The Holy Family' (Rijks-museum) and 'The Nativity' (National Gallery) are among the principal works ascribed to him, the last-named being a work of great charm and originality in its lighting.

Gellée, *see* CLAUDE.

Genre (Fr. 'kind', or 'variety'), originally denoted any one department of painting but is now a term specifically applied to painting which takes the familiar scenes of everyday life for its subject, in contrast to the lofty themes of religious, ideal or 'history' painting. An early master of *genre* is Pieter Brueghel the Elder, and the peasant life of the Netherlands inspired further brilliant examples of *genre* in the paintings of Teniers and Brouwer. Peasant life is also superbly represented in seventeenth-century France by the brothers Le Nain. Holland provides a wealth of *genre* pictures of burgher life in the works of Vermeer, de Hooch, Metsu, Ter Borch, Jan Steen and others. Chardin beautifully presents Parisian middle-class life in the eighteenth century. Hogarth extends *genre* into a cross-section of society, morally analysed. Various categories are found in English art: rustic, e.g. Morland; anecdotal and humorous, e.g. Wilkie; animal, e.g. Landseer. Paintings of Parisian life by Manet, Renoir and Degas demonstrate that *genre* is not necessarily inferior in beauty or quality to pictures with an ideal or more pretentious subject-matter.

GENTILE DA FABRIANO—The Adoration of the Magi—Uffizi Gallery, Florence.

Gentile da Fabriano (*b.* Fabriano, *c.* 1360; *d.* Rome, *c.* 1428), Italian painter associated with the Umbrian and Sienese schools, though he also painted in Florence, Venice, Brescia and Rome. He worked in Venice, 1408–14, on frescoes for the Doge's Palace and was the master of Jacopo Bellini (q.v.). His most famous work was 'The Adoration of the Magi', painted in 1423 for the church of Santa Trinità in Florence (Uffizi), which in gay colour and richness of detail and ornament is a masterpiece of what is known as the 'International Gothic' style. Other notable works are the altar-piece of the Quaratesi family, 1425, of which the centre panel, Madonna and Child, is in the English Royal Collection and the wings and panels in the Uffizi and Vatican galleries; and a 'Madonna with Saints' (Berlin). His last work was a series of frescoes (since destroyed) for San Giovanni in Laterano, Rome. These were finished by Pisanello (q.v.), on whom Gentile's Gothic manner was influential.

Gentileschi, Orazio (*b.* Pisa, 1565; *d.* London, 1638), Italian painter, who first studied with his brother, Aurelio, and as a youth went to Rome, where he worked for a succession of popes. He became the friend of Caravaggio, whose style greatly influenced him. In middle age he spent some time in Genoa and Paris and went to England at the invitation of the Duke of Buckingham when he was sixty, remaining there for the rest of his life and being handsomely rewarded by Charles I. His most noted picture is a large 'Annunciation', 1621 (Turin); his 'Joseph and Potiphar's Wife' is at Hampton Court. His daughter, Artemisia (*b.* 1597; *d.* Rome, 1651+), studied with her father and Agostino Tassi, spent a short time in England, 1638–9 (her self-portrait is at Hampton Court), but worked mainly at Naples in a heavily Caravaggesque style.

Gérard, François Pascal, Baron (*b.* Rome, 4 May 1770; *d.* Paris, 11 Jan. 1837), French painter, a pupil of the sculptor Pajou and later

O. GENTILESCHI—Judith with the Head of Holofernes—Pitti Gallery, Florence.

[293]

of David (q.v.). Unlike his master he took no part in the Revolution and avoided serving on the Revolutionary tribunal, to which he was assigned at David's wish, on the plea of illness. Changes of regime did not concern him and he had a busy career as a portrait painter both in the Napoleonic period and during the Restoration: some three hundred portraits of celebrities, including those of Napoleon, Talleyrand, Canova, Mme de Staël and Mme Récamier. Because the latter sat for Gérard when David's portrait of her was still unfinished, David never forgave either. Successful rather than of great note as an artist, Gérard as a portraitist is at his best in his picture of Isabey and his daughter (Louvre), and his 'Psyché et l'Amour' (Louvre) has considerable charm—which indeed caused Ingres to declare it 'the most beautiful thing since David'.

Géricault, Jean Louis André Théodore (*b*. Rouen, 26 Sept. 1791; *d*. Paris, 26 Jan. 1824), French painter of great originality and a leader of the French Romantic School. He studied first under the painter of hunting and racing scenes, Carle Vernet (q.v.), 1808–10, then under the classicist Guérin, 1810–11, though it was Baron Gros (q.v.) who really inspired him to the dash and spirit of his early pictures of Napoleonic cavalry officers. After an unhappy love-affair he left Paris for Italy, 1816–17, where he conceived ambitious projects of painting in the grand style of Michelangelo and Raphael, making studies for a large canvas suggested by the Barberi horse-race. On his return he painted his most famous picture, 'The Raft of the "Medusa"' 1819, showing the dead and the crazed and famished survivors of the frigate *Medusa* (marine calamity of 1815) on their raft, a painting in which the classic nude of David, realism of subject and a Romantic force of feeling were characteristically blended: it made a tremendous impression on the young Delacroix (q.v.), who incidentally posed for one of the figures. The visit to England which followed, 1820–2, marked a change of direction. The sporting print and English *genre* picture alike attracted him, 'The Derby at Epsom' (Louvre) being a striking result, while he made several lithographs of London life and character and in addition an equestrian portrait of the Prince Regent (Wallace Collection). In 1822–3, back in Paris, he executed a series of portraits, clinical in their veracity, of insane patients in the Salpetrière hospital. His career was cut short at an inconclusive point by a fall from a horse as a result of which he died, but his art, despite its various directions, gives him a brilliant place in the development of Romanticism. The horse especially, in his interpretation, is a symbol of Romantic sensibility and energy.

German Art Museums include the Kaiser Friedrich Museum (q.v.) and the National Gallery, Berlin, a collection of paintings from the nineteenth century to the present day. Important galleries are the Old Pinakothek, Munich (q.v.), the Dresden Gallery (q.v.) and the Kunsthalle, Hamburg (q.v.), Fine collections of modern painting are in the Wallraff Richartz Museum, Cologne; the Stuttgart Gallery; the Staedel Institute, Frankfurt; and Kunsthalle, Bremen.

German School, The. The first distinct phase of German pictorial

RHENISH MASTER, c. 1410–20—The Garden of Eden—Staedel Institute, Frankfurt.

art (Old German) is the mainly religious art of the fourteenth and
fifteenth centuries produced in a number of different centres from
Prague to Alsace and taking on characteristics of the 'International
Gothic' style (q.v.), a special development being the 'Soft Style',
mainly practised in Cologne. Paintings of the Madonna, tender in
sentiment and gentle in rhythm and figuration, are typical, and the
style is well represented by Stephen Lochner (q.v.). Master Bertram
and Master Francke in Hamburg, Konrad von Soest in Westphalia
and Lochner in Cologne (qq.v.) are leading early representatives of
Old-German art which in the course of the fifteenth century was
touched by Flemish, Burgundian and Renaissance influences. Hans
Pleydenwurff and Michael Wolgemut in Nuremberg, Lucas Moser and
Holbein the Elder in Swabia, Hans Multscher at Ulm, Michael Pacher
in Bavaria, Konrad Laib in Austria, Konrad Witz in Switzerland,
Martin Schongauer in Alsace, are representative (*see* individual
entries). Matthias Grünewald (q.v.) is a great master of the Old-
German style though belonging in date to the Renaissance period and
a contemporary of the great Dürer (q.v.). Gifted representatives of
the early Renaissance period were Altdorfer, Cranach, Burgkmair,
Baldung Grün, Süss von Kulmbach, Bernhard Strigel and Manuel

Deutsch (qq.v.), followed by the great Hans Holbein the Younger (q.v.) and Christoph Amberger (q.v.). The conflicts of the Reformation and the Thirty Years War put an end to the great period of German art, and the seventeenth and eighteenth centuries were an age of minor artists mainly living abroad, though Adam Elsheimer (q.v.) stands out in landscape. Rottenhammer, Mengs, Angelica Kauffmann and Tischbein (qq.v.) may be mentioned. Romanticism in the late eighteenth and early nineteenth centuries describes an effort to return to the religious past. The Nazarener (q.v.) movement represented by Cornelius and Overbeck (qq.v.) represents one phase and it is seen also in Runge, Caspar David Friedrich, Moritz von Schwind (qq.v.) and others. German nineteenth-century art did not achieve great European standing, though Böcklin (q.v.) in imaginative pictures, Menzel and Leibl (qq.v.) in realism, and Liebermann, Corinth and Slevogt (qq.v.) in an Impressionist style were distinguished. Developments of the twentieth century, however, have been of a remarkable kind, Expressionism (q.v.) being the main element. The artists associated with the 'Die Brücke' (q.v.) group and 'Der Blaue Reiter' (q.v.) represent it in vigorous fashion. Kirchner, Kandinsky, Klee, Beckmann, Nolde and Kokoschka (qq.v.) are now famous names. The First World War produced its reaction in the bitter social criticism of Grosz and Dix (qq.v.), and the feeling of revolt was crystallized in the idea of 'Die Neue Sachlichkeit' (q.v.). On the other hand the social and constructive possibilities of modern art were developed in the most famous of modern art schools, the Bauhaus (q.v.). The policy of Hitler and Goebbels condemned every aspect of modern art, in architecture, sculpture, painting and design, the suppression of 'degenerate art' leading to a wholesale dispersal of German artists in Europe and America. Since the Second World War there seems to have been no return to the satire or emotionalism of the 1920's but a growing cultivation of abstract art.

Gesso, prepared surface of plaster of Paris giving a smooth white ground for painting. It has been used especially for tempera painting on wooden panels and in the medieval altar-piece was sometimes moulded into required patterns before being painted and gilded.

Ghirlandaio, Domenico (*b.* Florence, *c.* 1449; *d.* 1494), Italian painter of the Florentine School, whose real name was Domenico di Tommaso Bigordi. He was styled Il Ghirlandaio or Grillandaio (garland-maker) after his father Tommaso, who was a goldsmith, and is notable not only as the master of Michelangelo but as one of the greatest Italian masters of fresco and a principal representative of the narrative art of the late fifteenth century. He studied under Baldovinetti and his style was influenced by Castagno, Masaccio and Verrocchio. His first major work was the 'Life of St Fina' in the Cappella Fina, 1475, and his frescoes in Florence include those for the Sassetti Chapel in Santa Trinità, 1485, and for the choir of Santa Maria Novella (the 'Life of St Francis', 1485, and the scenes from the life of St John the Baptist and the Virgin, his masterpiece, 1486–90). A prolific painter with a flourishing studio, Ghirlandaio produced not only frescoes and mosaics but many religious subjects on panel and portraits. Of the two frescoes he contributed to the Sistine Chapel to the order of Sixtus IV, 1481, the 'Calling of St Andrew and St Peter' remains. His altar-piece from Santa Maria Novella is at Munich. Ghirlandaio was assisted by his brothers, Davide (1452–1525) and Benedetto (1458–97). Davide helped in the mosaic of the 'Annunciation' over the north portal of Florence Cathedral and executed others

GHIRLANDAIO—Birth of St John the Baptist (Fresco)—Santa Maria Novella, Florence.

GHIRLANDAIO—Old Man
and Child—Louvre.

at Orvieto, Florence and Siena. The son of Domenico, Ridolfo (1483–1561), was also a painter and was a friend of Raphael. He too had a busy studio and was employed by the Signoria of Florence and the Medici. There are paintings by him in galleries at Berlin, Paris (Louvre) and Florence (Uffizi and Pitti).

Giacometti, name of a Swiss painter family. **Giovanni** (b. Stampa Grisons, 1868; d. there, 1933) studied in Munich and at Paris and was influenced by the colour of van Gogh in his paintings of the types and landscape of his native country. His cousin, **Augusto** (b. Stampa, 1877; d. Zürich, 1947), studied in Zürich and Paris and worked in Florence and at Zürich. From the 'Jugendstil' (see ART NOUVEAU) he advanced towards an early form of abstract expression, as in his 'Phantasy about a Potato-Blossom', 1917 (Chur, Kunsthaus). **Alberto** (b. Stampa, 10 Oct. 1901; d. Chur, Switzerland, 11 Jan. 1966), distinguished as a sculptor of lean figures, solitary in space, also painted and drew austere, phantom-like figures.

Gilbert, Sir John (b. Blackheath, 21 July 1817; d. there, 5 Oct. 1897), English painter and illustrator. He painted historical and literary subjects in oils and water-colour, Shakespeare and Scott providing many of them, and became R.A. in 1876. He is of note as a prolific Victorian illustrator rather than as a painter.

Gill, Eric (b. Brighton, 22 Feb. 1882; d. Uxbridge, 17 Nov. 1940), English sculptor, typographer and wood-engraver. Apart from the carved sculpture for which he is perhaps best known, his specialization in carved lettering equipped him to design some distinguished type faces and interested him in book decoration in general, his wood-engraving, e.g. for *The Canterbury Tales*, aiming at a close relation between text and design on the lines of William Morris's Kelmscott Press books.

Gillray, James (b. Chelsea, 1757; d. London, 1 June 1815), English

L. GIORDANO—Scene from the legend of Cupid and Psyche—The Feast of Psyche—
Reproduced by Gracious Permission of Her Majesty the Queen, Hampton Court.

caricaturist. After being a letter-engraver and actor, he was encouraged to become a caricaturist by the works of Hogarth, and his coloured etchings, fiercely satirical and topical, and directed against both the English court and France, made him celebrated. They compose an unconventional history of the late Georgian and Napoleonic period. He became insane in later life.

Giordano, Luca (*b*. Naples, 1632; *d*. there, 12 Jan. 1705), Italian painter of the Neapolitan School, nicknamed 'Luca fa presto' ('Hurry up, Luke!') from the precept of his father, Antonio, who first taught him to draw, and because of his own rate of production and astonishing facility. He was the pupil of Ribera at thirteen and was later taken by his father to Rome, where he studied under Pietro da Cortona (q.v.). He is an eminent representative of the baroque style in Naples of the later seventeenth century, in a lighter key than that of Ribera. He painted at Florence, Rome, Genoa and Madrid, mainly mural and ceiling decoration (e.g. the ballroom ceiling of the Palazzo Riccardi, Florence, 1682, and ceilings in the Escorial, Madrid, 1692), but also a large number of oil pictures and etchings. 'Christ expelling

[299]

the Traders from the Temple' (Church of the Padri Girolamini, Naples)
is one of his most famous works.

Giorgio, Francesco di, *see* FRANCESCO.

Giorgione da Castelfranco (*b.* Castelfranco, 1477–8; *d.* Venice, 25
Oct. 1510), Italian painter of the Venetian School, of whom few
things can be said with certainty save that his was a great and
individual genius. Giorgio Barbarelli, 'il maistro Zorzi da Castelfranco', called Giorgione after his death, seems to have been the pupil
of Giovanni Bellini at Venice, together with Titian, and to have
achieved early success there. In 1500, at the age of twenty-three, he
was chosen to paint portraits of the Doge Agostino Barberigo and the
condottiere Consalvo Ferrante. He decorated the façades of several
Venetian palaces, working with Titian on that of the Fondaco dei
Tedeschi, when it was rebuilt in 1504. He is described by Vasari as a
person of social charm, a musician and a romantic lover. Vasari
speaks of Sebastiano del Piombo and Titian as his 'disciples', and it is
supposed that the 'Venus' (Dresden), most probably one of Giorgione's last works, was finished by Titian, though the precise relation
of their art is still a matter of debate. That Giorgione died of the
'plague' in 1510 is certain. Four pictures are generally accepted as

GIORGIONE—Concert Champêtre—Louvre.

certainly his: the Castelfranco altar-piece, the 'Three Philosophers' (Vienna), the 'Portrait of a Lady' (Vienna) and 'The Tempest' (or 'Storm') (Venice, Accademia). To these are added with probability the 'Judith' (Leningrad), 'Portrait of a Young Man' (Berlin), 'Venus' (Dresden), 'Madonna with Saints' (Prado), 'Christ and the Adulteress' (Glasgow), the 'Judgment of Solomon' (Kingston Lacy), the Concert Champêtre' (Louvre) and 'Concert' (Florence, Pitti). The Castelfranco altar-piece, in its symmetrical composition, is related to the work of Bellini and may well be early, but otherwise Giorgione may be regarded as an innovator—in the development of the oil technique, in rich and warm colour and in a type of painting independent of a particular position or function—and to have set the course of sixteenth-century Venetian painting as represented by Titian, Sebastiano, Lorenzo Lotto and Palma Vecchio. A poetical and enigmatic beauty seems personal to him, and is clearly apparent in 'The Tempest' of about 1503. The dream-like quality of its impassive figures against the background of approaching electric storm has its eternal fascination. A like mysterious and contemplative beauty, with which the mature Titian's sense of drama and movement may be contrasted, is to be found in the 'Concert Champêtre' of the Louvre. Critical expertise, if it casts doubts on its authorship, must defer to the magic which inspired Manet to the reinterpretation of his 'Déjeuner sur l'Herbe'. (Colour)

Giottino (active mid-fourteenth century), Italian painter of the early Florentine School, called Giottino because he worked in the style of Giotto. His real name is uncertain, but he has been identified with both Tommaso di Stefano and Maso di Banco (q.v.). It is known that he worked in the Vatican. Works that have been attributed to him are 'Deposition' (Uffizi), 'Crucifixion' and 'Adoration' (Santa Maria Novella, Florence) and the 'Legend of Constantine and Pope Sylvester' (Santa Croce, Florence).

Giotto (Ambrogio di Bondone) (*b*. Colle, nr Vespignano, *c*. 1266; *d*. Florence, 8 Jan. 1337), Italian painter, the great progenitor of the Florentine School. There are few known facts about his life, but he was the son of a peasant landowner, probably of no great possessions but of reputable standing. A doubtful legend describes his discovery by Cimabue (q.v.) as a boy making drawings of his father's sheep. It seems likely that he was less influenced by Cimabue, whose fame according to Dante he eclipsed, than by the Roman School as represented by Pietro Cavallini (q.v.) and the sculpture of the Pisani, that is by forms of art which contained or revived something of the Western classical tradition as distinct from that of Byzantium. Often considered an early work (though its authorship has been the subject of controversy) is the series of the Life of Christ and Allegories of St Francis in the Upper Church of San Francesco at Assisi. He is recorded to have worked in a number of cities as well as in Florence— Rome, Naples, Padua, Rimini, Ravenna and Avignon. Working in Rome in 1298, he painted an altar-piece (no longer extant) for St Peter's and designed in mosaic the 'Navicella' (Christ saving St

GIOTTO—Virgin and Child with Angels—Uffizi Gallery, Florence.

Peter from the Waves) in the portico, though restoration has left little
of the original. His greatest undertaking was the series of frescoes
in the Arena Chapel, Padua, painted in 1303 and depicting the Life of
the Virgin and the Life of Christ in thirty-eight scenes. Majestically
simple in form, telling a story and conveying human expression
dramatically and with an economy of means that admits only
essentials, they display the genius of Giotto at its height, and already
forecast the achievements of the Renaissance. From Padua he
returned to Florence and Assisi, where he painted the allegorical
frescoes in the vault of the church, the 'Marriage of St Francis with
Poverty', 'The Triumph of Obedience', 'The Triumph of Charity'
and the 'Glorification of St Francis'. Of several panel pictures
attributed to him the 'Ognissanti' Madonna (Uffizi) is generally
admitted to be a masterpiece from his own hand. Giotto was appointed chief architect of the cathedral at Florence and in this
capacity designed the campanile (known as Giotto's Tower) begun in
1334. It was unfinished at the time of his death but completed
exactly in accordance with his plans, its relief decorations probably
being carried out by Andrea Pisano to his designs. He had many
pupils and followers, including Stefano Fiorentino, Bernardo Daddi,
Taddeo and Agnolo Gaddi, Giottino or Maso di Banco, and Orcagna,
and a main stream seems to flow from his workshop into the Florentine art of the fifteenth century, Masaccio for instance being in the
great line of succession.

Giovanni d'Allemagna, *see* VIVARINI, ANTONIO.

Giovanni di Paolo (*b.* Siena, *c.* 1403; *d.* there, 1482), Italian painter

G. DI PAOLO—St John the Baptist retiring to the Desert—National Gallery.

A. L. GIRODET DE ROUCY—The Burial of Atala—Louvre.

of the Sienese School, also known as Giovanni del Poggio from the
district of Siena where he lived. He ranks with Sassetta (q.v.), whom
he seems to have followed in style, though showing some points of
contact with his contemporary, Gentile da Fabriano (q.v.), and with
earlier Sienese art. He is individual in an imaginative simplification,
fantastic in effect, like that of his 'Miracle of St Nicholas of Bari', *c.*
1450 (Philadelphia Museum of Art). Six scenes from the life of John
the Baptist from a dismembered polyptych (Chicago and London)
are among his most striking works, a large number of which are
distributed among European and American collections.

Girodet de Roucy (-Trioson), Anne Louis (*b.* Montargis, 29 Jan.
1767; *d.* Paris, 9 Dec. 1824), French painter of imaginative subjects.
Left an orphan at an early age he was brought up by a Dr Trioson,
whose name he later added to his own. He was a pupil of David (q.v.),
won the Prix de Rome, 1789, and spent five of the revolutionary
years in Italy (not without danger in the riots at the French Academy
in Rome). He is of note as a man of complex and poetic mind in whom
the Romantic unrest clearly appears, and took, it was said, 'infinite
trouble to be original'. Romantic symptoms are the mysterious noc-
turnal light of his 'Sleep of Endymion' (Louvre), and the literary
tastes which led him to depict Napoleon's generals in the Halls of

[304]

T. GIRTIN—The White House, Chelsea (Water-colour)—Tate Gallery.

Ossian (ceiling for Malmaison, 1801) and to take from Chateaubriand 'The Burial of Atala' (Louvre).

Girtin, Thomas (*b*. Southwark, 18 Feb. 1775; *d*. London, 1 Nov. 1802), English landscape painter in water-colour. After desultory early training he spent a fruitful period in company with the young Turner, making copies from J. R. Cozens for Dr Monro and also copying and studying the drawings of Canaletto owned by Monro's neighbour, John Henderson. By 1796 he had begun to develop a personal style, replacing the tinted topographical drawing by water-colour paintings in which free brushwork, strength of tone and broadly handled masses brought a new vigour into the art, and indeed suggested new possibilities for landscape in either water-colour or oil. Turner set himself to rival Girtin in this development of water-colour, and Constable, who saw examples of Girtin's work in Sir George Beaumont's collection, was at once impressed by the technical suggestion they offered. To views of the English country-side, such as the splendid 'View on the Wharfe', he added, 1801–2, some excellent views of Paris (subsequently made into soft-ground etchings), and on his return from his Parisian visit worked on a panorama of London (the 'Eidometropolis'), six sketches for which are preserved in the British Museum. Though he died of tuberculosis at the age of twenty-seven he is, in both achievement and influence, an artist of importance.

Glackens, William James (*b*. Philadelphia, 13 Mar. 1870; *d*. Westport, Connecticut, 22 May, 1938), American painter, one of the group of Eight who brought freshness of outlook into American art. In early life he worked as an illustrator, studying also at the Pennsylvania Academy of Fine Arts, and in 1895 for a year in Paris. Able eventually

[305]

to devote himself exclu-
sively to painting, he
produced a number of
scenes of city life and
of portraits and nudes
influenced in style by
Renoir.

Glaze, in oil-painting
a thin film of trans-
parent colour spread
over an area of solid
pigment, modifying and
enriching its effect. The
solid pigment has to be
lighter in tone than the
glaze, thus giving a
luminous result. It was
an important aspect of
the elaborate technique of European old masters, Titian being famous
for the depth and glow of colour thus obtained.

Gleizes, Albert (*b.* Paris, 1881; *d.* 23 June 1953), French Cubist
painter, who began by painting Impressionist landscapes but took
part in the first Cubist exhibition at the Salon des Indépendants and
evolved a decorative and geometrically simplified style. His work
attracted much attention at the Armory Show in New York, 1913.
In later life he applied his flat geometrical technique to religious
subjects, with debatable success. He illustrated Pascal's *Pensées*
1948–50, with a series of etchings.

Goerg, Edouard (*b.* Sidney, 9 June 1891), painter and etcher, born
of French parents in Australia, who went to Paris in 1910 and settled
there. He was the pupil of Maurice Denis, but Rouault (as well as
Goya and Daumier) was a strong influence on his work. He painted
young girls in a well-defined and attractive style, also flower-pieces,
and illustrated many books with his etchings.

Goes, Hugo van der (*b.* probably Ghent, *c.* 1440; *d.* Roode-Clooster,
Brussels, 1482), Flemish painter who worked at Ghent and later at
Bruges. One of the greatest fifteenth-century masters, he began with
small panels warmly coloured and detailed in the van Eyck fashion,
but from about 1474 he worked on a larger scale, using cool and
translucent colour and often expressing great emotional intensity.
His most famous work is the Portinari altar-piece, *c.* 1475 (Uffizi),
executed for the agent of the Medici at Bruges, Tommaso Portinari,

H. VAN DER GOES—The Adoration of the Shepherds (Portinari Altar-piece)—Uffizi, Florence.

which made a great impression on the Florentines, being closely studied by Ghirlandaio (q.v.), while its author was favourably mentioned by Vasari (q.v.). Other great works are the 'Adoration of the Magi' (Berlin), 'Death of the Virgin' (Bruges) and 'Monk meditating' (New York, Metropolitan Museum). He became a monk in the Roode-Clooster, Brussels, in 1475 but continued to paint, though suffering intermittently in the last years of his life from a kind of mania or despairing melancholy which one seems to see reflected in the look of suffering in some of the faces he painted and makes one think of Vincent van Gogh.

Gogh, Vincent van (*b.* Groot Zundert, North Brabant, 30 Mar. 1853; *d.* Auvers-sur-l'Oise, 29 July 1890), Dutch painter and one of the greatest artists of the Post-Impressionist period, the son of a Dutch pastor. He did not take to art seriously until he was twenty-seven, having by that time failed in various projected careers, in the firm of Goupil & Co., art dealers at The Hague and in London and Paris, as an usher in schools at Ramsgate and Isleworth, and as lay preacher among the miners of the Borinage. The first stage of his career as artist may be dated 1880–6 in Holland and Belgium.

VAN GOGH—The Potato Eaters—Kroller-Müller Museum, Otterlo.

Supported by an allowance from his brother Theo, he took drawing
lessons in Brussels, was with the painter Anton Mauve for a while at
The Hague and for a year in the Academy at Antwerp. 'The Potato-
Eaters' of 1885 was the remarkable product of this period. There
follows the Paris period, 1886–8, in which he was much influenced by
Japanese prints, by Impressionism and the division of colour as
practised by Seurat and Signac. His famous 'Boots' was a last effort
in his early dark, proletarian style; his new sense of colour and design
found wonderful expression in 1888 at Arles, to which period belong
such famous pictures as his views of Arles, 'The Drawbridge', 'Or-
chard in Blossom', 'Boats at Saintes-Maries', 'The Chair and Pipe',
'The Café at Night'. 'The Zouave Officer' and his several 'Sun-
flowers'. Following the mental crisis of 1888, when after a quarrel
with Gauguin he mutilated his ear, his genius struggled with the
depression of mental illness and hospital surroundings. The year 1889
at St-Rémy produced his free copies after various artists and his
paintings of cypress-trees; 1890 at Auvers-sur-Oise (with Dr Gachet)
the last agitated paintings of cornfields before he shot himself. Both
the number and the splendour of his pictures produced during a
short and unhappy span of life remain astonishing, and his influence
on modern art in the conception of colour and individual expression
has been immense. His letters to his brother Theo are an illuminating

VAN GOGH—Cypresses—Tate Gallery.

commentary on his work and ideas. His work is to be found in a number of galleries, and great collections are those of his nephew, Ir. V. W. van Gogh, and at the Kröller-Müller Museum. (Colour)

Golden Section. Proportion obtained by dividing a line unequally, so that the smaller section is to the larger as the larger to the whole, the ratio thus obtained having been often considered by artists as 'ideal', i.e. infallibly producing harmony of proportion, wherever applied. The idea of such an ideal proportion inspired the 'Section d'Or' Cubist exhibition in 1912.

Gonçalves, Nuno (active 1450–67), Portuguese painter, now recognized as a fifteenth-century master of outstanding quality. Francisco de Hollanda in his *Dialogues*, 1548, mentions him among the great European painters of his time, though subsequently he was forgotten. Of his few surviving works the six panels (in tempera and oil) of the polyptych 'The Veneration of St Vincent' (Lisbon, Museu de Arte Antiga) are the most important. The polyptych painted 1465–7 for the monastery of St Vincent, Lisbon (and recognized as the work of Gonçalves in 1908), represents members of court and society in the great age of maritime discovery and expansion. The influence of

NUNO GONÇALVES—The Veneration of St Vincent (detail)—Museu de Arte Antiga, Lisbon.

J. GOSSART (Mabuse)—The Adoration of the Kings—National Gallery.

Flemish painting and Gothic wood sculpture is present but the artist's individual power in composition and portraiture is manifest.

Gonzales, José, see GRIS.

Gossart (Gossaert), Jan (called **Mabuse**) (*b.* château of Duurstede, nr Utrecht, *c.* 1472; *d.* Antwerp, *c.* 1536), Flemish painter of a Maubeuge family. He painted religious and mythological subjects and portraits and after a visit to Italy in the retinue of his patron, the Duke of Burgundy, worked at Antwerp. At first a follower of Gerard David (q.v.), he turned to Renaissance models, being influenced by both Albrecht Dürer (q.v.) and Italian masters, his 'Adam and Eve' (Berlin) being a typically Renaissance study of the nude. His 'Adoration of the Magi' (National Gallery), imperfect as a composition, contains a wealth of well-painted incident and is an outstanding illustration of his earlier manner. His portraits, in a somewhat hard style, have considerable merit.

Gothardt, Matthias, see GRÜNEWALD.

Gothic Painting, art flourishing from the twelfth to sixteenth centuries in Europe, parallel with the rise of Gothic architecture and the associated arts of design. It is distinct from the preceding Romanesque style in its interest in the individual human being, in a new delight in nature, in richness of detail and love of bright colour and ornament. These characteristics are symptomatic of social change, the passing of a rigid order, monastic and feudal, and the growth of urban centres where the artist had lay as well as ecclesiastic patrons and where the independent craft guild gave him a freedom and status unknown to the monastic painter. Gothic painting technically had two points of origin: it was a development of the illuminated manuscript, retaining its minuteness of finish even on a larger than book scale; it was also derived from Gothic sculpture in the sense that many paintings imitated the carved figures standing in canopies and the sharply angular folds of dress made by the sculptor's chisel. It had several regional developments before and after the beginning of the fifteenth century, but there then flourished what is known as the International Gothic style (q.v.), France being the chief centre of influence, which extended from Germany to Italy. The famous manuscript of the brothers Limbourg, 'Les Très Riches Heures du Duc de Berry' (end of fourteenth century), beautifully represents the International style. Comprehensively regarded, Gothic painting comprises (1) Anglo-French work, e.g. Wilton Diptych; (2) in France, the work of miniaturists and such painters as Jean Malouel, Jean Fouquet and the Maître de Moulins; (3) in the Netherlands, van Eyck, van der Weyden, Hugo van der Goes, Gerard David; (4) in Italy, the early School of Siena, Lorenzetti, Martini, Sassetta; the Umbrian painter Gentile da Fabriano, Pisanello; (5) in Spain, Pedro Serra, Jaime Huguet, Luis Dalmau, and in Portugal Nuno Gonçalves; (6) in Germany, the School of Cologne, Stefan Lochner and others; also Schongauer, Michael Pacher, Altdorfer and finally Matthias Grünewald.

Gouache, water-colour made opaque by the admixture of Chinese white. In this definition it is identical with 'body colour', though *gouache* more conveniently describes a painting executed in this medium as well as the medium itself, and may also imply the addition of gum to water-colour and body-colour. It lacks the special brilliance of transparent water-colour through which the ground of white paper is visible, but is more substantial in effect. The colour dries lighter than when first applied, with a matt surface, often somewhat resembling a matt oil sketch. It was used by the painters of miniatures in manuscripts and subsequently by many European masters, including Dürer (in his studies of landscape and animals), Rubens and van Dyck. Modern French artists have favoured it, e.g. Utrillo. It has had fewer practitioners in England than pure water-colour but was effectively employed by Paul Sandby (q.v.).

Goya, y Lucientes, Francisco José de (*b.* Fuentetodos, 30 Mar. 1746; *d.* Bordeaux, 16 April 1828), Spanish painter, one of the greatest European artists. He showed early promise and was apprenticed at fourteen to a painter in Saragossa, José Luzán y Martinez. When nineteen, as legend has it because of some amorous escapade, he left for Madrid, where he worked for the painter Francisco Bayeu (q.v.). He married Bayeu's sister, Josefa, in 1773, after a short visit to Rome, and settled in Madrid. His brother-in-law's connections helped him to gain an important commission in 1775 for a series of forty tapestry designs. These were not strictly 'cartoons' but large paintings on canvas depicting various aspects of Spanish life in a decorative style which owed something to rococo art and particularly to Tiepolo, though such examples as 'The Four Seasons' were essentially Spanish in type and landscape setting and individually brilliant in execution. He worked on these designs for a number of years as well as on wall-paintings for churches, and by 1786 was court painter to Charles III. In 1799 he was the king's first painter and an artist of recognized eminence. He had devoted patrons in Charles IV and the Duchess of Alba, but his life was troubled. In 1792 he became deaf as the result of a serious illness and his position during and after the Napoleonic invasion of Spain was uneasy. When Ferdinand VII was driven out he continued to work for the usurper Joseph Bonaparte. When Ferdinand was restored he was not penalized but seems to have found the restored court uncongenial and sought permission in 1824 to retire to France, spending the last few years of his life in Bordeaux. It is part of the complexity of Goya's life and work that he enjoyed court life; that he was at the same time a revolutionary in taking an intensely critical view of institutions; that he hated war; that he was

F. DE GOYA—Nude Maja—Prado.

F. DE GOYA—Majas on a Balcony—Metropolitan Museum of Art, New York, Havemeyer Collection.

F. DE GOYA—The Firing Party, 3rd May 1808—Prado.

a patriot yet one with an artist's detachment. His portraits of Charles IV and his queen were mercilessly unflattering, though the royal family is grouped in splendour in the famous masterpiece, the 'Family of Charles IV', in the Prado. Yet other portraits show that in his passionate desire for truth he did not refuse to recognize the existence of masculine dignity or feminine charm. Masterly examples of the one are the 'Don Sebastian Martinez' (New York Metropolitan Museum) and the portrait of Francisco Bayeu in the Prado; of the other the exquisite Doña Tadea de Enriquez (Prado) and the sultry beauty of Doña Isabel de Porcel (National Gallery). His paintings of Spanish life-festivals, religious processions and bullfights reveal his passionate interest in and yet critical analysis of human behaviour. They include sombre representations of the madhouse, the prison cell and scene of execution. His revolutionary spirit appears in the famous etched and aquatinted series of graphic works, the 'Caprices', published in 1797, with their covert attack on the corruption of court and clergy, the 'Proverbs' and the 'Disparates' or 'Extravagances' of 1819, with their further sardonic comment on human absurdity. The 'Disasters of War', 1808–20, was a more direct impeachment of the cruelty and horrors perpetrated during the French invasion. They have their equivalents in the later paintings. War inspired the grim masterpiece, 'The Firing Party, 3rd May

[315]

1808' (Prado), which incited Manet to paint the execution of the Emperor Maximilian. The paintings in Goya's own villa, 'La Quinta del Sordo' ('The Deaf Man's House'), conjured up such dreadful visions as his 'Saturn', 'The Witches' Sabbath' and the weird pathos of the 'Pilgrimage to San Isidro'. Here his deafness seems to have heightened his sensitivity to the strangeness of human grimace. His religious pictures count for less in the estimate of his art. His frescoes for the church of San Antonio de la Florida in Madrid are inappropriately mundane, yet, as Goya constantly surprises us by unexpected bursts of genius (one of them the famous nude study, the 'Nude Maja' of the Prado), he was capable also in his late years of a work as full of spiritual emotion as his 'Communion of San José' (Bayonne). Technically, Goya attained brilliant effects by thin painting over a red earth ground. Influenced by Rembrandt ('Rembrandt, Velasquez and Nature' were, he said, his guides), he turned in later years to a dusky near-monochrome. His skill, however, seemed to increase with age, and the 'Milkmaid of Bordeaux', one of his last paintings, shows him using colour with great freedom. His portrait of Wellington, stolen from the National Gallery in 1961, was recovered in 1965.

Goyen, Jan van (*b.* Leyden, 13 April 1596; *d.* The Hague, April 1656) Dutch painter of landscape, marine and river views, also an

⅃. VAN GOYEN—Landscape with Two Oaks—Rijksmuseum, Amsterdam.

D. GRANT—The Lemon Gatherers—Tate Gallery.

etcher. He worked with Esaias van de Velde (q.v.) at Haarlem, after
some study with other masters, and settled at The Hague. His art was
creative in the development of Dutch landscape painting, gradually
replacing the incidental interest of boats, figures and buildings in his
river scenes by a larger concern with space, light and atmosphere
conceived in what was virtually a warm monochrome. Rembrandt in
landscape derived some inspiration from him.

Gozzoli, *see* BENOZZO DI LESE.

Graf, Urs (*b.* Solothurn, *c.* 1485; *d.* 1527–8), Swiss painter-engraver
and goldsmith. He was trained and worked at Basel, being mainly
noted for his drawings and engravings of the fantastically costumed
military types of the time. Like his Swiss contemporary, Hans Leu,
painter and engraver of Zürich, he was one of the Swiss mercenaries
or landsknechts and may, like him, have taken part with the imperial
forces in the sack of Rome, 1527.

Grand Style, The, English term with equivalents in French (*beau
idéal*) and Italian (*gusto grande*), used in the past to indicate a
superior excellence in painting, especially of the High Renaissance in
Italy. As defined by Sir Joshua Reynolds in his *Discourses*, it consists
in the creation of generalized forms which approach perfection in
correcting the accidental effects of nature and rising above 'par-
ticularities and details of every kind', e.g. local modes and manners
and fashion in any form. A debatable division was thus established
between 'higher' and 'lower' spheres of art (automatically relegating

[317]

a Brueghel or a Teniers to the lower category), though the criterion, if suitably reinterpreted, has not lost all its point. See also CLASSICISM, HISTORY PAINTING, IDEAL, IDEALISM.

'Grande Jatte, La', painting by Seurat (q.v.), more fully titled as 'Après-midi de Dimanche sur l'Île de la Grande Jatte', exhibited at the last Impressionist exhibition of 1886. It depicts members of the Parisian bourgeoisie strolling in their Sunday best, though the composition is notable mainly for a studied formality for which the subject was a pretext. The artist made many preliminary sketches on the spot. It is now in the Art Institute of Chicago.

Grant, Duncan (b. Rothiemurchus, Inverness, 25 Jan. 1885), painter of Scottish birth. He studied art in London, Italy and Paris and was among the British artists first influenced by Post-Impressionism. A decorative aspect of his talent appears in work done c. 1913 with Roger Fry in the Omega Workshops. His oil landscapes, portraits and still lifes show a sensitive ability in representation.

Graphic Art, drawing as distinct from painting, a term which also comprises the various forms of engraving.

Greaves, Walter (b. Chelsea, 4 July 1846, d. London, Nov. 1930), English painter, son of a boat-builder. He took to art under the influence of Whistler, whose handyman and assistant he was for nearly twenty years. A famous early work is 'Hammersmith Bridge on Boat Race Day', 1862 (Tate Gallery), unusual in its 'primitive' quality, but most of his paintings are views of the Thames in a

W. GREAVES—Hammersmith Bridge on Boat Race Day—Tate Gallery.

EL GRECO—The Agony in the Garden—National Gallery.

Whistlerian style. In old age he was admitted as Poor Brother to the Charterhouse, where he died.

Greco, El (*b.* Crete, 1541; *d.* Toledo, 6 or 7 April 1614), Spanish painter by association, though of Greek origin, his real name being Domenikos Theotokopoulos. He was known to his contemporaries as El Griego ('the Greek'), was trained by Greek monks in his native island of Crete as an icon painter in the Byzantine tradition and habitually signed his paintings in Greek characters. As a young artist he went to Italy and, Crete being then a Venetian possession, Venice was his first objective. He is stated to have been a pupil of Titian, though his early work seems to owe more to Bassano and Tintoretto, and it is possible that he was also influenced by Correggio. In 1570, as recorded by his friend, the Dalmatian miniature painter Giulio Clovio, who gained him an introduction to Cardinal Farnese, he went on to Rome, where he stayed for six years. It is said that he spoke in somewhat contemptuous terms of Michelangelo's 'Last Judgment', though his 'Christ driving the Traders from the Temple' (in several versions) shows him to have borrowed figures and details of composition not only from the Venetians but also from Michelangelo and Raphael. He settled in Toledo in 1577, his aim no doubt in going to Spain being to work for Philip II, the great amateur of

EL GRECO—The Burial of
Count Orgaz—Santo Tomé,
Toledo.

Venetian art, but fail-
ing to please the king's
taste he did not take
up residence in the
royal capital, Madrid.
Toledo, however, was
still much the larger of
the two cities, a centre
of industry and crafts-
manship and also the
ecclesiastical capital,
headquarters of the
Jesuits and the Counter-
Reformation. A foreigner
when he arrived, speak-
ing only Greek and
Italian, El Greco stayed
at Toledo for the rest of
his life, and the religious and spiritual character of his works links
him inseparably with the spirit of the time and place. His work was
evidently much approved and in demand, though the decay of the
city seems to have brought him to poverty in his later years. His
complex inheritance as an artist, his Spanish background and
personal genius, combine to give a unique greatness to his achievement. Italian influences remained in his work until about 1580, and
in his first commissions at Toledo. These included a now dismembered
altar-piece for Santo Domingo el Antiguo, the 'Trinity' (Prado) and
'Assumption' (Chicago), the latter based on the 'Assumption' of
Titian, and the 'Espolio', or 'Disrobing of Christ', for Toledo
Cathedral. From 1580 onwards his Byzantine inheritance regained
dominance, yet was combined with a passionate insistence on rhythm
and movement, a vehement desire for intensity of expression which
is conveyed by the elongation and distortion of figures and unusual
and disturbing colour schemes with calculated discords of crimson,
lemon yellow, green and blue, and livid flesh tones. Perspective and
normal effects of lighting were disregarded and the significance of the
young El Greco's remarks to Giulio Clovio, that the daylight blinded
him to the inner light, becomes apparent. In a modern and 'expressionist' fashion he was projecting a vision conceived in the mind and
emotions. The characteristic El Greco is already to be seen in the
'Martyrdom of St Maurice', 1581–4 (Madrid, Escorial), of which
Philip II disapproved. The huge masterpiece, the 'Burial of Count
Orgaz' (Santo Tomé, Toledo), painted c. 1587 (q.v.), marvellously

EL GRECO—View of Toledo—Metropolitan Museum of Art, New York, Havemeyer
Collection.

combined austere Spanish dignity with rapturous sublimity. Great
later compositions are the 'Agony in the Garden' (National Gallery
and other versions) and the soaring vertical ascent of the 'Pentecost',
'Resurrection' and 'Adoration of the Shepherds' (Prado). The later
period includes portraits superbly characterized (and refuting the
absurd supposition that El Greco's elongations in other works were
due to some defect of eyesight). 'Cardinal Niño de Guevara' (New
York, Metropolitan Museum) is one of his great portraits, and a
remarkable collection is in the Prado. His famous and single pure

[321]

landscape, 'View of Toledo' (Metropolitan Museum), typically selects the intense and abnormal atmosphere of storm. It may be noted that El Greco, as in his 'Boy blowing on Coals' (Naples), was the first of those painters who exploited the mysterious and rich effects of shadow produced by artificial light.

The many duplicates, revisions and versions of his paintings suggest a busy studio, though the part played by assistants does not seem clear and he had no follower of note. This is hardly surprising in view of his essential individuality. While he is identified with Spain in his fervid mysticism and his appreciation of the sombre dignity of the grandee, he was not a realist in the same sense as the native Iberian. On Spanish painting his influence was small, though Velazquez studied his portraiture and method of design. Yet he sums up in a wonderful fashion the spiritual aspect of a civilization with which by the happiest of coincidences he found a true affinity.

Greek Painting is represented by (1) vase painting, (2) wall and picture painting on representational lines not unlike those followed by artists of more recent times. The vase painting constitutes a brilliant form of graphic art notable for its expressiveness of line and balance of black and white. After the Dorian invasions of about 1100 B.C. the naturalistic art of the Aegean civilization was lost (*see* AEGEAN PAINTING), though the black glaze of the Minoan potter was still used in the early Greek 'geometric' style that arose about the end of the tenth century B.C. Between the eighth and sixth centuries oriental and geometric elements were blended and representations of deer and other animals appear as well as mythological and battle scenes. Rhodes, Crete and Corinth were centres, Corinth being noted for its exquisite tiny perfume pots. From the sixth century the Attic

painters come into prominence with a new technique by which figures were not painted in black on the clay of the vase but left in the colour of the clay, the background being painted black. This 'red-figure' style is accompanied by a new skill and power in rendering the human

GREEK VASE PAINTING, Fifth Century B.C. (attributed to Douris) — Two Women putting away Clothes, (Kylix in red-figured style) — Metropolitan Museum of Art, New York.

MOSAIC AFTER PHILOXENOS—The Battls of Issus—Museo Nazionale, Naples.

GREEK VASE PAINTING (Attic, c. 425 B.C.)—Alcestis in her Bridal Bower (from a clay epinetron (carder's knee-guard) from Eritrea)—Athens Museum.

GRAECO-ROMAN PAINT-
ING (from Stabia)—Flora—
Museo Nazionale, Naples.

GRAECO-ROMAN PAINT-
ING (Herculaneum)—
'Sappho'—Museo Nazion-
ale, Naples.

figure. Famous painters now sign their works and can be individually recognized, e.g. Euphronios, Klitias, Exekias, Douris and Brygos (? painter-potter) (qq.v.). Painting as an individual and representational art dates from the fifth century B.C. and with its rise vase painting sinks to a less eminent position. Polygnotos (q.v.) was the first great Athenian mural painter and the style of his composition is indicated by some copies on vases. Otherwise we can only form an idea of what Greek mural and 'easel' painting was like from ancient description and copies made in the Roman period. Apollodoros (q.v.) developed light and shade. Zeuxis and Parrhasios carried realism a stage further. Ancient critics considered the great period of Greek painting the fourth century B.C. and Apelles its supreme master. The art of Philoxenos (q.v.) can be gauged from a mosaic copy. The copies or imitations of Hellenistic painting at Pompeii and Herculaneum convey that the Greek painters had achieved a great mastery of elaborate composition and dramatic action. *See also* ROMAN PAINTING. Byzantine art shows some continuance of the classical tradition, though fused with oriental elements.

Greuze, Jean Baptiste (*b.* Tournus, 21 Aug. 1725; *d.* Paris, 21 Mar. 1805), French *genre* and portrait painter. He studied art at Lyons and first made his mark with his 'Lecture de Bible' at the Salon in 1755. He became famous after 1769, when the pretty but wanton girl he had married began to appear in pictures which delighted his public. Praised by Diderot for what he took to be ideas of moral purity, a number of Greuze's paintings are suspect for an appearance of innocence suggestive of its opposite. Reproof of his false sentiment must except paintings of children, which have a simple charm, though as an artist he has many shortcomings, in drawing and execution as well as idea, and his storytelling *genre*, e.g. 'La Malédiction Paternelle' (Louvre), has no great significance. The Revolution ended his vogue.

J. B. GREUZE—The Broken Jug—Louvre.

J. GRIS—Wine Bottle and Newspaper—Photo, Marlborough Fine Art.

Gris, Juan (*b*. Madrid, 1887; *d*. Boulogne-sur-Seine, May 1927), Spanish painter whose real name was José Gonzales, mainly noted as a painter of Cubist still lifes. He went to Paris in 1906, meeting Picasso (q.v.), whose disciple he became, and began to paint about 1910. First trained as an engineer, he had a precise and scientific outlook and delighted in variations of geometric form effectively combined with an imitative rendering of substance, e.g. the grain of wood and the use of *papiers collés*—pieces of wallpaper, etc. 'With a mind as precise as mine', he said, 'I can never smudge a blue or bend a straight line.' In addition to oil-paintings he produced some etchings and lithographs as book illustrations.

Grisaille, monochrome painting carried out in tones of grey. It has been used variously as an underpainting over which colour was laid or as an imitation in a picture of the effect of architectural and sculptural detail (early Netherlandish art providing examples) and as a feature of mural decoration. The term is also applied to stained-glass painting.

Gromaire, Marcel (*b*. Noyelle-sur-Sambre, 24 July 1892), French painter of Expressionist tendency. He studied law in Paris but then

[326]

M. GROMAIRE—New York, Central Park—Musée d'Art Moderne, Paris.

began to attend art classes in Montparnasse. A series of war paintings produced after the 1914–18 war first displayed a characteristic, somewhat sombre and heavy style which he later applied to landscape, figure studies and scenes of working-class life. He has produced a number of etchings, closely related to his paintings in character.

Gros, Antoine Jean, Baron (*b.* Paris, 16 Mar. 1771; *d.* 25 June 1835), French painter, the son of a miniaturist and one of the most original of the pupils of David (q.v.). Stranded in Italy during the events of the Revolution and the beginning of the Napoleonic regime, he was befriended by Josephine, who introduced him to Bonaparte. Gros became his official painter and witnessed battle at first hand. 'Bonaparte at the Bridge of Arcola', 1796 (Louvre), was followed by an epic series which gained him many honours, famous being 'Napoleon on the Battlefield of Eylau', 1808 (Louvre), and 'The Plague-stricken at Jaffa', 1804 (Louvre). The latter is a key picture in early nineteenth-century French art, the dramatic contrasts of its groups of figures inspiring Delacroix (q.v.), while it first turned artists' eyes towards the 'oriental' subject later so popular. In reviving in painting the sense of movement and emotional colour (in which he followed Rubens rather than David) Gros was a herald of Romanticism. In the anticlimax of the Restoration he turned back with poor success to the

[327]

A. J. GROS—The Plague-stricken of Jaffa—Louvre.

Davidian classicism, his failure being seemingly in part responsible for his suicide by drowning in a tributary of the Seine.

Grosz, George (*b.* Berlin, 26 July 1893; *d.* there, 6 July 1959), satirical draughtsman and painter, born in Germany but settled since 1933 in the United States. He was associated with the Dadaists of 1917 in violent protest against war and the society that countenanced it, and his early work, during the 1920's, consisted of brilliant pen drawings satirizing the generals, industrialists, profiteers, Junkers and churchmen and the vices and follies of a night-club era. His work was pilloried in the Nazi exhibition of 'Degenerate Art'. In the United States, where he became naturalized, his style lost its early incisiveness, though some works of a milder character were again followed, with the renewal of war, by elaborate representations of evil and suffering.

Grotesque (It. *grottesco*, from *grotesca*, a style of painting found in the 'grottoes' or ruins of ancient Roman buildings), form of decoration in which human figures, imaginary monsters, animals, flowers and fruit were capriciously mingled. Excavations in the Baths of Titus and Roman palaces provided examples which stimulated the fancy of Italian Renaissance artists and were copied and freely elaborated in painting and architectural ornament. A famous instance is given by the medallions and panels of the Loggie of the Vatican carried out by Giulio Romano and Giovanni da Udine to

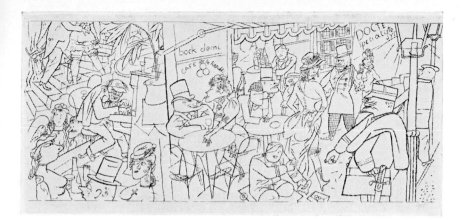

G. GROSZ—Café—Museum of Modern Art, New York.

Raphael's designs. It is easy to understand how the word has come to be applied to any extravagant representation of objects. *See also* ARABESQUE.

Ground, prepared surface of the canvas or panel on which a painter works, either white oil paint (over which a warm tone such as that of Indian red is sometimes laid) or plaster (*see* GESSO). In etching the ground is the wax coating of the metal plate through which the artist draws with the etching needle.

Gruber, Francis (*b.* Nancy, 1912; *d.* Paris, 1948), French painter who studied art under Othon Friesz, Charles Dufresne (qq.v.) and Henri de Waroquier. He came into prominence after the Second World War by reason of the austere realism which gave impressiveness to his sad and wasted figures and desolate landscapes.

Grünewald, Matthias (*b.* Würzburg, 1460 or 1475–80; *d.* Halle, 28–9 Aug. 1528), German painter, the greatest of Germany's artists with the exception of Dürer. He was called Grünewald by his posthumous biographer, Joachim Sandrart, but his real name was Matthias Neithardt, though he himself substituted that of Gothardt, *c.* 1516, his (rare) signature having the initials M.N., M.G. or M.G.N. To his contemporaries he was 'Matthis of Aschaffenburg'. He was trained in the style of Martin Schongauer (q.v.) (though unlike the latter he produced no engravings), and is first mentioned, 1501, in the archives of Seligenstadt. From 1508 to 1514 he was painter to the Archbishop of Mainz at Aschaffenburg and after 1514 to the Elector of Mainz, Albrecht von Brandenburg. His master work, the altar-piece for Isenheim in Alsace, was painted 1513–15. His later years were occupied by a series of paintings ordered by the Elector of Mainz for the cathedral of Halle (where Grünewald also had the function of hydraulic engineer). Apart from the Isenheim altar his remaining work is fragmentary: the 'Christ Mocked' (Munich); a Crucifixion

[329]

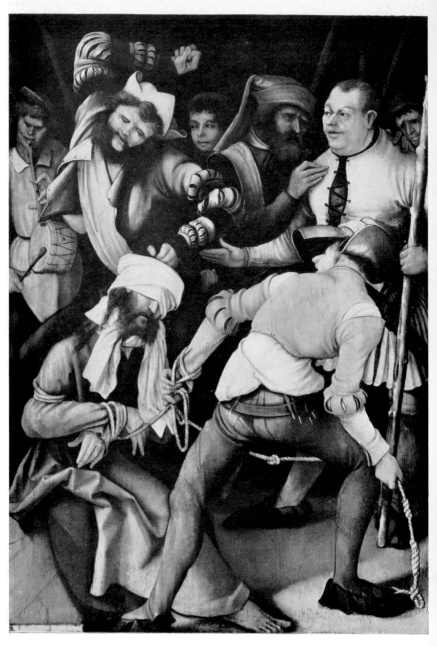

M. GRÜNEWALD—Christ Mocked—Pinakothek, Munich.

F. GUARDI—Fantastic Scene—Bergamo.

F. GUARDI—The Rialto—Wallace Collection.

M. GRÜNEWALD—The Isenheim Altar—Colmar, Unterlinden Monastery Museum.

(Basel); parts of altar-pieces at Stuppach (church), Freiburg-Breis-
gau, Karlsruhe and Aschaffenburg; a fine late work (part of the Halle
commission) being the 'Meeting of St Erasmus and St Maurice'
(Munich). The Isenheim altar-piece, now at the Unterlinden Monastery, Colmar, has, however, its whole majestic sequence of paintings
comprising the Crucifixion of the closed shutters, the Mourning of the
predella, the Nativity and Concert of Angels, the Annunciation and
Resurrection; when fully opened showing St Anthony and scenes of
his temptation and his visit to St Paul in the desert. This complex
work might be compared to a great organ composition ranging from
most exalted passages to profundities in the expression of suffering
and wild bursts of fantastic invention. It adds a new emotional range
to the Old-German art to which it may still be said to belong. Unlike
his contemporary, Dürer, he was untouched by the spirit of the
Renaissance, yet he seems in his own way to open up to art prospects
hitherto unknown in the intensity of tragedy and pathos he achieves.

Guardi, Francesco (*b.* Venice, 5 Oct. 1712; *d.* there, 1 Jan. 1793),
Italian painter, son of a minor Venetian artist, Domenico Guardi. He
began as a figure painter, collaborating with his brother Gian Antonio, but in middle age, i.e. from about 1760, devoted himself to
views of Venice, being influenced by the example of Canaletto and
the demand of visitors for paintings of the city. A figure of 'Hope',
1747 (Sarasota, Ringling Museum), and five large canvases (based on

[332]

illustrations by Piazzetta to Tasso), discovered in Ireland in 1959 and
identified as his, show his decorative skill in rococo figure painting, in
which, however, he does not challenge comparison with his brother-
in-law, Tiepolo (q.v.). His views of Venice and the islands of the
lagoon are his main product. His output was large and he seems to
have been assisted by his son Giacomo (1764–1835), who produced
gouache views in a style of his own. Guardi painted not only famous
buildings and splendid occasions like Canaletto but insular byways
and architectural caprices with ruins, with a sparkling touch and a
sense of atmosphere that might be called Impressionist.

Guercino, Il ('squint-eyed'), nickname of Giovanni Francesco Barbieri (*b.* Cento, Ferrara, *c.* 1591; *d.* Bologna, 22 Nov. 1666), Italian
painter, one of the leading baroque masters. He first studied at Cento
and worked in Rome, Venice and Bologna, forming a powerful style
by study successively of the Carracci, Caravaggio and Guido Reni.
His work in Rome, 1621–2, when he was employed by Pope Gregory
XV, included his 'Petronilla', which was placed in the Capitol, and
his ceiling decoration 'Aurora' for the Casino Ludovisi, which rivals
Guido Reni's famous version of the same subject. From 1623 to 1642
he worked at Cento, then removed to Bologna, where, following Reni,
he produced many vapid religious paintings which show a decline
from his early work. He was a prolific and able draughtsman and his
drawings were highly prized in eighteenth-century England, many
fine examples being among the 600 in the Royal Collection at Windsor
Castle.

'Guernica', painting
by Picasso, made in
1937 after the Basque
town of Guernica was
reported destroyed by
German bombers flying
for General Franco in
the Spanish Civil War.
Carried out entirely in
black, white and grey,
this huge canvas, 11
feet 6 inches by 25 feet
8 inches, expresses an
overwhelming anguish
and horror, though not
all details of its bullfight
symbolism are clear. It

GUERCINO—The Libyan
Sybil—Royal Collection,
Windsor Castle.

[333]

PABLO PICASSO—Guernica—Museum of Modern Art, New York.

was exhibited in the Spanish building of the Paris World's Fair, 1937, and is now in the Museum of Modern Art, New York.

Guggenheim Museum, New York, art collection of the Guggenheim Foundation established in 1937 by the University of the State of New York and endowed by Solomon R. Guggenheim. Primarily formed to illustrate the progress of non-figurative art, represented for example by Kandinsky, Delaunay and Mondrian, it now constitutes an outstanding collection of modern art from Cézanne and Seurat to Jackson Pollock and Riopelle. It is now housed in a cylindrical gallery with a spiral ramp, designed on original lines by Frank Lloyd Wright.

Guido da Siena (13th century), Italian painter who worked in the Byzantine style, a forerunner of Duccio and the Sienese School, though dates are uncertain. The date 1221 appears on a Madonna signed by him in the Palazzo Pubblico, Siena. Some authorities, however, on stylistic grounds and by comparison with other paintings at Siena attributed to him, assign it to *c.* 1270.

Guilds. The associations for mutual aid and the maintenance of standards in various trades and crafts which grew up in the Middle Ages included guilds of painters or guilds to which painters belonged. They mark the change from monastic craftsmanship to that of lay and urban communities first observable in the twelfth and thirteenth centuries in France, the Netherlands and Italy. Siena had its guild of painters in 1335, Ghent about the same time. Painters in Florence belonged to the Doctors' and Apothecaries' Guild (which Giotto, for instance, duly entered), but elsewhere the guilds were trade unions of artists alone. They maintained an apprenticeship system, and determined the admission of a painter as a master, one capable of employing pupils and assistants, his 'masterpiece' being the work which secured him this right and the full privileges of the guild. Guild records are of value in tracing the career of many artists. Guilds flourished especially in the cities of the Netherlands, north and south, and remained strong until the seventeenth century. They declined as

C. GUYS—Rue de la Lune
(Ink and Colour)—Photo:
Marlborough Fine Art.

the painter acquired a
prestige, a status and
an individualistic out-
look which increasingly
separated him from the
craftsman pure and
simple. The rise of
academies is a symptom
of this change.

Guttuso, Renato (*b.*
Bagheria, Palermo, 1912),
Italian painter whose
work contains social
comment and is Expres-
sionist in style. In the
Second World War he
took part in the resist-
ance to the German
occupation of Rome and
published a book of anti-Nazi drawings, *Gott mit uns*. He works
in Rome.

Guys, Constantin (*b.* Vlissingen, 3 Dec. 1802; *d.* Paris, 13 Mar.
1892), French draughtsman, famous for his brilliant studies of life in
the Victorian and Second Empire period. Details of his career are
scanty, but at the time of Queen Victoria's accession he was French
tutor in the family of Dr T. C. Girtin (son of Thomas Girtin), when it
was remarked he was constantly drawing. He became a reporter-
illustrator for the *Illustrated London News*, in which his drawings of
the Crimean War were engraved. London was his headquarters until
the 1860's, but afterwards he worked in Paris. He depicted bourgeois
society and the *demi-monde*, military occasions, horses and carriages
and women of various degree in pen and wash drawings and water-
colours of remarkable character. Baudelaire's magnificent study of
his art, *Le Peintre de la Vie Moderne*, if irrelevantly literary in some
respects, justly called attention to his genius.

[335]

H

Hals, Dirck (*b.* Haarlem, baptized 19 Mar. 1591; *d.* there, buried 17 May 1656), Dutch *genre* painter, the brother of Frans Hals and the pupil of Abraham Bloemaert (qq.v.). He was among the first to develop the 'conversation piece', painting cavaliers and ladies either indoors or taking part in *fêtes champêtres*, his brother's feeling for gaiety appearing in these conversation pieces in another form.

Hals, Frans (*b.* Antwerp, 1580–1; *d.* Haarlem, 29 Aug. 1666), painter of the Dutch School, though born at Antwerp of Flemish parents. He settled in Haarlem, where his brother Dirck was born, being trained in the studio of the painter and biographer of art, Karel van Mander, and became, next to Rembrandt, the greatest of the Dutch portrait painters, developing a broad and fluent method of painting, disciplined by great economy of colour, with which he inimitably rendered liveliness of expression. A famous example is the 'Laughing Cavalier' (Wallace Collection) (q.v.), though this shows capacity for laughter rather than open merriment. His work comprises the group portraiture of the Military Guilds, composed with remarkable skill to provide variety of interest while paying equal attention to each person represented; individual commissioned portraits; and the studies of common and Bohemian types which appealed to him ('La Bohémienne'—Louvre, 'Hille Bobbe'—Berlin). Late works in which he was most penetrating and nearest to Rembrandt were the groups of 1664 depicting the regents, male and female, of the Old Peoples' Almshouse. He and his wife in old age were inmates of the almshouse which is now the Frans Hals Museum, contains his great groups and is mainly a memorial to him, though including other works by Haarlem artists. His seven sons were all minor painters. *See* 'LAUGHING CAVALIER'.

Hampton Court Gallery. The remarkable collection of pictures in the famous palace (which dates from 1514) contains works from Charles I's and later royal collections, notable among them Mantegna's nine cartoons of the 'Triumph of Julius Caesar', Lely's 'Windsor Beauties' (ladies of Charles II's court) and Kneller's 'Hampton Court Beauties' (ladies of William and Mary's court).

Harnett, William Michael (*b.* Ireland, 1848; *d.* 1892), American still-life painter. He was brought from Ireland to Philadelphia as a child and studied art at the Pennsylvania Academy of Fine Arts and in New York, where he eventually settled after some years in Europe. His still lifes were skilful examples of *trompe l'œil* illusionism, depicting books, papers, musical instruments, etc., extremely popular in his

FRANS HALS—The Repast of the Officers of the St Jorisdoelen—Frans Hals Museum, Haarlem.

FRANS HALS—The Lady Governors of the Old Men's Home, Haarlem—Frans Hals Museum, Haarlem.

own day and revived in popularity at the present time with the vogue for some kind of 'magic realism'.

Harpignies, Henri (*b.* Valenciennes, 28 July 1819; *d.* St Privé (Yonne), 28 Aug. 1916), French landscape painter. A follower of Corot and the Barbizon School (qq.v.), he travelled widely in France, his best-known oil-paintings being those of the valley of the Loire. He painted also in water-colour in an English style.

Hartley, Marsden (*b.* Lewiston, Maine, 1877; *d.* 1943), American Expressionist painter, who studied in Cleveland and New York, painted in Maine and from 1912 spent much time in Europe. He was influenced both by Cézanne and the 'Blaue Reiter' group (q.v.) of Munich, making various abstract experiments, though his later paintings of landscape, figures and exterior still life in Maine, e.g. his 'Log Jam' (Detroit), are considered his best.

Hartung, Hans (*b.* Leipzig, 1904), German-born abstract painter. Brought up on German Impressionism and Expressionism, he turned to non-figurative painting by 1922. It earned him Nazi disfavour and he fled to France, serving in the Foreign Legion during the Second World War and becoming a French citizen in 1942. Typical of his work are free improvisations in monochrome.

Hassam, Childe (*b.* Dorchester, Massachusetts, 17 Oct. 1859; *d.* New York, 27 Aug. 1935), American painter and graphic artist. He studied in Boston and Paris, where he was influenced by Impressionism. Returning to New York, he was a pioneer in depicting its street life in a fresh, Impressionist fashion, though he also painted some New England landscapes. He produced also a large number of etchings and lithographs.

Hatching, lines parallel or crossed ('cross-hatching') by which a draughtsman or engraver gives a linear equivalent of tone or shadow. It is also found in the form of brushwork in tempera painting and fresco, being used to convey a depth or gradation of tone otherwise difficult to obtain in these media.

'Hay-wain, The', painting by Constable of East Anglian landscape, the building in it being Willy Lott's house near Flatford Mill,

[338]

M. HARTLEY—Log Jam, Penobscott Bay—Detroit Institute of Arts.

B. R. HAYDON—Punch or Mayday—Tate Gallery.

which appears in other works by him. It is signed 'John Constable pinx. London, 1821' and was exhibited in the Academy of 1821 and at the Paris Salon of 1824, where its freshness and luminosity made a great impression. Delacroix is said to have extensively repainted his 'Massacre of Scio' after seeing it. A full-sized sketch for the picture (which was acquired by the National Gallery in 1886) is in the Victoria and Albert Museum and shows an even greater sense of atmosphere and technical freedom. (Colour, *see* list.)

Haydon, Benjamin Robert (*b.* Plymouth, 26 Jan. 1786; *d.* London, 22 June 1846), English subject painter, trained in the Royal Academy Schools under Fuseli. He aspired to excel in 'High Art' and painted huge biblical and classical compositions. Pinning great hopes to his cartoons for paintings in the new Houses of Parliament, he was bitterly disappointed in their being passed over and in other unsuccessful projects. A lifelong struggle with debt and misfortunes real, exaggerated or imagined ended in his taking his own life. Haydon's real talent can be seen ironically enough not in his grandiose style but in two admirable *genre* pictures, 'Punch or Mayday' and 'Chairing the Member', now in the Tate Gallery. He was an impassioned advocate for the purchase of the Elgin Marbles by the nation, but his chief title to posterity's regard is perhaps the vividly written *Autobiography and Journals*.

Hayman, Francis (*b.* Exeter, 1708; *d.* London, 2 Feb. 1776), English painter, perhaps best known as decorator of Vauxhall Gardens. He also designed book illustrations and painted portraits

and small portrait groups with which the youthful work of Gainsborough shows some affinity, though the tradition that Gainsborough was his pupil seems without support. He was a friend of Hogarth, whom he accompanied on the visit to France that incited 'Calais Gate', a founder member of the Royal Academy and its first librarian.

F. HAYMAN—Self-portrait—Royal Albert Memorial Museum, Exeter.

W. C. HEDA—A Study of Still Life—National Gallery.

Heckel, Erich (*b.* Döbeln, 31 July 1883), German Expressionist painter and engraver, associated with Schmidt-Rottluff and Kirchner (qq.v.) in founding the 'Die Brücke' group, 1905 (q.v.). He studied architecture in Dresden, saw active service, 1915–18, and afterwards worked in Berlin. In 1949 he was appointed to the Academy of Karlsruhe. To the forceful colour and angular forms of Expressionism (q.v.) he adds a feeling for German Gothic art.

Heda, Willem Claesz (*b.* Haarlem, 1594; *d. c.* 1680), one of the leading Dutch still-life painters, who depicted with great skill such objects as pewter tankards, clay pipes and wineglasses, set usually against a neutral background. He trained his son, Gerrit Willemsz Heda (*c.* 1620–?1670) in the same branch of art.

Heem, Jan Davidz de (*b.* Utrecht, 1606; *d.* Antwerp, 1683–4), Dutch painter of still life, the son and pupil of David de Heem (*c.* 1570–1632), whom he surpassed in this branch of art. He worked at Leyden, 1628–32, Utrecht, 1632–5 and again 1667–72, and finally at Antwerp. Dutch interest in floriculture contributed to the great demand for his paintings of vases of flowers executed with polished skill. He is well represented in German and Dutch galleries, the Louvre and the Wallace Collection. His son Cornelis (1631–95) was also a painter.

Heemskerk, Maerten Jacobsz van (often called **Maerten van Veen**)

[341]

J. D. DE HEEM—Fruit and Flowers—National Gallery.

M. J. VAN HEEMSKERK—Self-portrait with the Colosseum—Fitzwilliam Museum, Cambridge.

(*b.* Heemskerk, 1498; *d.* 1574), Dutch painter who studied in Haarlem with Cornelisz Willemz and Jan Scorel (q.v.). In his early work he imitated Mabuse and imbibed Italian influence both indirectly and by study of the masters on his visits to Rome, 1532–5. A self-portrait with the Colosseum as background is in the Fitzwilliam Museum, Cambridge; other works are a 'Crucifixion' (Ghent), 'Judgment of Momus' (Berlin), 'Triumph of Silenus' (Vienna) and 'St Luke painting the likeness of the Virgin and Child' (Haarlem).

Hellenic, Hellenistic, terms descriptive of the culture of ancient Greece but in two separate aspects. 'Hellenic' comprises the development from archaic to classical Greek art, i.e. from *c.* eighth century B.C. to the end of the fourth century B.C. 'Hellenistic' (Gk *hellēnizein,* to speak the language of the Greeks) is now commonly used of Greek culture from the period of Alexander's conquests to the final passing of the ancient world. As applied to art it refers not only to the greater naturalism and emotional effects sought in sculpture of the post-classical age but in general to the spread of Greek influence in the Mediterranean countries and eastwards. Thus hellenized districts of Egypt show this influence in the naturalistic portraits that replaced the conventional painted head on mummy cases and are alternatively described as 'Greco-Roman'.

[343]

B. VAN DE HELST—Banquet of the Civic Guard, 18 June 1648—Rijksmuseum, Amsterdam.

Helst, Bartholomeus van der (*b.* Haarlem, 1613; *d.* Amsterdam, buried 16 Dec. 1670), Dutch portrait painter, pupil of Nicolaes Elias at Amsterdam and one of the founders of the Amsterdam Painters' Guild. Though he does not rank with Rembrandt and Hals in portraiture, his smoothly painted, well-composed works had great success in his time, most notable being the large group 'Banquet of the Burgher Guard', 1648 (Rijksmuseum), with its twenty-four full-length figures.

Hermitage, Leningrad, founded by Catherine the Great, the principal Russian collection of European paintings, in which Rembrandt is splendidly represented. Part of the collection of the Moscow Museum of Modern Western Art is now included in this museum.

Herrera, de, Spanish painters, father and son. **Francisco the Elder (El Viejo)** (*b.* Seville, 1576; *d.* Madrid, 1656) was a painter of frescoes and history pictures, etcher and medallist. He worked in a coarse and forcible style of which some trace may be discovered in the early 'kitchen pictures' of Velazquez, whose first master he was. He was a man of such difficult temper, however, that neither his children nor his pupils would stay with him. His enemies accused him of coining false money and he took refuge in the Jesuits' College at Seville, where he painted the 'St Hermengild in Glory' which won him the pardon of Philip IV. **Francisco the Younger (El Mozo)** (*b.* Seville, 1622; *d.* Madrid, 25 Aug. 1685) was the second son and pupil of his father but fled to Rome to escape his cruelty. He became celebrated for his pictures of still life, flowers, fruit and fish. He also painted frescoes and, in later life, portraits. He became subdirector of the academy at Seville under Murillo in 1660. His painting of St Francis is in Seville Cathedral, and his 'Assumption of the Virgin' in the Atocha church in Madrid won him appointment as painter to the king.

Heyden, Jan van der (*b.* Gorkum, 1637; *d.* Amsterdam, 28 Sept. 1712), Dutch painter who worked mainly at Amsterdam. The designer of a fire-engine and a system of street lighting, he is noted as

J. VAN DER HEYDEN—The Approach to the Town of Veere—Reproduced by Gracious Permission of Her Majesty the Queen, Buckingham Palace.

an artist for his town views in Holland and Germany (e.g. his 'Street in Cologne'—National Gallery) and in particular for his rendering of the picturesque gables and canals of Amsterdam.

Hicks, Edward (b. Bucks County, Pennsylvania, 1780; d. 1849), the most famous of American folk artists of the early nineteenth century, a sign and carriage painter and also a travelling Quaker preacher. His favourite subject, of which he made many delightful variations, was 'The Peaceable Kingdom', derived from the eleventh chapter of the Book of Isaiah, in which, as the prophet foretold, wolf, leopard, lion, calf, lamb, kid, cow and bear dwell peaceably together. Many of his paintings were signs for the inns of his native Bucks county, taken from prints of such subjects as 'Washington on Horseback', 'The Declaration of Independence' and 'William Penn's Treaty with the Indians', the last-named scene constantly appearing in the background of 'The Peaceable Kingdom'.

Highmore, Joseph (b. London, 1692; d. 1780), English portrait painter, a pupil of Kneller and a nephew of Thomas Highmore (d. 1720), who was serjeant painter to William III. Good examples of his work are his portrait of Samuel Richardson (National Portrait

[345]

J. HIGHMORE—Illustration to 'Pamela'—Mr B. finds Pamela writing—Tate Gallery.

Gallery) and the series of illustrative 'conversation pieces' suggested by Richardson's *Pamela* (now divided equally between the Tate Gallery, the National Gallery of Victoria and the Fitzwilliam Museum), which have delicacy and charm.

'Hilanderas, Las', 'The Tapestry Weavers', late masterpiece of Velazquez, painted about 1656 and in the Prado, Madrid. It is a view of the interior of the state tapestry works, full of light and movement, in which the artist contrasts the peasant spinners of the foreground with the aristocratic visitors and luxurious tapestry to the rear. The tapestry shown represents Titian's 'Rape of Europa' (which was in the Spanish Royal Collection) and its inclusion was no doubt a sign of Velazquez's homage to the Venetian master.

Hilliard (Hillyarde), Nicholas (*b.* Exeter, *c.* 1547, *d.* London, Jan. 1619), English master of the miniature portrait, the son of a goldsmith, trained as goldsmith and 'limner'. Settling in London he became a favourite artist of Queen Elizabeth I and her court, painting with exquisite skill, somewhat influenced by Holbein but distinctly Elizabethan in poetic feeling. His pupils and followers in the art of miniature were his son Lawrence (1581/2–1640+) and the French

[346]

N. HILLIARD—Portrait of a Young Man (Miniature)
—Victoria and Albert Museum.

Huguenot Isaac Oliver (Ollivier) (*d.* 1617). Hilliard wrote an informative *Treatise concerning the Art of Limning*, *c.* 1600. A number of his small masterpieces, including portraits of the Queen, are now in the Victoria and Albert Museum.

Hiroshige (Ando Tokitaro) (1797–1858), Japanese artist, one of the chief members of the Ukiyo-e or popular school of Japan, especially

VELAZQUEZ—Las Hilanderas—Prado.

HIROSHIGE—Boats returning to Yabase (Colour Print)—Victoria and Albert Museum.

occupied in making colour prints. Hiroshige and his pupils (two of whom adopted his professional name) applied the process of colour block printing for landscapes with a skill and harmony of effect only equalled in Japan by Hokusai (q.v.). Most of his subjects were taken from the vicinity of Yedo or were scenes on the old highway between Tokaido and Kyoto. He produced also some bird and flower prints. He was an influence on nineteenth-century art in Europe and Whistler was evidently influenced in his Thames nocturnes by Hiroshige's style of design.

History Painting, now an archaic term, referring to the ideal presentation of incidents taken from biblical or classical history or classical mythology, as exemplified in the work of the Renaissance masters and of later artists seeking to emulate them. The definition clearly distinguishes it from the painting of historical subjects as introduced by West and Copley. In this the particular detail, of portraiture, accurate costume and accessories and surroundings, is opposed to the generalized conception which belongs to 'history painting' proper or in the earlier sense of the term.

Hobbema, Meindert (b. Amsterdam, 1638; d. there, 7 Dec. 1709), Dutch landscape painter, presumed the pupil of Jacob van Ruisdael (q.v.), with whose work Hobbema's has several points of relation, though he did not possess Ruisdael's range. He was the outstanding

M. HOBBEMA—The Avenue, Middelharnis—National Gallery.

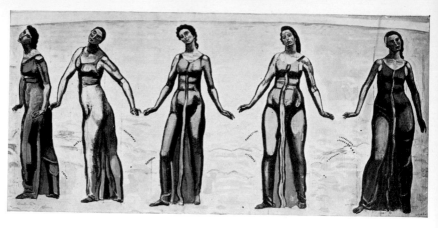

F. HODLER—Towards the Infinite, Kunsthaus, Zürich.

interpreter of the Dutch rural picturesque in the second half of the seventeenth century, painting woods, water-mills, winding tracks, streams and cottages with delightful sympathy. There is much that is obscure about his career and the chronology of his work. He obtained a post in the Excise at the age of thirty and it has been assumed that he then gave up painting, with the superb exception of his masterpiece, 'The Avenue, Middelharnis' (National Gallery), signed and dated 1689. If, with this one exception, he did not paint during forty years of his life, it cannot have been because of the security given by his post, since he died in poverty and was buried in the pauper section of an Amsterdam cemetery. His works are now widely distributed in the world's galleries, the nine paintings in the National Gallery reflecting the admiration which English connoisseurs had for his work in the eighteenth and nineteenth centuries, while his influence on English landscape is exemplified in Crome's reputed dying words: 'Hobbema, Hobbema, how I have loved you.'

Hodler, Ferdinand (*b.* Bern, 1853; *d.* Geneva, 1918), Swiss painter who studied art at Geneva with Barthélémy Menn and by copying old masters. He competed successfully for the decoration of the national museum at Zürich. Beginning as portrait and landscape painter he turned to historical themes and finally evolved a decorative and symbolic style, as in his 'Towards the Infinite', which made a great impression in his lifetime and caused him to be regarded as the most distinguished of the purely Swiss school. There was a strong element of 'art nouveau' (q.v.) or 'Jugendstil' in his work.

Hofer, Karl (*b.* Karlsruhe, 11 Oct. 1878; *d.* Berlin, 3 April 1955), German painter, a pupil of Hans Thoma (q.v.). In figure compositions, landscape and still life he combined simplicity of form and charm of colour with a desire to add an emotional content that may be called Expressionist (*see* EXPRESSIONISM). He was appointed head of the Hochschule für Bildenden Künste, Berlin, in 1945.

W. HOGARTH—Lord George Graham in his Cabin—National Maritime Museum, Greenwich.

Hogarth, William (*b*. London, 10 Dec. 1697; *d*. there, 26 Oct. 1764), English portrait and subject painter and one of the greatest personalities in British art, the son of a poor schoolmaster from Westmorland. He was apprenticed as a boy to the silver-plate engraver Ellis Gamble, and first became known as an engraver by his plates for Butler's *Hudibras*. He then turned to painting, which he seems to have studied under Sir James Thornhill at the academy in St Martin's Lane (making a runaway marriage, 1729, with Thornhill's daughter). His early paintings were small family groups or 'conversation pieces', e.g. the 'Wanstead Assembly' and the 'Fountaine Family' (Philadelphia). A stepping-stone between these and his famous pictures of the social scene was his rendering of the 'Beggar's Opera', *c*. 1730, of which three versions exist (showing both actors and distinguished spectators on the stage). He then turned to the larger stage of London life in the series 'A Harlot's Progress', 1731, painted and engraved, though the paintings no longer exist. In engraving the series won immediate popularity. There is subsequently no consecutive pattern in his work. 'A Rake's Progress', 1735 (Soane Museum), was followed by an attempt at the 'great style of history painting', the biblical compositions (coolly received) for St Bartholomew's Hospital, and thereafter by individual subjects of social or satirical import, painted

W. HOGARTH—The Graham Children—Tate Gallery.

or engraved or both; portraits; further series, 'Marriage à la Mode' and 'The Election' (Soane Museum) being the most outstanding; and a final attempt, 1759, to outdo Correggio in the 'Sigismonda Mourning over the Heart of Guiscardo' (Tate Gallery), much derided at the time and since and somewhat unfairly. His genius was at its height in the 1740's, with the best of the story series, the 'Marriage à la Mode', 1744 (Tate), the 'March of the Guards towards Scotland', 1746 (Foundling Hospital), and his 'O the Roast Beef of Old England' ('Calais Gate'), 1748 (National Gallery). Though he inveighed against 'phizmongering' he produced one of the world's masterpieces in his oil sketch, the 'Shrimp Girl' (National Gallery), and one of the best studies of English types in his 'Heads of his Servants' (National Gallery). Hogarth has been misrepresented in various ways. He was not an enemy of the old masters but of darkened varnish and of affected connoisseurs who depreciated native talent and over-praised foreign mediocrities (a habit still prevalent). His handling of paint seems to show an intelligent study of eighteenth-century French art. The moralizing for which he is often aesthetically blamed

was a simple device enabling him to give a wonderfully comprehensive picture of an age. 'Gin Lane', for instance, is a masterpiece
of graphic art apart from its 'lesson'. In 1751 he retired to his house
at Chiswick (in Hogarth Lane, now a museum), producing in 1753 his
Analysis of Beauty with its exposition of the value of the double
curve ('line of beauty') and serpentine spiral ('line of grace'),
traceable as rococo devices of composition in his own work. He was
given a minor official status by George III in 1757 but his later years
after 'Sigismonda' were unproductive and he was drawn into the
follies of controversy against Wilkes and Charles Churchill. He
left no school yet in many ways is supremely representative of his
country.

    Hokusai, Katsuhika (Nakajima Tet-Sujiro) (1760–1849), Japanese
painter and graphic artist, born in Tokyo of an artisan family. He
practised early as a wood-engraver and studied with a well-known
painter and designer of colour prints, Shunshó, but after quitting his
studio worked for a long time in poverty. He was a prolific book
illustrator and the leading representative of the Ukiyo-e or popular
school, being equally noted for his intensely vivid drawings and for
his colour prints. He added art teaching and designing to his many
labours. His works include the *Mangwa* or *Ten Thousand Sketches*, a
pictorial encyclopaedia of all aspects of Japanese life in fifteen
volumes, the *Hundred Views of Mount Fuji* (1835, three volumes,
monochrome) and the famous *Thirty-Six Views of Fujiyama* in
colour prints of striking design and novel combinations of colour. A

HOKUSAI—The Hollow of the Deep-Sea Wave off Kanagawa—British Museum.

famous colour print is his 'The Wave', Like Hiroshige (q.v.) he influenced European artists in the nineteenth century by his prints, and in the European view he is one of the world's greatest artists.

Holbein the Elder, Hans (*b.* Augsburg, *c.* 1465; *d.* Isenheim, 1524), German painter mainly of religious works, belonging to the school of van der Weyden and Memlinc in his early paintings but showing Renaissance influence in such a work as the 'Basilica of St Paul', 1502 (Augsburg). His principal painting is the altar-piece, 'St Sebastian', 1515–17 (Munich). Financial failure ended his career as artist at Augsburg and ill success then seems to have pursued him at Isenheim and elsewhere. He had a strong sense of character in portrait drawings, as in the sketch-books preserved at Berlin, which reappears in his great son, Hans Holbein the Younger.

Holbein the Younger, Hans (*b.* Augsburg, 1497; *d.* London, 29 Nov. 1543), German painter and designer. He was trained by his father and Hans Burgkmair (q.v.) and worked in the family studio as a boy, together with his brother Ambrosius. In 1515 he went to Basel with Ambrosius (a painter of promise who died prematurely in 1519) and for some years found constant employment in the prosperous German-Swiss city (the centre of Humanism), of which he became a naturalized Swiss citizen in 1520. Working for the printer-publishers, Amerbach and Froben, he showed himself a remarkable designer for books. His illustrations for Erasmus's *Praise of Folly* were as popular as the book itself. Later he designed a title-page for More's *Utopia* as well as for Luther's German translation of the New Testament, while the

HANS HOLBEIN (The Younger)—Portrait of a Lady — Reproduced by Gracious Permission of Her Majesty the Queen, Windsor.

HANS HOLBEIN (The Younger)—The Ambassadors—National Gallery.

'Dance of Death' series, in the woodcuts made from his designs by Hans Lutzelberger, ranks with Dürer's 'Apocalypse' as one of the masterpieces of European graphic art. He made numerous designs for goldsmith's work and stained glass, was much occupied with mural decoration (a celebrated 'Peasants' Dance' for a house in Basel and paintings for the Rathaus) and also executed some religious works (the 'Dead Christ', 1521—Basel; the 'Madonna', 1522—Solothurn), though his mastery of portraiture was already most in evidence. It appears in his portraits of Burgomaster Meyer and his wife, 1516, and Bonifazius Amerbach, 1519 (Basel), while the 'Madonna of the Burgomaster Meyer' (Darmstadt) is in effect a magnificent portrait group. Erasmus lives in the portraits of 1523 (Louvre; Longford Castle), which have the essence of the humanistic spirit. Holbein had a passing contact with Italy in a journey to Milan, 1518, and with

HANS HOLBEIN (The Younger)—Portrait of Anne of Cleves—Louvre.

France, 1524, when he visited Bourges and may have seen works by
Jean Clouet (at this time he adopted a method of chalk drawing com-
parable with that of the French portraitist), but a cardinal event was
his introduction to Sir Thomas More in England, 1526, on the
recommendation of Erasmus. He stayed until 1528, painting the
More family (an informal group of which copies and an original
drawing exist); portraits of Warham, Archbishop of Canterbury, and
Bishop Fisher; and making a superb series of portrait drawings
(Windsor). He then returned to Basel to finish his work at the
Rathaus, painting also a portrait of his wife and children in which one
may perhaps discern her anxiety at their separation and the strain of
the religious strife and disturbances from which Basel was suffering.
From 1532 London was definitely his headquarters. He painted the
German merchants of the steelyard, e.g. Jörg Gyze (Berlin), the
famous portrait of 'The (French) Ambassadors' (National Gallery),
1533, remarkable in technical skill and curious detail though not his
greatest triumph, and in 1536 became court painter to Henry VIII.
The dynastic group for the Privy Chamber at Whitehall, including
Henry VII, Henry VIII, Jane Seymour and Elizabeth of York, was
destroyed by fire in 1698, but in other works Holbein has left an
imperishable record of the Tudors. Of his numerous portrayals of
Henry VIII an authentic example is in the Thyssen Collection. He
was compelled to paint elaborate details of court dress but his later
work is remarkable for an exquisite refinement of line and essential
simplicity of design, as in the portrait he was sent to make at Brussels
of the Duchess of Milan, 1537 (National Gallery), and that of Anne of
Cleves, 1539 (Louvre). His other work in England included ornamental design (e.g. the drawing for the 'Jane Seymour Cup'—
Bodleian Library) and miniatures, beautiful examples of which are in
the Victoria and Albert Museum. Holbein, though he may have
inspired the miniaturist Hilliard in some degree, stands alone in
the history of the English School and may be called a great inter-
nationalist of portraiture.

Homer, Winslow (*b.* Boston, 24 Feb. 1836; *d.* Prout's Neck,
Maine, 27 Sept. 1910), American painter in oils and water-colour who
excelled in distinctively American scenes of popular life and marine
and landscape subjects. He had his training as an illustrator and an
illustrative bias remains in his work as a painter. His first oils were
taken from the Civil War and from 1873 he painted in water-colour,
developing a sense of light and open air. After a visit to the North Sea
coast of England, 1881, he settled on the coast of Maine, painting the
fishing boats and incidents and hazards of seafaring life. Later he
explored the continent from the Canadian forests to the Caribbean.
'Country School', 1871 (St Louis), 'Fox Hunt', 1893 (Pennsylvania
Academy), and 'Gulf Stream', 1899 (New York, Metropolitan
Museum), represent the wide range of his art.

'Hommage à Delacroix', painting of great documentary interest by
Fantin-Latour (q.v.), signed and dated 1864 and now in the Louvre.
Grouped round a portrait of Delacroix, who had died in 1863, are

[357]

W. HOMER—Long Branch, New Jersey—Museum of Fine Arts, Boston.

painters, including Manet (standing at right), Bracquemond (to Manet's right), Whistler (leaning on his cane in the centre) and Legros (to Whistler's left). The writers, seated, are Champfleury (centre), Baudelaire (at right) and Duranty (left). Fantin-Latour portrays himself palette in hand.

Hondecoeter, Melchior d' (*b.* Utrecht, 1636; *d.* Amsterdam, 3 April 1695), Dutch painter and engraver, the pupil of his father, Gisbert Hondecoeter, and his maternal uncle Jan Weenix (q.v.), noted especially for his paintings of birds. He worked at The Hague, 1659–1663, and then at Amsterdam. His most famous picture is 'The Floating Feather' (Rijksmuseum).

Honthorst, Gerard van (*b.* Utrecht, 4 Nov. 1590; *d.* 27 April 1656), Dutch painter and engraver, a pupil of Abraham Bloemaert (q.v.) at Utrecht. He spent some years in Rome and was much influenced by the violent effects of light and shade of Caravaggio, though Honthorst, unlike Caravaggio, specifically represented candlelight, becoming known in Italy as 'Gerard of the Night' (Gherardo delle Notti). His patron in Rome was the Marchese Vincenzo Giustiniani, who owned a large picture collection (including works by Caravaggio), and for him Honthorst painted the impressive 'Christ before the High Priest' now in the National Gallery. He is noted not only for chiaroscuro but for bringing northwards the Italian style of illusionist wall painting, coming to London in 1628 to paint 'Apollo and Diana' for the Banqueting Hall, Whitehall (representing Charles I

G. VAN HONTHORST—The Nativity—Uffizi Gallery, Florence.

and Henrietta Maria seated on clouds 'receiving the Liberal Arts', and now at Hampton Court). He was later court painter at The Hague.

Hooch, Pieter de (*b.* nr Rotterdam, baptized 20 Dec. 1632; *d.* Amsterdam, *c.* 1683), Dutch painter who worked at Delft for the greater and more fruitful part of his career, being stimulated by the art of his great contemporary there, Vermeer. He is something more than a *genre* painter, for though his courtyards and interiors with their domestic figures and visitors give fascinating glimpses of everyday life, the beauty of these compositions primarily depends on the sense of space, the effect of light and exquisitely calculated arrangement, as e.g. in the 'Courtyard of a Dutch House' (National Gallery) and the 'Boy bringing Pomegranates' (Wallace Collection). An unfortunate change came over his work after 1657 and his move to Amsterdam, when his efforts to depict fashionable society in luxurious surroundings retained little trace of his earlier quality; but at his best he comes near to Vermeer.

Hoogstraten, Samuel van (*b.* Dordrecht, 2 Aug. 1627; *d.* there, 19 Oct. 1678), Dutch painter, a pupil of Rembrandt at Amsterdam. He painted portraits, biblical compositions and interiors and experimented with perspective in *trompe l'œil* illusion, characteristic of which are peep-show boxes in various collections (National Gallery, The Hague,

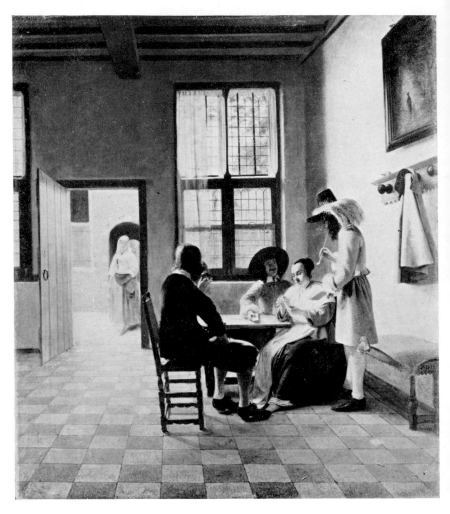

P. DE HOOCH—The Card Players—Reproduced by Gracious Permission of Her Majesty the Queen.

J. HOPPNER—Portrait of Mrs Williams—Tate Gallery.

Detroit). He also wrote, 1678, a work on painting, discussing Rembrandt's art and theory.

Hopper, Edward (*b.* Nyack, New York, 22 July 1882), American painter and etcher. He studied at the Chase School in New York and also in Paris, afterwards devoting himself to interpretations of the American city background painted with stark fidelity, as in his 'Early Sunday Morning', 1930 (New York, Whitney Museum of American Art).

Hoppner, John (*b.* Whitechapel, 4 April 1758; *d.* London, 23 Jan. 1810), portrait painter, born in England of German parentage. He studed at the Royal Academy Schools and became portrait painter to the Prince of Wales, 1789, R.A., 1795, and in popularity a rival to Lawrence (q.v.), though in quality and technique by no means of the same rank. His 'Mrs Williams' (Tate Gallery) shows him at his best.

Hsia Kuei (fl. early thirteenth century), Chinese painter, a native of Ch'ientang, Chekiang province, and contemporary of Ma Yuan (q.v.), with whom he ranks among the greatest of the Sung landscape painters. He was the court painter of the Emperor Ning Tsung, by whom he was held in great honour. He excelled in rendering mountains rising above mist and the varied aspects of the Yangtse river.

Huber, Wolf (*b.* Feldkirch, *c.* 1490; *d.* Passau, 3 June 1533), German painter and graphic artist mainly noted for his woodcuts, who shares with his contemporary Albrecht Altdorfer (q.v.) a principal place in the Danubian School. He worked at both of its headquarters, Ratisbon and Passau (where he was court painter to the Prince Bishops), and expresses its feeling for Romantic landscape. A fine series of his landscape drawings is in the British Museum.

Hudson, Thomas (*b.* Devon, 1701; *d.* London, 1779), English portrait painter, the son-in-law and pupil of Jonathan Richardson the elder, and, 1741–3, the master of Reynolds. Stiff and conventional

W. HUBER—Rocky Landscape with Bridge (Pen and Wash)—University College, London.

T. COLE—Sunny Morning on the Hudson River—Museum of Fine Arts, Boston.

in style, he was fashionable for a period. Handel was among his many sitters.

Hudson River School, American nineteenth-century painters of landscape who were mainly, though not exclusively, inspired by the mountain and river scenery of the Catskills and the Hudson. The Romantic love of wild nature in general, combined with the thrilling discovery of America's own natural wonders, inspired some of the most original paintings produced in America during the century. The most famous representative of the school was Thomas Cole (q.v.), who set up his studio at Catskill in 1826. To the same generation and direction of effort belong Thomas Doughty, Asher B. Durand, Samuel F. B. Morse, Alvin Fisher and Henry Inman. Painters of somewhat later date continue the history of the school to the end of the nineteenth century. Albert Bierstadt (q.v.) is notable among them, others being John W. Casilear, John F. Kensett, Worthington Whittredge, Jasper F. Cropsey and Frederick C. Church.

Hue, though often applied to any shade of colour, means, strictly speaking, the colour obtained by mixing a primary with a secondary colour.

Huet, Paul (*b.* Paris, 3 Oct. 1805; *d.* there, 9 Jan. 1869), French landscape painter, a pupil of Gros (q.v.). He was a friend of Delacroix and Bonington, an admirer of Constable (qq.v.) and one of the leaders in the direct approach to nature.

Hughes, Arthur (*b.* London, 27 Jan. 1832; *d.* there, 22 Dec. 1915), English painter and illustrator. He studied under Alfred Stevens and

W. HOLMAN HUNT—The Scapegoat—Lady Lever Art Gallery.

at the Royal Academy
Schools and was an
associate of the Pre-
Raphaelites, contribut-
ing to their Oxford Union
decorations in 1857 and
being of note for the
Pre-Raphaelite charm
of his ' April Love ', 1856
(Tate Gallery).

Huguet, Jaime (*c.*
1420–*c.* 1490), Spanish
painter of altar-pieces, a
leading artist of the
Catalan Gothic School.
Among his remaining
works are the retable of
Sts Abdon and Sennen,
1460 (church of San
Miguel de Terrasa); that of the Corporation of St Stephen, 1462 (part
of the predella, Museum of Barcelona); of St Augustine (six large
panels at Barcelona); and of the Constable de Porting (Santa Agueda,
Barcelona). The wealthy city guilds kept him busily employed on
these offerings to the Church and his altar-pieces were also exported
to Sardinia, then under Spanish dominion. He had a number of
collaborators, among whom the brothers Vergos were producers of
independent works. Huguet's richly patterned altar-pieces are
distinct in tranquil, poetic feeling.

Hunt, William Holman (*b.* London, 2 April 1827; *d.* there, 7 Sept.
1910), English painter of religious and literary subjects, trained at
the Royal Academy Schools. He met Millais and Rossetti and together with them was a founder of the Pre-Raphaelite Brotherhood,
remaining the most loyal adherent to its canon of 'truth to nature'
throughout his career. The success of his 'Light of the World'
(versions in Keble College and St Paul's Cathedral) induced him to
pay visits to Palestine in a search for circumstantial accuracy in his
religious works, with such remarkable results as the painting of the
Dead Sea in his 'The Scapegoat' of 1856 (Lady Lever Art Gallery).
His scrupulous detail can be well appreciated in this and the earlier
'A Hireling Shepherd', 1852 (Manchester). He received the Order of
Merit in 1905 and in that year published his *Pre-Raphaelitism and
the Pre-Raphaelite Brotherhood*, a personal view of the ideals and inner
history of the movement.

[364]

Huysum, Jan van (*b*. Amsterdam, 15 April 1682; *d*. there, 7 Feb. 1749), Dutch flower painter, the pupil of his father, Justus, also a flower painter. He worked throughout his life at Amsterdam and painted both in oil and water-colour, his oils being noted for their elaborate composition and lavishness of minute detail and gaining in colourful effect from the light background he usually favoured.

I

Icon, representation of Christ, an angel or a saint in the form of a panel painting as used in the Greek Orthodox Church, a development from Byzantine painting (q.v.). Parts of the painting are often covered with gold or silver plates. Russia was a great centre of their production (*see* RUSSIAN PAINTING).

Iconography, classification and description of the images and symbols of pictorial art associated with some particular subject. Thus Christian iconography includes an account of symbols such as the Lamb, Dove and Fish and their meaning. The word, however, may also refer to portraiture and to pictures and prints illustrating the appearance and career of some famous person, e.g. Napoleonic and Shakespearian iconography. Van Dyck's famous series of etched portraits of his contemporaries was grouped under the heading 'Iconography'.

Iconostasis (Gk literally 'image-stand'), in Byzantine architecture a screen separating the chancel from the nave of a church and serving as a stand on which religious paintings or icons were hung. In the Eastern Orthodox Church it is ornate, completely shutting off the sanctuary from the nave and hung profusely with rows of icons.

Ideal, Idealism, in pictorial art the conception that a beauty superior to that found in nature is the artist's true aim. This may be purely an exercise of the imagination. 'Phidias contemplated only that image [of Jupiter] which he had conceived in his mind from Homer's description' (Proclus, as quoted by Sir Joshua Reynolds). Or it may be, as Reynolds puts it in his *Discourses*, a correction of what is imperfect in nature, 'the idea of that central form from which every deviation is deformity'. To depict the perfect human figure is one resultant aim, and classical Greek sculpture has always been a model in this respect for those followers of the ideal who are called classicists (*see* CLASSICISM). An ideal landscape, however, is also conceivable, as in the work of Poussin (q.v.), or a type of pictorial composition perfect in dignity and harmony, as in the art of the High Renaissance. The 'grand style' (q.v.) analysed by Reynolds is the expression of Idealism. Art has pursued many different aims, no less valid, e.g. Realism (q.v.), but Idealism remains in modern art in the conception of an abstract beauty distinct from the representation of any organic and natural form.

Illumination of Manuscripts, art of embellishing manuscripts either by pictorial ornamentation or with decorated letters and designs in gold and colours, much practised in the Middle Ages and especially applied to devotional works. The materials used were the ancient

[366]

form of paper, papyrus; parchment (made from sheepskin); and vellum (made from calfskin). A form of body colour or *gouache* (q.v.) was usual, combined with a precious metal, gold or silver, the use of which, strictly speaking, constitutes 'illumination'. The art appears to have evolved from the classical methods of decorating or illustrating books of the second and third centuries A.D. with pictures either in outline or with gilt shading. It developed into the Byzantine art of adorning manuscripts of the Gospels with brilliantly painted ornamental designs, gilt or silver lettering and finely executed miniatures with gilt backgrounds; and the ornamentation of the Franco-Lombards of the so-called Carolingian school, the characteristics of which were a liberal use of gold and profusely embellished initial letters. The earliest extant example is said to be the fragmentary copy of the *Iliad* on vellum (Milan, Ambrosian Library, fifth century). Its sobriety of decoration is in striking contrast with the brilliant miniatures (a technical term from the Latin *miniare*, to colour with red ochre, meaning a picture in an illuminated manuscript and not a small portrait) of Byzantine art. Byzantine illumination extends from the age of Justinian (reigned 526–64) to the fall of Constantinople, A.D. 1453. It was marked by an oriental richness of colour and a conventional treatment of the figure, the tendency to rigid stylization being increased by the Iconoclastic period of the eighth century. The most brilliant period was that of the ninth century, when the patronage of art revived under Basil I. Examples of the early period are rare, but a fragment of the Eusebian canons (British Museum) is attributed to the age of Justinian and was probably of the kind that furnished a model for the early illuminators of France and Ireland. The ninth century shows some return to the spirit of ancient Greek art, e.g. in

[369]

JEAN TAVERNIER—
Philip the Good Kneeling
before the Enthroned Vir-
gin (Miniature from Jean
Mielot, 'Les Miracles de
Notre Dame')—Bodleian
Library, Oxford.

S. BENING—The Cruci-
fixion — Fitzwilliam
Museum, Cambridge.

THE MASTER OF MARY OF BURGUNDY—Sts Anthony and Paul in the Desert (Book of Hours, c. 1480)—Bodleian Library, Oxford.

the *Menologium* (a calendar and lives of the saints) in the Vatican Library and the beautiful Paris Psalter (Bibliothèque Nationale). An important independent development was that of Celtic illumination in the seventh to ninth centuries, notable for its interlaced ornament, deriving from pre-Christian Celtic art, and the decorative emphasis given to initial letters. Famous examples are the *Book of Kells* (Dublin, Trinity College Library) and the Lindisfarne Gospels (British Museum, Cotton Collection). The Franco-Lombard art combined the best elements of Celtic and Byzantine together with a lavish use of gold. Beautiful examples of Carolingian illumination are the Alcuin Bible (British Museum, *c.* 800), the Evangeliary of Lothair (Paris, Bibliothèque Nationale, *c.* 850) and the Golden Gospels of Charles the Bald (Munich, *c.* 850). Various monastic styles preceded the great transition at the end of the twelfth century to Gothic illumination and the golden age, the change being marked by the development of the decorative border and the use of large initials as a frame for picture or miniature, together with a new realism in pictorial treatment. England, France, Germany and the Netherlands give a wealth of examples from the thirteenth to fifteenth centuries, the manuscript painting providing a model for the painting as an independent work on a larger scale. Famous painters who were also miniaturists were the van Eycks and Gerard David in the Netherlands and Jean Fouquet in France. Famous examples of Gothic illumination are the fourteenth-century East Anglian Luttrell Psalter (British Museum),

[371]

J. FOUQUET—The Taking of Jericho (Miniature from Manuscript of Josephus, 'History of the Jews', 1470–5)—Bibliothèque Nationale, Paris.

THE BROTHERS DE LIMBOURG—Les Très Riches Heures du Duc de Berry (month of June, showing the Duke's palace and Ste Chapelle)—Musée Condé, Chantilly.

the fifteenth-century Bedford Book of Hours (British Museum) and 'Les Très Riches Heures du Duc de Berry' (Chantilly, Musée Condé, *c.* 1410), attributed to three brothers from Limbourg. A final richness of effect was achieved with the advent of the Renaissance and the return to classical modes of ornament and pictorial style, especially in Italy and France. As a form of painting on the book scale illumination for some time survived the invention of printing and continued in the sixteenth century, finally disappearing with the rise of printed illustration. An analogy with Gothic illumination may be found in oriental art. *See also* MINIATURE; PERSIAN PAINTING; INDIAN PAINTING.

Illusionism, aim of representing objects in such a way that they seem to exist as real objects in three dimensions. The baroque ceiling in which figures appear to detach themselves in space (like the sculpture with which they are often combined in effect) gives an example. The device is here theatrical and its value is to be considered in terms of 'theatre'. A more vulgar form of illusionism is the *trompe l'œil* picture of still life or small objects. *See* TROMPE L'ŒIL.

Illustration, form of art which is not completely self-explanatory or self-sufficient. Paintings are sometimes criticized as 'illustrative' when they rely too much on the spectator's presumed knowledge of some associated story or sequence of events. Illustration, however, in the modern sense may be defined as the pictorial presentation of an idea expounded in an accompanying text, and from this point of view what might be a defect in an independent painting becomes a virtue.

ORIENTAL MINIATURE PAINTING (Mughal, Akbar Period)—Hamsa's Son, Rustam, with his Mistress—Victoria and Albert Museum.

The earliest examples are to be found in block-prints, such as the *St Christopher*, 1423, which made their first appearance in Europe about the same time as the invention of printing. Both text and design were cut in wood and printed from the same block. At a later date the prints were pasted together to form books, an example being the *Biblia Pauperum, c.* 1465. One of the earliest books to contain woodcut illustrations was Aldus's *Hypnerotomachia Polifili*, 1499. Soon afterwards Botticelli made his admirable designs for Dante's *Divina Commedia*. The history of illustration is closely bound up with the development of the graphic processes of reproduction (*see* separate articles on AQUATINT; ETCHING; LINE-ENGRAVING; MEZZOTINT; WOODCUTS AND WOOD-ENGRAVING). An early classic of woodcut illustration is the younger Holbein's *Dance of Death*, 1538. In France fine woodcuts were made for Books of Hours in the early sixteenth century. Line-engraving was much used from the seventeenth century onwards. The various forms taken by illustration in works of fiction, books on natural history, travel and topography, art and archaeology, etc., can only be briefly signalized here, but its great period may be said to date from the late eighteenth century, and a variety of excellent and even great works is to be noted. Among them are the magnificent works of William Blake (q.v.), including the great *Illustrations of the Book of Job*, 1825, and the woodcuts for the *Pastorals* of Virgil, 1821. Thomas Bewick (q.v.) gave wood-engraving new life in his illustrations of the *General History of Quadrupeds*, 1790, and *History of British Birds*, 1797. Classics of their kind are *The Birds of America* by Audubon (q.v.), 1827–38, and P. Reinagle's illustrations, mezzotinted and aquatinted, to R. J. Thornton's *Temple of Flora*, 1797–1807. Notable illustrations by Rowlandson (q.v.) are those to the *English Dance of Death* by W. Combe, 1815–16.

The novels of Dickens, Lever, Harrison Ainsworth, Trollope and others gave much scope for the illustrator in England, as also did the rise of the illustrated magazines such as *Good Words, Cornhill* and *The Leisure Hour*. The etchings of Cruikshank (q.v.) are outstanding and the English school of illustration in the sixties is justly famous, though the work of artists such as Boyd Houghton, Pinwell, Frederick Walker, Millais and others was translated from drawings into wood-engravings by engravers, among whom the Dalziel Brothers are notable. Germany had a great illustrator in Adolph Menzel (q.v.). In France the nineteenth century produced such illustrators as the brilliant 'Grandville' (Jean Ignace Isidore Gérard, 1803–47) and Gustave Doré (q.v.). Of special note in England is the Pre-Raphaelite urge towards beauty in illustration first signalized by Ruskin in the illustrations to *Modern Painters* and *The Stones of Venice*. A landmark was the Moxon edition of Tennyson, 1857, illustrated by Rossetti (q.v.) and others. A final product was the Kelmscott Press set up by William Morris in 1891, which reintegrated pictorial design and text as in the famous Kelmscott *Chaucer*. The efforts of Morris had a profound effect on the modern conception of a beautiful book in which illustration has a decorative rather than informative role.

[375]

Mechanical means of reproduction created new possibilities, e.g. in line illustration, brilliantly cultivated by Aubrey Beardsley (q.v.) and by the Spanish artist Daniel Vierge (1851–1904) in the sparkling black and white of his pen drawings to *Pablo de Segovia* and *Don Quixote*. In this century, however, there has been a tendency to revert to the traditional processes of graphic reproduction which can be used to original purpose by the artist himself. Among many notable products of the artist-engraver are the wood-engravings of Eric Gill and Robert Gibbings for the Golden Cockerel Press books in England; the wood-engravings of Rockwell Kent to *Moby Dick* and other works in America; the etchings by Segonzac for Virgil's *Georgics*, the aquatints of Picasso to Buffon's *Natural History*, as well as illustrations to various fine editions by Chagall, Matisse, Rouault and other artists of the School of Paris. In Belgium Frans Masereel produced an original form of woodcut book telling a story without words.

Impasto, in oil-painting the physical substance of pigment as the artist applies it to the canvas, particularly when heavy enough to be somewhat raised above the surface, thus catching the light and throwing a slight shadow of its own and so adding to the liveliness as well as solidity of effect. It is often heavily loaded in the light areas, only the shadows being left transparent, but some painters, e.g. van Gogh, have used it with uniform emphasis.

Impressionism, in a general sense the replacement of outline and chiaroscuro by broken colour designed to convey the natural effect of light and of its incidence on objects under given atmospheric conditions. Suggestions of the method are to be found in European art before the nineteenth century, e.g. in the paintings of Velazquez, Watteau, Guardi, Goya and especially the landscapes of Constable and Turner, but the term more specifically refers to the beautiful phase of painting in France which developed *c.* 1860–70 and reached its maturity after the Franco-Prussian War, 1871–80. The group of young painters who were later to be called Impressionists were influenced in the earlier of these periods by a number of landscape painters who had already made the direct study of nature their aim. Corot was a great inspiration; so too were such painters of open-air effect as Boudin, Daubigny and the Dutch painter Johann Barthold Jongkind (qq.v.). In perceiving the direction to which their work pointed Claude Monet (q.v.) was already a leader as a young man and an influence on his friends and fellow students Alfred Sisley, Auguste Renoir and Frederic Bazille (qq.v.). A more definite impulse of doctrine was given by the Realism of Courbet (q.v.), which insisted on the importance of painting everyday life and scenes without recourse to ideal or unusual subject-matter. Edouard Manet (q.v.) succeeded him as the daring realist of the 1860's, notably with his famous 'Déjeuner sur l'Herbe', and as the object of popular hostility and the great *refusé* of the Salon he became the hero of a youthful circle which met at the Café Guerbois in Paris. It included Monet, Renoir, Camille Pissarro, Paul Cézanne and a number of others, and

[376]

C. MONET—La Grenouillère—Collection of Mrs M. S. Woltzer.

A. SISLEY—Horses being watered at Port-Marly—Buhrle Collection.

their exchange of ideas was fruitful. Manet was a leader in being the object of their admiration, though it was not from him that Monet and his friends acquired the idea of painting open-air effects. The study of the mystery and beauty of light and the rendering of 'impression', i.e. the reproduction of a transient effect seen in a momentary vivid glimpse as opposed to a systematic reproduction of detail, was pursued by the younger men in the outskirts of Paris and along the Seine. In the years up to 1870 and before Impressionism had gained its name the main elements of its theory and technique were already decided. It was desirable to paint swiftly and directly from nature *en plein air*; to discard the conventional tonality of brown and the use of all browns, ochres and black, translating light and shade into terms of pure colour (the vibrant blue observed in Japanese prints was not without effect in this emancipation from dark and muddy tones); to modify any local or descriptive colour, e.g. a red dress, a yellow sail, by the observed effect of light upon it; to paint in a fashion optically correct, i.e. rendering in a blurred fashion the surroundings of an object on which the gaze was focused; and to convey with equal accuracy the blurring of definition produced by bright sunlight, mist and distance. It is possible that Monet and Pissarro gained some confirmation of or stimulus to their aims during a sojourn in London in 1870 when they made acquaintance with the work of Turner, but their essential programme was previously well defined. It was vigorously prosecuted after the interruption of the Franco-Prussian War. The exhibition held in 1874, to which Monet, Renoir, Sisley, Pissarro, Degas, Cézanne, Boudin, Guillaumin and Berthe Morisot contributed, included the 'Impression-Sunrise' by Monet which caused a Parisian critic to coin the word Impressionism in ridicule. It was defiantly adopted by the artists for the second exhibition of 1876 and the six further exhibitions which followed at intervals, the last being held in 1886. Manet never exhibited with the group, though through the influence of Monet and Berthe Morisot he adopted Impressionist methods. The most consistent of the Impressionists were Monet, Pissarro and Sisley. Renoir, Degas and Cézanne departed from the movement in their individual ways, yet its theory not only produced works of great beauty but was the spring-board of fresh effort. The Neo-Impressionism of the 1880's, as practised by Seurat, Signac and (for a while) Pissarro, was a scientific and logical extension of the Impressionist method (*see* DIVISIONISM). Post-Impressionism (q.v.) stemmed from it. In England the influence of Impressionism led to the foundation of the New English Art Club in which the work of Wilson Steer and Walter Sickert (qq.v.) was notable. In Germany it affected such artists as Max Liebermann and Lovis Corinth (qq.v.). The nearly abstract colour of Monet's last period has been the object of renewed enthusiasm and study at the present day.

Indian Painting is first represented by the mural decoration of Buddhist temples, the great example being the frescoes of the cave-temple of Ajanta in the Deccan, painted over a period from 200 B.C.

A. RENOIR—The First Evening Out—Tate Gallery.

RASHID (Bikaner, 1693)—Maharaja Anup Singh Hunting Lions—Collection of H.R.H. The Maharaja of Bikaner.

to the seventh century A.D. They depict realistic scenes from Buddhist life and parables from the Buddhist religion and as compositions are among the great works of art of the world. Long subtle curves, bold and vigorous lines of uniform thickness, give them majestic breadth and rhythm. In the 'golden age' of the Guptas, fourth to fifth centuries A.D., other frescoes were produced at Ellora and Bagh. Related in style to the Ajanta frescoes are those of Sigirya in Ceylon (late fifth century). The subsequent history of Indian painting is that of pictures on a small scale produced in various local schools and many of them depicting episodes from the numerous myths and legends of Hinduism. The Jain sect of the western districts of Upper India, an offshoot of Brahminism and Buddhism, fostered a type of religious painting, bold and stylized in outline and with flat colour. The complex history of religion in India is reflected in the development of its art. During the period of Moslem domination, from the thirteenth century onwards, Hindu schools of painting continued to flourish at Benares, in the Punjab, the Deccan and South India. Tradition was especially strong in Rajputana, and Rajput painting derived from the traditional mural art and was devoted to illustrating the stories of legend and religious epic. A special development was

[380]

RAJASTHANI PAINTING (Malwa, c. 1650)—Girl walking with Peacocks, Illustration of the musical mode Gauri Ragini—G. K. Kanoria Collection, Calcutta.

INDIAN PAINTING (Malwa, c. 1680)—Lady with Garlands among Deer—Victoria and Albert Museum.

that of the Rāg-mālas or melody pictures in which Indian music was translated into pictorial terms, in love scenes or representations of emotional contact with nature such as the forest by moonlight. Buddhist schools continued to flourish in Nepal, Sikkim, Bhutan, Tibet and Burma. The Mughal emperors, however, Humayun, Akbar and Jehangir, gave a new impetus to painting in the sixteenth century. Humayun, father of Akbar, spent some years of exile in Persia and on returning to the throne brought with him Persian painters who influenced the Hindu School, Mir Sayyid Ali from Tabriz and Abd al-Samad of Shiraz having both Hindu and Moslem pupils. Akbar had a number of artists working for him, many of whose names are known, and there resulted an intermingling of styles, though it is possible to distinguish the Hindu and Moslem strains. Representational art being condemned by the Prophet, calligraphy was valued more highly than the picture and the Moslem painter tended to combine calligraphy with illustration and in the latter to be more realistic, secular and matter-of-fact than the Hindu.

[381]

INDIAN PAINTING (Mughal, c. 1660)—Jungle Folk Hunting at Night—Victoria and Albert Museum.

USTAD MANSUR (Mughal, Early Seventeenth Century)—Turkey Cock—Victoria and Albert Museum.

AJANTA CAVE WALL PAINTING, c. A.D 500—Copy in Victoria and Albert Museum.

INDIAN PAINTING (Sikh with Guler and Jammu Influence)—Sikh Ruler receiving a Deputation—Victoria and Albert Museum.

INDIAN PAINTING (Rajput, 1710)—Rajah Jaswaul Singh of Jaisalmer carried in State—Victoria and Albert Museum.

BICHITR (Mughal, 1633)—Emperor Shah Jahan
—Victoria and Albert Museum.

INDIAN PAINTING (Mughal)—Akbar lost when
hunting (Outline by Mahesh, Portraits by Kisu)—
Victoria and Albert Museum.

KANGRA PAINTING (Early Nineteenth Century)—Lady with Pet Animals and Birds—
Indian Museum, Calcutta.

MANOHAR DAS—Attendant leading an Indian Black Buck—Victoria and Albert
Museum.

INDIAN PAINTING (Jammu, c. 1750)—Raja Balwant Singh inspecting a Horse—Victoria and Albert Museum.

INDIAN PAINTING (Kangra, 1790)—The Gathering Storm—Victoria and Albert Museum.

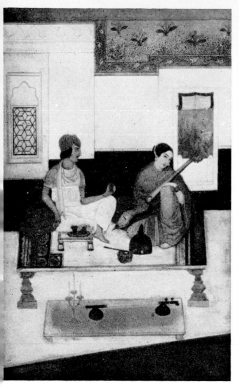

A. N. TAGORE—Summer — Indian Museum, Calcutta.

INDIAN PAINTING (Kangra, c. 1800)—Toilet of a Rajput Princess—Victoria and Albert Museum.

In the painting of birds and flowers, however, the Moslem master Mansur in the reign of Jahangir (1605–27) showed an exquisite sense of nature. He was rivalled by the Hindu Manohar Das, whose 'Attendant leading a Black Buck' (Victoria and Albert Museum) is a masterpiece of animal *genre*. Mughal painting declined during the reign of Aurangzeb, who discouraged the arts for religious reasons and banished the Hindu painters from his court. The latter, however, continued to find patronage at the Hindu courts, and Rajput painting continued into the eighteenth and nineteenth centuries. It is seen at its best in the Palahari art, named from the hill country of the Punjab where it flourished, and was divided between the schools centred at Jammu and Kangra, Kangra being noted for grace of line and softness of colouring. In the nineteenth century art declined, though portrait painting was encouraged by the Sikh rulers of the Punjab. The influence of European painting had already appeared in the time of Jahangir, who encouraged his artists to copy European works, and in the nineteenth century under the East India Company

[387]

Ingres   Ingres

and as part of the British Empire India's native tradition weakened. In the early twentieth century there was a movement to restore it in which the Tagore family was prominent, and a renaissance was encouraged by the work of Dr Abanindranath Tagore. With a revival throughout India are associated the names also of Gagendranath Tagore, Jamini Roy, D. P. Roy Chowdhury and many others.

Ingres, Jean Auguste Dominique (*b.* Montauban, 29 Aug. 1780; *d.* Paris, 14 Jan. 1867), French painter and draughtsman and famous protagonist of Classicism in art. He was the son of a tailor (who was also a versatile amateur in painting, sculpture and music). He became a pupil of David (q.v.), won the Prix de Rome in 1801 and studied and worked in Rome, 1806–20, and in Florence until 1824. This long absence from Paris, repeated 1834–41, when he was again in Rome, partly explains his lack of sympathy with French contemporaries, notably Delacroix (q.v.), who had breathed the atmosphere of Romanticism. Ingres's view of what was classic in art was founded on Raphael rather than David, his homage to Raphael being paid in the 'Vow of Louis XIII' (cathedral of Montauban), Salon success of 1824, and the 'Apotheosis of Homer', 1827, commissioned by Charles X for a ceiling in the Louvre. In subject Ingres was as various as any of his contemporaries, his works including a Romantic, moonlit 'Dream of Ossian', both antique and medieval themes, paintings of ceremonial functions, religious paintings, portraits and nude compositions oriental at least in the suggestion of title, 'La Grande Odalisque' and 'Le Bain Turc'. His quarrel with the Romantics and the nature of his own Classicism could be simply stated as a preference for drawing rather than colour, though his work needs to be considered apart from labels. The exquisite pencil portraits, many executed during his

J. A. D. INGRES—La Grande Odalisque—Louvre.

first Italian stay, give him an assured place among the world's great draughtsmen. In the painted portrait, such as those of M. de Norvins (National Gallery) or Mme de Sennones (Musée de Nantes), he could produce masterpieces. The paintings of the nude of his later years have a sensuous beauty. It would be easy to call him academic and reactionary on the strength of prejudices obstinately maintained to the end of his long life, yet his basically realistic genius outweighs his defects. The Musée Ingres, Montauban, founded in 1843, received the contents of his studio by bequest, including four thousand of his drawings and numerous paintings.

Innes, James Dickson (b. Llanelly, 1887; d. Swanley, late in 1914), English landscape painter, of Catalan descent on his mother's side. He studied at the Slade School and painted in South Wales, often in company with Augustus John, and later on the Mediterranean slopes of the Pyrenees. His small landscapes in oil and water-colour (mainly exhibited at the New English Art Club and product of an all too short career) had a force of design and colour which made a considerable impression on his artist contemporaries in England.

Inness, George (b. Newburgh, New York, 1 May 1825; d. Brig of Allan, 2 Aug. 1894), American landscape painter, largely self-taught, though he profited by the study of Corot and the Barbizon painters on his frequent visits to Europe. This influence seems to have directed him away from the spacious panoramas of American Romantic landscape to a more intimate naturalistic approach. 'The Lackawanna Valley', 1855 (Washington, National Gallery), and 'Peace and

GEORGE INNESS—The Lackawanna Valley—Washington National Gallery of Art.

Plenty', 1865 (New York, Metropolitan Museum), are among his best works. He died during a visit to Scotland.

Intaglio, strictly speaking a gem on one surface of which a design has been hollowed out so that when this side is stamped on some material such as wax the design is impressed and stands out in relief. The term is now commonly used to describe the engraving and printing processes where the matter to be reproduced is below the general surface of the printing plate. See ENGRAVING.

International Gothic, style of late medieval painting which spread throughout Europe in the fourteenth and fifteenth centuries. It had its origin in the illuminated manuscript, transferring to the panel picture the brilliant colour, the fine detail and rich sense of pattern and the individual characterization of the painters of miniatures in manuscripts. The style was practised notably by the Franco-Flemish school of painter-illuminators, including the three brothers 'de Limbourg', whose masterpiece was the 'Très Riches Heures du Duc de Berry', Jean Malouel, who worked at Paris and Dijon, Henri Bellechose, who followed Malouel at Dijon, and Melchoir Broederlam of Ypres, who became painter to Philip the Bold, Duke of Burgundy. It was represented in Spain by Ferrer Bassa, Jaime and Pedro Serra, Luis Borrassa (qq.v.) and others; in Italy by the Sienese painters Simone Martini and Lippo Memmi, by Gentile da Fabriano and Pisanello (qq.v.); in the Germanic lands by Stefan Lochner and Master Bertram (qq.v.). The style forecasts the course taken by the painting of the southern Netherlands in its first great period.

Intimism, neither a movement nor a theory but a term resulting from a French proclivity for general ideas, applied to the work of two of the least theoretic of painters, Bonnard and Vuillard (qq.v.). It refers to their affection for simple and familiar themes, and in particular for the domestic interior and its intimate detail and quiet routine.

Isabey, Louis Gabriel Eugène (b. Paris, 22 July 1803; d. Lagny, 26 April 1886), French painter and lithographer, the son of the miniature painter, Jean Baptiste Isabey (1767–1855). His landscapes and seascapes link him with the Barbizon School (q.v.).

Isenbrant, Adriaen (d. Bruges, June 1551), painter of the early Netherlandish School at Bruges, whose place and date of birth are unknown but who was enrolled as a master in the Painters' Guild of Bruges in 1510 and was probably a pupil of Gerard David (q.v.). 'Our Lady of the Seven Sorrows' (Church of Notre Dame, Bruges) is a notable work attributed to him in which Renaissance detail conjoins with Netherlandish style.

Isenheim Altar, masterpiece of Matthias Grünewald, executed, 1510–15, for the convent of the order of St Anthony at Isenheim, Alsace, and now in the Unterlinden Monastery Museum at Colmar. It is a polyptych showing in its original complete form a collaboration between painter and wood-carver, the work of the latter, Backoffen, being a centre-piece of St Anthony enthroned, with St Augustine and

St Jerome, and carvings in the predella of Christ and the Twelve
Apostles. The painted scenes by Grünewald, presented by the opening or closing of the several panels, are: St Anthony assisting the
hermit Paul; the temptation of St Anthony; the Annunciation; the
Virgin among angelic musicians; the Virgin and Child; the Resurrection; the Crucifixion; and on the predella, when closed, a Pietà.
In two wings flanking the closed centre-piece (Crucifixion) are St
Anthony and St Sebastian, the latter the supposed portrait of the
artist. This majestic series of paintings represents the final achievement of the medieval spirit in German art.

Israels, Josef (*b.* Groningen, 27 Jan. 1824; *d.* The Hague, 1911),
Dutch painter of Jewish parentage who studied in Paris under Picot
and then settled at The Hague. A period spent among poor fishing
folk made him the champion, in his pictures, of the toiler and earned
him the title of the 'Dutch Millet'.

Italian Art Museums. The great art collections of Italy are:
Florence, the Uffizi and Pitti Galleries (qq.v.); *Rome*, the Vatican
(q.v.) and the gallery of the Palazzo Borghese (famous among its
Renaissance paintings being Titian's 'Sacred and Profane Love');
Venice, Accademia delle Belle Arti (q.v.); *Milan*, Brera. Other
galleries of note are the Pinacoteca (q.v.), Siena, and the Museo
Nazionale of Naples, with its paintings from Pompeii and Her-
culaneum.

Italian Painting ranges in an amazing wealth of production over a
period of some five hundred years, from the thirteenth century to the
eighteenth. The origins of this development may be found in the
fragmentary continuance of the classical or Greco-Roman tradition
(*see* EARLY CHRISTIAN ART; ROMAN PAINTING; ROME) and also in the
Byzantine art of the Eastern Roman Empire, represented on Italian
soil by settlements of Greek artists or by Italian artists working in
the same style (*see* BYZANTINE PAINTING). It is usual, however, to
associate the emergence of a truly Italian art with the effort to shake
off the Byzantine conventions, a transitional stage in this process
being shown by the thirteenth-century painters Cimabue and
Duccio and the new line of painting being triumphantly established
by Giotto (*c.* 1266–1337). From his time onward it is possible to see a
steady development of painting on a grand scale continuing until the
height of the Renaissance is reached at the beginning of the sixteenth
century. In this development the rise of the Italian city-states,
virtually independent in the absence of any centralized authority,
was a most important factor. The cities grew wealthy by trade and the
rivalry between them took the form not only of strife but of a
competition in splendour which produced beautiful buildings and the
need for works of art to adorn them. The history of the cities is also
bound up with the rise of princely families who exercised a discerning
patronage, the Medici family of Florence being the supreme example.
The cities had their own distinctive character in art and Italian
painting must necessarily be studied in terms of its many regional
schools. *See under* BOLOGNA; FERRARA; FLORENCE; MILAN; NAPLES;

PADUA; PARMA; SIENA; UMBRIA; VENICE. There are, however, certain overall stages which define the progress of Italian painting in general. The fourteenth century is the pre-Renaissance stage, in Italian description the *trecento*. To some extent Italy was affected at this period by the International Gothic style (q.v.), as in the work of Simone Martini, Gentile da Fabriano and Pisanello. The fifteenth century, *quattrocento*, is the early Renaissance, a period of growing technical mastery; the sixteenth century is the High Renaissance, the *cinquecento*, when Rome (q.v.), now revived in religious authority and splendour, made full use of the genius that had been locally fostered elsewhere. The forms of art which subsequently flourished, Mannerist and baroque (q.v.), had a wide influence and from the sixteenth century onwards Italy was the school and training ground of Europe. In the course of Italian painting religious art for church or monastery was a constant theme, but the emergence of the secular subject is also impressive. The classical studies of the Renaissance prince called for elaborate compositions based on mythology. The 'grand style' (q.v.) was an Italian invention and Italy was the seat of Classicism (q.v.). Technically Italian achievement was supreme in fresco and tempera, and though oil painting was an importation it arrived at its full technical fruition in Venice. The eighteenth century was a kind of epilogue to Italian greatness in art and the nineteenth century was a fallow period, though modern times have witnessed a revival of painting. Italian Futurism of the early twentieth century was an effort of a somewhat desperate kind to dispel the idea that Italy was no more than a country of museums and past glories and to encourage a contemporary spirit. Individual painters such as Modigliani and de Chirico (qq.v.) have made a distinctively Italian contribution to modern art.

END OF VOLUME ONE